DJ Screw

AMERICAN MUSIC SERIES

Jessica Hopper and Charles L. Hughes, series editors

David Cantwell, *The Running Kind: Listening to Merle Haggard*
Stephen Deusner, *Where the Devil Don't Stay:*
Traveling the South with the Drive-By Truckers
Eric Harvey, *Who Got the Camera? A History of Rap and Reality*
Kristin Hersh, *Seeing Sideways: A Memoir of Music and Motherhood*
Hannah Ewens, *Fangirls: Scenes from Modern Music Culture*
Sasha Geffen, *Glitter Up the Dark: How Pop Music Broke the Binary*
Hanif Abdurraqib, *Go Ahead in the Rain: Notes to A Tribe Called Quest*
Chris Stamey, *A Spy in the House of Loud: New York Songs and Stories*
Holly Gleason, editor, *Woman Walk the Line:*
How the Women in Country Music Changed Our Lives
Adam Sobsey, *Chrissie Hynde: A Musical Biography*
Lloyd Sachs, *T Bone Burnett: A Life in Pursuit*
Danny Alexander, *Real Love, No Drama: The Music of Mary J. Blige*
Alina Simone, *Madonnaland and Other Detours into Fame and Fandom*
Kristin Hersh, *Don't Suck, Don't Die: Giving Up Vic Chesnutt*
Chris Morris, *Los Lobos: Dream in Blue*
Eddie Huffman, *John Prine: In Spite of Himself*
John T. Davis, *The Flatlanders: Now It's Now Again*
David Menconi, *Ryan Adams: Losering, a Story of Whiskeytown*
Don McLeese, *Dwight Yoakam: A Thousand Miles from Nowhere*

Peter Blackstock and David Menconi, founding editors

Lance Scott Walker

DJ Screw

A Life in Slow Revolution

UNIVERSITY OF TEXAS PRESS ᐊᐅ AUSTIN

Requests for permission to reproduce material from
this work should be sent to:
 Permissions
 University of Texas Press
 P.O. Box 7819
 Austin, TX 78713-7819
 utpress.utexas.edu/rp-form

♾ The paper used in this book meets the minimum
requirements of ANSI/NISO Z39.48-1992 (R1997)
(Permanence of Paper).

LIBRARY OF CONGRESS CATALOGING-IN-
PUBLICATION DATA

Names: Walker, Lance Scott, author.
Title: DJ Screw : a life in slow revolution / Lance
 Scott Walker.
Other titles: American music series (Austin, Tex.)
Description: First edition. | Austin : University
 of Texas Press, 2022. | Series: American music
 series | Includes bibliographical references
 and index.
Identifiers: LCCN 2021040676
ISBN 978-1-4773-2513-1 (cloth)
ISBN 978-1-4773-2117-1 (paperback)
ISBN 978-1-4773-2514-8 (PDF)
ISBN 978-1-4773-2515-5 (ePub)
Subjects: LCSH: DJ Screw, 1971–2000. | DJ Screw,
 1971–2000—Homes and haunts. | African
 American disc jockeys—Texas—Houston—
 Biography. | Rap musicians—Texas—Houston—
 Biography. | Chopped and screwed (Music)—
 History and criticism.
Classification: LCC ML429.D548 W35 2022 |
 DDC 782.421649092 [B]—dc23
LC record available at https://lccn.loc.gov/2021040676

doi:10.7560/321171

For Red

The Screw sound is when I mix tapes with songs that people can relax to. Slower tempos, to feel the music and so you can hear what the rapper is saying. When I am mixing, I might run across something a rapper's saying which is important. I may run it back two or three times to let you hear what he saying — so you can wake up and listen, because they are telling you something. I make my tapes so everyone can feel them.

DJ Screw, as told to Bilal Allah for *Rap Pages*, November 1995

Contents

Preface

This is folklore. DJ Screw is a Texas legend. He is bona fide hip-hop royalty and a pioneer of his discipline who left us with a rich archive of music that both documented and shaped a culture, remaking the fabric of Houston itself in the process. Robert Earl Davis Jr. has been gone for two decades now, but the sound of his chopped and screwed mixing technique has left an indelible mark on contemporary music. His Screw tapes continue to sell and get sampled by other artists, and unearthed volumes of his recordings still materialize each year, adding to the mystique of the underground cassettes that have sold into the millions all over the world.

When I moved to Houston in 1992, Geto Boys were local heroes, breaking nationally the summer before. Shortly thereafter, it was DJ Screw who would emerge to define the sound of the city. You heard it first in the streets, and it was heavy. It was enchanting. It was mystical. It made Houston feel different from anywhere else on the planet. By the mid-1990s, you couldn't open a window in the big, hot city without hearing a car drive by playing slowed down hip-hop. You still can't.

A decade later, I was years into working on a book chronicling Houston rap music with photographer Peter Beste, and DJ Screw's name was omnipresent in nearly every interview I conducted. The stories people told about him were larger than life, more than just posthumous remembrances. He was the lifeblood of a huge swath of the city, and it was clear that his innovation, wisdom, and love for the people of Houston and Smithville forged a legacy deserving of its own book.

This is part of a greater library, an expanding fount of knowledge about an independent artist who came from nothing and dreamed up something bigger than his city. To tell the story of DJ Screw is to illuminate the history of Houston, a place that still reverberates with his vibe a full generation after his time. The artists who collaborated with him on that huge catalog are still at work—the same voices who crafted timeless stories from rounds of the ranking game The Dozens, from freestyles recounting their lives, or from the magic they created in the room with those turntables spinning—their testimony filling in the puzzle that is the life of Robert Earl Davis Jr.

No matter how many interviews I do with the people who knew him, I'll still be an outsider in DJ Screw's life. I didn't know him personally; I'm a white punk rocker from Galveston Island. This hybrid oral history format is intended to open the aperture past my own eyes, ears, and experience, centering on the recollections of those who knew him, loved him, and drew inspiration from his work. Beyond my own research, I called on the reporting and scholarship of the authors and journalists who preceded me, so that DJ Screw and those who lived alongside him are the ones retelling this epic story.

I am eternally grateful to Screw's family and friends for blessing this project and for their commitment, cooperation, and help throughout, and to the 153 people who have given their time and attention through multiple interviews since 2005. Recollections open old wounds; the candor and confidences of our conversations over the years have been invaluable in gathering material for this project. For all of you, on and off the record, I hope you are reminded of Screw in these pages. This is your book.

A traditional biography this is not, but none of us live traditional biographies anymore. The future is behind us before we can ever live it. No one can keep up. But DJ Screw *slowed down the world*, and over the years his music has continued to grow and prove more relevant and influential across generations. Screw set off a wave. May that wave circle the world forever.

Lance Scott Walker
NEW YORK

DJ Screw

1. Screw York City
1999

If ever there were a moment under the lights, it was in December of '99, on a cold Tuesday night in Midtown Manhattan. Folks had packed themselves eight hundred deep into Club Downtime's three levels for Justo Faison's Fourth Annual Mixtape Awards, where DJ Screw was an honored guest. The Justos were a big deal for DJs, and in the house were New York luminaries like mixtape king Mister Cee, Tony Touch of the Rock Steady Crew, DJ Clue, and Yonkers rapper DMX (who released his third album that day)—all of them present when Harlem native Kool DJ Red Alert, one of hip-hop's founding fathers, called Screw up to the microphone to present him with a diamond-studded ring recognizing his work on the homemade mixes he called Screw tapes.

Those in the room that night witnessed an enigma, a Southern icon whose music they might have heard but who had always been as much a mystery himself as the city and state from which he'd brought his sound. It was Screw's first look at *them*, too. Back home, he didn't leave the house all that much. This was the twenty-eight-year-old's first trip to hip-hop's origin city. His first time on the East Coast. His first and only trip on an airplane.

The day before, he missed his first flight out of Houston, then fell hard asleep on the second because he'd been working straight through for days. When he got to New York, Funkmaster Flex picked him up from the airport and took him over to Hot 97, where he slept a little on the air, too. He could respect the hustle of the big city because he was a student of hip-hop—even if West Coast gangsta rap was his genre of choice—but Screw still moved at the speed of Screw. Always.

By the dawn of the 2000s, he had been carving out space inside of that speed—that slowness—for a decade, working from home all night while the members of his Screwed Up Click stepped through the gate around his front porch and on back into the "wood room," where they recorded the tapes that tell a prolific story of the sound of DJ Screw. The microphone he passed around that room recorded them rapping freestyle, and with it the sound that emanated from his speakers as it echoed off the wood-paneled walls around them, crossing into the aural palpitations he was chopping between records. Folks have called the effect psychedelic, and they would be right. But really, what he was recording was what was on everybody's mind on any given night, heavy ideas rattling the tile floor beneath their feet, big shoes and huge voices in there for hundreds of sessions.

The setting was everything. Screw and his turntables at the center, facing the wall, bass pouring out of his system and expanding around the people behind him in real time before being slowed down to tape. Plenty of those recording sessions only really got going in the small hours of the night, when Screw did his best work, still rolling well into the Houston sunrise, everybody lost in the loop with him. What coalesced when he slowed it down further and dubbed it from the master cassette was the drone of a thundering freight train, exacting and volcanic like nobody else could manage even with the very same tools.

Outside of the house, Screwheads were a congregation in the streets, his music throbbing out of their open windows as they drove the big avenues of Houston down into the deepest corners of its neighborhoods, hidden streets in dense and barren parts of the city alike, banging Screw tapes around every corner. They drove down his street and waited in line to step up to his gate and buy cassettes from the hand of the man himself, taking those tapes back to their neighborhoods for everybody to hear while holding on to the hope of one day making a tape in the wood room themselves. Folks celebrated Screw because he played what they wanted to hear in Houston, or maybe *showed* them what they wanted to hear in Houston. Either way, he knew, and when he opened his record store, they followed him there, and the culture evolved.

Screw's house was bigger than rap music in Houston because life stories intersected when that microphone moved around the room. Whether family or not even friendly with one another, they all drew from his magic, and the music they grew up knowing—rap, maybe R&B, reggae—and from the energy of making something from that at *home*, bringing a sound to the voices of their streets, painting a picture of where they were from under the brightest light they knew: DJ Screw's.

But the recording session was only the first part. Everyone's perception of what a Screw tape sounded like when they recorded it live at his house was one thing, but they were made to believe in his touch when they finally heard Screw slow it down to where he was hearing it in his head. And then there was the swing in his chopping, as only he could employ, at the same time deconstructing a song's relationship with its lyrics, shaking the linear story within, all the while cutting new rhythms into the cloth of the sound.

When he ran things back—to double tap the drums, repeat words or whole phrases—Screw was emphasizing what *he* wanted to hear. He drove whatever he was hearing out of the weeds through repetition, revisiting lyrics, surgically, from a slice of music echoing between two turntables, one record playing a little behind the other, usually the same song, but maybe not. Screw made it sound like two songs went together even if they didn't, and that told you what he was feeling. He was going way further than just slowing down the speed. He was changing how you understood the song.

Whatever it meant to the folks in the New York club that night, "chopped and screwed" had by then become synonymous with Houston rap. But Robert Earl Davis Jr. didn't just fly up there to represent his name, DJ Screw, or his business, Screwed Up Records & Tapes. He was going on behalf of his beloved big city of Houston, for his tiny hometown of Smithville, Texas, and for his family and the village of friends around him, many of whom he'd opened doors for—literally, the doors to his own house—and helped lift into real careers.

Their passage through his house fed into the electricity of his work at the turntables, where he dug for rhythms that spoke to his energies, tore into the flesh of the beat, laid down a heavy undertow and then handed off the microphone. The result was a broadcast, a transmission of voices into every neighborhood, Screw's work channeling currents around him. Plenty of his people were able to build their own thing because they appeared on Screw tapes. That was what he wanted the whole time.

Most of that work was done in the streets, but by the time he got to New York, DJ Screw had been interviewed by *The Source*, *Murder Dog*, and *XXL*, profiled on BET and the local news station, and had made an appearance on the *Billboard* 200 with his album *3 'N the Mornin'*. Some got their first shot with him and launched careers, while others were established and found a whole new lane with Screw in their lives. Botany Boys, Fat Pat, Lil' Keke, Big Hawk, Big Pokey, Big Moe, E.S.G., Mike-D, Yungstar, Mr. 3-2, Z-Ro, Trae Tha Truth, Lil' Flip. Some weren't even rappers before they stepped in his house (besides, the Screwed Up Click was a lot more than just rappers), and others still got out of the streets because Screw encouraged them to focus on their music. What mattered to him was that everyone around him could eat.

By 1999, the Screwed Up Click was a collective roar, even if its biggest voice, Fat Pat, was already gone—his murder the first of many tragedies to befall the S.U.C. For Pat's brother Big Hawk, and for Screw, it was a hurt that never went away. But Pat's voice, his hooks, his cadence, swagger, and slang had already been embossed on the Screwed Up Click, as was Southside style icon Corey Blount's influence on the car culture around them before he went to prison around the time of Pat's death.

Screw was no bystander in the way their legacies played out. He helped keep their names in people's ears. Every tape was a diary, from his selections to his cuts to the parts where he talks in that cool, calm voice—unflappable, real, and big hearted. The people in the recordings wouldn't be around forever, but their voices were kept alive on the tapes—hundreds of tapes, maybe thousands—because no one else could see them but Screw. That was his fabled generosity at work—the product of a youth spent in the country, no doubt. Screw captured that rawness— the banter, the freestyles, the long stretches of testimony pouring from their hearts—because he made room for them to have a voice. It was as if he foresaw that either they wouldn't be here forever or *he* wouldn't be here forever, and recorded as much of them as he could—cementing his own legacy in the end. After all, DJ Screw *is* on every tape.

In the Bayou City, a generation of hip-hop artists preceded him, and there were people in Screw's life who nurtured his passion at every stage of his growth. Rap-A-Lot Records and Geto Boys had set the template and put Houston on the map. DJ Darryl Scott started with mixtapes and the clubs and eventually opened his own shop, as Screw would do a decade later. Screw had forefathers and peers and brothers and sisters all around him. In a way, it was *Houston* they were honoring that night in New York, a gumbo history boiling over with R&B, blues, funk, boogie, zydeco, and H-Town's own multiple hip-hop thoroughfares.

So Screw took that ring with him back to Houston, where it was twenty degrees warmer, and he showed it around. He knew—as they did—that back in New York, no one had ever heard anything like what he was doing on those tapes. He had done so much of his thing, his way, that it could no longer be ignored. The music had distilled. He was proud of having pushed it that far.

But he was still the same person, all the time. Everybody tells the same story there. The whole of his life had taken place in Texas. A nod from up north wasn't going to get to his head. Screw was the same to the stranger freestyling for him on the sidewalk as he was to the people who had been there when he started scratching on the turntable as a middle schooler back in Smithville, or even when he crossed paths with the famous rappers who called on him when they came to town. He'd built a Screwed Up family, and anybody who got close to him was made to feel like they were his best friend.

The guy with the Dickies shirt and pants and the quiet, breathy voice that made everybody listen close when he spoke stood there at the club that night with a track record behind him thick enough to hold up to the light. But his real glimmer came from behind the wheels, where he'd crafted an eddy of sound with his ears and hands and heart, leaving everyone room to express themselves and outgrow him at the same time. New York City wasn't the peak. Screw music doesn't peak. It just grinds.

DJ Screw had less than a year to live at that point. Nobody knew it, least of all Screw himself, but he always worked like he was running out of time anyway, and in his last year he burned it at both ends. He had a lot on the horizon.

In December of 2001, Screw was posthumously honored with the Pink House Award at Justo's Sixth Annual Mixtape Awards at the Apollo Theater in Harlem. It was a rowdier, much larger event full of drama and the stresses of life in New York City after 9/11—an event Robert Earl Davis Jr. never lived to see. The world had changed, and by then a lot more people knew about the work of DJ Screw. They needed it, even if they didn't know it yet.

"I wanna Screw the whole world," he told Cheryl Smith for *The Source* in 1995. During his lifetime, Screw put in the work, but it was his influence that would go on to keep the promise. In the years that followed his death, DJ Screw's sound reverberated in his home city and beyond, entering the mainstream when fresh new voices would rush onto the charts carrying his style in their music. That was *going* to happen eventually. Screw had left the floodgates open, and just like he predicted, the sound he created in a Southside Houston bedroom would go worldwide.

2. Robert Earl
1971

The Colorado River snakes its way southeast through the Texas Hill Country from its genesis out near Lubbock in the Llano Estacado plains, looping through Austin on down past Bay City, where the river's lower course spills out into the Gulf of Mexico. If you take a ride out to where Highway 71 and Highway 95 converge, you'll be pretty well near the middle of a triangle between Austin, San Antonio, and Houston, and there at the bottom of one of the river's many bends is where you'll find the town of Smithville.

There is a Main Street like you'll see in most old Texas towns, and sidewalks lined with a nineteenth-century drugstore, barbershop, bank, bakery, saloon, and a windowless Masonic lodge. Smithville was founded in the 1820s as an outpost that sprung up around a store, followed by a church, post office, and then finally a railway, which brought more businesses, hotels, and even a doctor. Folks on the north side of the tracks live near the highway and the river, and folks on the south side live next to the country. Flanked on all sides by hills sprawling for miles along farm-to-market roads, cars and trucks weave around folks on horseback while cattle gather all around them in pastures where the heat is relieved by the shade of cypress, cedar, mesquite, and all manner of prairie oak. The railroad line is still there, dividing the town in two right across the belly north to south, with a half dozen freight trains passing throughout the day. At one time they had a passenger train and a bus passing through, but the ridership couldn't keep them coming around. Smithville has only ever swollen up to a few thousand people.

In August of 1969, one of Smithville's own returned home from a stay on the West Coast. Ida Mae Deary had been living near Los Angeles with her sister, whose brother-in-law she became close to, and while she was in California, Ida gave birth to a daughter, Michelle. After she returned to Smithville with the baby, the twenty-one-year-old met and fell in love with a man named Robert Earl Davis, who came from an even smaller town about fifteen minutes up the road called Winchester, where the population numbered in the dozens and *everybody* knew each other. Robert and his brothers all carried a mean pool stick.

Michelle "Red" Wheeler (sister) "My Auntie B—she actually moved to California with her husband she had married, which his name was James Martin. And so my biological father is my auntie's brother-in-law. [*laughs*] That's how I was born in California. Once my mom had me, she waited until I was six months old and then came back to Texas, because I don't think she was ready to be settled down yet. And I don't think *he* was ready, either—they just created me. And then she got with Robert when I was a diaper baby, as they would say. So he's what I knew as a dad."

Ida Mae and Robert married in January of 1970, and by October of that year, Ida was pregnant. On July 20, 1971, they drove to a hospital thirteen miles up the highway in Bastrop, where she gave birth to a baby boy. They named him Robert Earl Davis Jr., bringing him home to a house Robert's mother owned in Center Union, out in the country to the east of Smithville. For a while, that was where the four of them lived, just long enough to imprint the country on baby Robert Earl.

Ida Mae Deary Davis (mother, as told to Matt Sonzala for *Murder Dog*) "My son was musically inclined before he could walk. Yes sir. Because I'd be playing my blues on Fridays and Saturdays and he'd just stand up and jump to the beat . . . Before he could walk he could dance. He could move his little body."

Robert Earl Davis Sr. (father, as told to Reggie "Bird" Oliver) "We was livin' on a farm out there, and there wasn't much to do but raise crops and so forth. So we decided to move to Houston, and I end up becoming a truck driver."

The story of DJ Screw begins in Smithville because that's where his family was from, but his first memories would actually be from the big city a hundred miles away. When Robert Earl was still a baby, his family picked up and moved to a neighborhood on the east side of Houston, just north of downtown. The area had its reputation, but it also played a crucial role in the musical history of what was then the sixth-largest city in the United States.

HOUSTON, TEXAS

The Davis family—Robert, Ida, Michelle, and baby Robert Earl—moved into an apartment in a small complex about a mile north of Fifth Ward near the intersection of Collingsworth and Lockwood, in Kashmere Gardens. Robert drove trucks for the chemical distribution company Van Waters & Rogers, dispatching from just west of Hobby Airport on the Southside, and Ida worked a handful of jobs all around town. Michelle started school at Isaacs Elementary while Robert Earl was still a toddler.

Michelle "Red" Wheeler "My uncle Donnie was the one who did the out-of-state driving, but my dad mostly stayed in Texas. When he would do the lil short runs to Beaumont, that's when me and Screw would go. I was the one who was always excited and ready to go. Screw was never ready to go. For *me*, that was exciting, because I wanted to be a truck driver. When he got us up at three or four o'clock in the morning to leave, we were in our pajamas! We put on our house shoes and we was out the door. We ain't get dressed. We'd stay in the sleeper and he'd go pick up his trailer and we'd gone on to Beaumont, unload, and come on back! That was our journey."

In the early 1970s, the cost of living in Kashmere Gardens was low, but it wasn't an easy place for any young family to land. The entirety of northeast Houston—Fifth Ward, Kashmere Gardens, Settegast, Denver Harbor, Port Houston, East Houston, and Trinity / Houston Gardens— was then facing tremendous economic hardships, and crime in the area earned Fifth Ward a reputation citywide as the "Bloody Nickel." But those conditions were a product of stresses the community had been facing by then for generations, most of which had been brought on by people from outside of the ward.

The lines that demarcated Houston's old political divisions fell off the map a hundred years ago, but people still call all six of them by name. Fifth Ward, Fourth Ward, and Third Ward were gutted and devalued in the '50s and '60s when Houston developers came through with a couple of big highways (I-10 and the Eastex) that they just happened to have planned right through mostly Black communities. Years later, local manufacturers were caught sneaking into Fifth Ward to dump their chemicals. In place of a true sewage system, Fifth Ward and its surrounding areas are lined with deep drainage ditches to take the runoff, and when toxic waste—creosote, paper sludge, asbestos mining waste— is dumped into those ditches, it leeches into people's front yards, and that has driven up the cancer rates all around northeast Houston. Going back to its immigrant beginnings in the nineteenth century as Frenchtown, and through its evolutions ever since, long before and after the ward divisions in Houston, Fifth Ward and its surrounding communities have been systemically marginalized.

Plenty was shining from that community in the early 1970s, though. Boxer George Foreman, who in '73 beat Joe Frazier in Kingston, Jamaica, for the heavyweight title, was from Fifth Ward. It was also home to Barbara Jordan and Mickey Leland, both of whom ascended through Texas politics and then on to US Congress in the early and mid-'70s.

But nothing in the area's backstory could compare with the richness of its musical history, which had been boiling over for decades by the time the Davis family arrived. Blues, R&B, boogie, zydeco, and jazz were being played by musicians from neighborhoods all over Houston, and the very best of them were playing in the cafes and clubs of the Northside.

The Davis family had set down in Kashmere Gardens at the end of a couple of gilded musical eras. Just down the street from where they lived was the Fifth Ward institution Houston's original Black (and Jewish) music entrepreneur Don Robey had built through his Bronze Peacock Dinner Club, launching the high-profile Peacock label (which later merged with the Memphis label Duke). Robey was Houston's original-gangster music-industry man, running a complex operation with champagne and white tablecloths along with security guarding back rooms reserved for illegal gambling.

The club was just one part of the Duke-Peacock empire. Robey also owned a record store on Lyons Avenue and several other labels, including Sure-Shot, Back Beat, and Song Bird. And then there was his roster—Bobby "Blue" Bland, Big Walter "Thunderbird" Price, Willie Mae "Big Mama" Thornton. Thornton moved to Houston from Alabama and in 1952 released "Hound Dog," preceding Elvis Presley's version and establishing her—and Peacock—as some of rock 'n' roll's earliest pioneers.

But it was Robey's business partner, Louisiana native Evelyn Johnson, who became the architect of his longevity in the entertainment world when she took over booking tours for artists who were on the label (and plenty who weren't), curating a roster full of talent for their Buffalo Booking Agency that included Clarence "Gatemouth" Brown, Johnny Otis, and B.B. King. Really they were progenitors of what became the 360 deal, where a label or agency manages every part of an artist's career: putting out their records, owning the club where they played, and then booking them elsewhere around the country.

Robey sold off the operation to ABC Dunhill before he died in 1975, by which point a younger entrepreneur named Ray Barnett was the one taking on the task of bringing in talent for Houston audiences in a time of Jim Crow pressures—police raids, red tape, legal hurdles—levied against Black businesses. Barnett booked artists from all over, but he didn't have to look far. In the late '60s and early '70s, lots was going on in Houston. Bubbha Thomas and his Lightmen were concocting a new kind of funky jazz in Fourth Ward, while Lightnin' Hopkins and other Houston blues artists were still getting plenty of work—recording and gigs—in Third Ward and beyond. At Fifth Ward's Silver Slipper they were playing zydeco—an East Texas adaptation of Louisiana la la music that was still growing through the trek of its biggest star, Opelousas's Clifton Chenier. In its original form, la la is just accordion and washboard, but when jobs in the oil refineries brought those musicians east to Texas, where they worked (and eventually played) alongside Houston blues and jazz musicians, the mix of cultures became known as zydeco.

Two miles north up Lockwood, in Trinity Gardens, was the home of Conrad "Prof" Johnson's Kashmere Stage Band, which Johnson had taken over direction of in 1969. He shaped the all-Black Kashmere High School band into an airtight funk and jazz hybrid that cut six albums and traveled the world winning competitions, with many of its young musicians going on to lengthy careers. Johnson's run with Kashmere Stage Band came to an end in 1978, when Robert Earl was in the second grade and maybe just then becoming aware of his musical DNA.

Robert Sr. was on the road a lot, and so it was mostly Ida Mae who was home with the children at the apartment on Lockwood. They did travel to Smithville to see Ida's mother on occasion, and even had a stay in Los Angeles for a funeral, but Robert Earl mainly stuck close to home. He went to school right around the corner at Isaacs, going through a back fence with his sister to get there, and he spent time in the apartment around his mother, who became his main musical influence because she was always playing records and eight-tracks in the house. There were record shops in Fifth Ward and nearby Third Ward, and Ida Mae dropped in frequently, priding herself on her good taste. By the time Robert Earl was finishing up elementary school in the late '70s, he'd been getting a musical education right at home for years.

DJ Screw (Robert Earl Davis Jr., as told to Desmond Lewis) "My mom really got me into this music. 'Cuz when we was little, we'd sit around the house and she'd play music all day, and that's what kinda stuck with me."

Ida Mae (as told to Michael Hall for *Texas Monthly*) "I had three jobs. I cleaned at the washateria, I cleaned at the school, and I worked for a lady on lunch breaks. And I made tapes at night when I lived in Houston. I used to sell eight-track tapes out of my house, make tapes from my records on Friday nights. People would come to my house. It started with a girlfriend, *Can you make me this tape?* He would stand there and watch me. He watched what I did. He said, *I can do that.*"

Her selections were Robert Earl's musical upbringing: Tower of Power,

Switch, Blue Magic, Teddy Pendergrass, Bobby Womack, Deniece Williams. Young Robert Earl absorbed all of it, including his mother's ritual of recording those records to tape. Even if he didn't realize it yet, the seeds of his creative future were surrounding him, both in the history of the neighborhood where he was growing up and in the records Ida was playing on the living room stereo. But before he came of age, their living situation was going to change, and the entire musical landscape around him with it.

"BUNNYTOWN"

In 1980, Robert Earl and Michelle's parents separated, and Ida Mae took the kids with her back to Smithville. Even though Robert Sr. was often gone on the road, this was the first time the family unit had been broken up. Ida Mae moved the three of them in with her mother, Jessie, into her three-bedroom, one-bathroom house on the south side of Smithville in an area known as Buntetown. The neighborhood was called that because of a part of Smithville settled in 1895 known as the Bunte Addition, initially to accommodate those who were priced out of the rest of town. As Smithville became more segregated and created new social and racial divisions, white folks started calling it "Bunnytown."

Shorty Mac (cousin Trey Adkins) "When we grew up, Blacks stayed on one side of the track, whites stayed on one side of the track, and you *never would* hardly see too many Black people that got even a chance to live over there."

Michelle "Red" Wheeler "My grandmother, her place is further down the road. The man grew corn in her part of the field, and we just would run through those cornfields, and we weren't scared of any bugs! We'd run into spiders and you'd just knock them out of the way. We used to try to catch snakes out the pond, and *now* I am scared of every bug livin'!"

Ida Mae went to work for the school district there in Smithville, doing janitorial work at both the middle school and the high school, where her mother also worked. Things were different out there, but it turned out Red and Robert Earl had been country folk all along. Smithville was home, and in middle school, Robert Earl would meet the kids who would confirm that.

Larry B (cousin) "We used to do work for his mother. She used to be janitorial, and he would always go check in. He would always communicate with her, and tell her where he was gonna be, hang out or whatever. Sometimes she'd ask us to help out just a little. And then she would have these sandwiches. He *loved* his Spam. No nothin', just Spam and bread. He would put that on a sandwich and get a big glass of iced tea and he would sit there boy like it was a gourmet meal. And we'd just sit there and eat our lil Spam and be playin' the music. He was like a brother to me, man. We just like brothers. Me, him, and Shorty Mac."

There were any number of reasons a young Robert Earl was happy to be in Smithville. His grandmother "Gessie" was there, for one, but he also had plenty of cousins. Back in Houston was Big Bubb, Chris Cooley was out in San Antonio, and in Smithville were ACT, D-Ray, Lil' Doug, and Big Baby. Those were just on his father's side. On his mother's side, there was his cousin Trey Adkins, who had gone by the name Sugar D in elementary school but by then was known as Shorty Mac.

Shorty Mac "I didn't *know* him until he moved back. I wouldn't have seen him before that, because hell, I pro'ly couldn't even leave out of my yard. But then, once he moved *back*, then that's when me, him, and Larry connected. Because my house was like the house that all the *kids* came to, and stayed all day, all night. And unless you got in trouble and got sent home, *e'rebody* came to my mama house. And so when he moved *back*, we was all of the same age. And then they had a lil store here behind us called Marlon's that everybody used to hang out at and play video games."

DJ Big Baby "His dad and my dad are first cousins, so that's basically how I know him. He was like probably about like four or five years older than me. I used to see him walkin' down the street every now and then. You know, he used to have a big boom box he would carry around."

D-Ray (cousin, as told to Jason Culberson for *Screwville*) "My first memory of Screw down here in Smithville . . . actually Screw and his sister, Michelle, Red, stayed with us on Walker Street, at 401 Walker Street, and I remember us stayin' together in that house for a while. I can't recall how long. Probably about a year or so, not too long, but they did—Screw and Michelle stayed with us on Walker Street. It was me, my grandmother, Jessie Deary, Eula Mae Deary, Ida Mae Deary, Doug, Michelle, and Robert, which y'all know as DJ Screw. We all stayed in the same house about a year. I was small. I was a lil kid . . . Michelle my big cousin, Screw was my big cousin. But he wasn't *Screw* then. You know what I'm sayin'. He was just . . . big cousin Earl."

Robert Earl also had an older half brother on his dad's side, Charles Oliver, who lived in La Grange, and a half sister, Tammy Gayton, in West Point. His third cousin was Adrian Washington, who would become known as ACT, or ACTION, and whose mother was related to Robert Earl on his dad's side. Robert Earl played on a Little League team with Shorty Mac called the Smithville Pirates as their third baseman, but he didn't have a whole lot of baseball in him.

Ida Mae (as told to Michael Hall) "He wasn't into sports. He was into music."

Shorty Mac "I don't think Screw made it through the whole year. This is why he didn't make it—because he *was* playin'! One day, somebody was hittin' it to him—it might have even been the coach was hittin' the ball to him—and it took a bounce and hit him in the mouth. I guess he was goin' for a ground ball, and the ball jumped up and hit him in the mouth. And after that, like maybe a week later, the same thing happened, and he had to get stitches. So if you ever look at Screw lip, and you see a little thang—he had to get stitches in his lip. And he never played again after that. After he got them stitches."

Big Bubb (cousin) "In Smithville they had a lot of gopher holes, and he got hit in the mouth with the ball and it busted his lip wide open and his shit got like real big. So it took forever for it to heal up and go back down to normal. It happened *again*. The same thing happened again, busted it big wide open. So if you look at Screw, you see how his top lip kinda big like? That's from that. And we were young! He used to have the big-ass Afro where you put the hat on and the hair still stickin' out. Old Screw bob. Our other cousin Ray—he crazy—the one just passed not too long ago, the one from Cali, he say, *Boy you s'posed to catch it witcha hand, not witcha mouth! Put the glove up there!*"

HARRIS STREET

In 1983, Ida Mae moved the family out of Gessie's house on Walker Street and into an apartment on the other end of Smithville. She was still working at the school with her mother, but had been taking on other jobs, too, because she was putting money away. One morning she got the family into the car and drove them over to an empty lot on the corner of Harris Street and MLK, where Robert Earl and Michelle could see a group of people standing around under the trees.

Michelle "Red" Wheeler "We all came down here and I was like, *Mama, what are you doin' down here?* There were contractors and everybody, they were here, and she got out of the car, she said, *Come on!* We all got out and we came and my grandmother, you know, she walked around here. And she [Ida Mae] didn't tell *anybody* what she was doin'. Nobody knew she was tryin' to build this house. We was like, *What are you doin'?* And they was like, *Hey, Mrs. Davis, how you doin'?* It was about seven or eight people that were waiting on us to get here, and so when we got here they said, *Okay, Mrs. Davis—go on ahead and dig your first hole!* And she looked at us, and she put the shovel down and she put her foot on it, and she said, *This is* our *land now.* And my grandmother, she immediately started to cry, because she knew my mom was tryin' to fix her life after Robert. And it was hard. We went through a lot of things when it came to Robert, but you learn, you get over it, and you go on. We went through a lot. We went through a lot, and for her to make that accomplishment and establish herself, it was a really good feeling."

The house on Harris Street was completed in 1984, when Robert Earl was in middle school. The 1,200-square-foot brick house had three bedrooms, two bathrooms, and a carport, with a huge corner lot right next to it. Robert Earl had his own room, and soon there was a drum set and a piano in the living room, with a growing collection of records to spin on the turntable. Robert Earl played a little bit of piano—his mother even got him lessons—and he and his cousin Chris Cooley would both beat on the drums, but it was the turntable in that living room that would prove to be his primary distraction.

Shorty Mac "Our seventh-grade year, we got in trouble *every day*. When they do the announcements early in the morning time—I think they do like the Pledge of Allegiance, then the announcements? And then they'll call me, Larry, and Screw to the office. And seven out of ten times we used to get what we call "pops," where they hit you with a paddle, 'cuz somethin' we did the day before. Like we wasn't gettin' in trouble for stealin' or none of that kinda stuff. We'd just get in trouble *actually* for clownin' in class! If we was in the classroom, lunchroom, out on the playground—nine times out of ten we got in trouble for clownin' in class, or walkin' between the buses when they'll say it on the intercom, *Do not walk between the buses.* The bell rings, we walk straight between the buses to go home instead of walkin' around like e'rebody else. I think the only thing that might have kept me from not failin' seventh grade, was I think my daddy came home—'cuz he used to work in Corpus Christi—he came home like halfway through the middle of our seventh-grade year, and he looked at my report card, and he told me if I didn't pass that he was going to beat me. At the end of the year—I don't even know how I made it through. I probably failed two or three classes. Like in math class, with calculators we was puttin' in the numbers backwards because we wasn't doin' the work at home. We was just doin' other stuff! Listenin' to music and just not payin' attention."

RADIO

In the early '80s, most of the radio stations within range of Smithville were playing country music. But at night, Robert Earl and Shorty Mac could just barely receive a signal from Austin public radio station KAZI.

That was huge, because the only access they really had to hip-hop then was what they could pick up on the radio. Nobody had MTV, and the channel didn't touch rap music in its early days anyway. So the best means for obtaining new music meant getting their hands on an audio cassette—sometimes a tape that had been dubbed over several times—and recording songs off the radio with a tape recorder, sometimes just by holding it up to the speakers. Robert Earl paid attention to how the DJs mixed the songs, so he could pause the tape while recording and catch a song right where he wanted, and he listened to how the songs followed one another.

Shorty Mac "You could pick up a radio station outta Austin named 88.7, and then on *weekends* for some reason, we used to pick up Majic 102. When you got to the back of my house and you put your antenna right, you could pick up Majic 102. It depends on what part of the house you was in. In the front, if you had your antenna right, you could pick up 88.7 on a clear night outside. You go to the *back* of the house, you put your antenna right, it's a clear night, you could pick up 102. They used to have the Mastermix on there and we would sit up and listen. But can't nobody come around the radio! You gotta stay away from the radio, because if anybody come around the radio, you gonna lose your signal. Put it in the corner, turn it up. We used to put the antenna out, tinfoil, even a clothes hanger on it. Everything else was blues and stuff like that. Like my daddy was into Ray Charles and B.B. King and all that stuff, the newer blues, Earth, Wind & Fire. We had all that kind of music around us."

DJ Screw (as told to Bilal Allah for *Rap Pages*) "When break-dancing was the shit, I heard scratching on the radio and I just wanted to try it. My ol' lady listened to old records, so I was always around the music because of her. Then I started messing with the turntables, trying to learn all about it."

Ida Mae (as told to Matt Sonzala) "I always thought he was going to be a break-dancer. And then I gave him piano lessons. I wanted him to be a pianist, too. But when it got down to the music, I knew what he was up to. I felt it. He felt it, too. We gave him music lessons and everything, but he didn't want to be no piano player. He would rather mess with turntables, and that's exactly what he did."

THE GLOVE

The summer they moved into the house on Harris Street was when hip-hop broke. Some of the first movies about the culture, *Beat Street* and *Breakin'*, were in theaters; Run-DMC, Fat Boys, and Whodini were on the charts; and the genre's audience was widening. Robert Earl persuaded his mother to drive him and Shorty Mac to see *Breakin'* in Austin, and while everybody else chewing popcorn in the theater that night was mesmerized by the skills of a young rapper named Ice-T and the break-dance moves of Shabba Doo and Boogaloo Shrimp, Robert Earl couldn't keep his eyes and ears off the hands of DJ Chris "the Glove" Taylor.

Shorty Mac "We left out of the movies and the only thing he noticed was the DJ that Ice-T had with him. The whole way home, he was sayin', *Man, I could do that. I could do that.*"

Nothing in Screw's life had yet changed him as much as seeing that film. He held the black vinyl of his mother's records up to the light to read where the grooves told him the songs began and ended, where they were quiet and where they were loud. Screw developed a different clock for himself on his mother's turntable, where he could take forever going through records because he was a kid and he had the time. When he put the needle down, he could feel those grooves he'd seen in the light, sliding the needle back and forth between them. Everything was a moving part, turntable and records together as one instrument.

Ida Mae (as told to Matt Sonzala) "I'd be at work and then he'd disconnect all of my stuff and hook it up in his room and by the time he'd think I was coming home he'd put it back where it belonged."

Shorty Mac "We was walkin' down the street. He had a jam box, and the handle broke on it. He took the jam box home, took his mama turntable, and connected it to the jam box some kinda way, and he made like the

AM/FM lil fader thing, he turned *that* into a fader. There was a guy up the street that was deejayin' at the local club named DJ Daryal Butts—he [Robert Earl] would run down there and borrow one of his turntables and he would connect that up, and he put six by nines—speakers that go in cars—all around his room, and he had 'em all spaced out, and no headphones. He would just sit there and be mixin' and takin' a little bitty jam box and recordin' his mixtapes on that, without headphones. So it was like we had our own lil radio station or somethin'. At that age we was twelve, thirteen years old, but it was kinda just really amazin' to see him mixin' without headphones on, and it just . . . that's how he basically started."

Ida Mae (as told to Matt Sonzala) "I was in the bedroom I think and I said, *Boy, what are you doing?* That's what I said. And I said, *Plus you scratching up all my records!* And it sounded like it was dragging it, like when there's no needle on the thing, it sounds like it's dragging. But it worked out fine for him. It didn't work out fine for me and my records, but he said, *Mama one day this is gonna make us rich.* And I looked at this little ol' cute face and I said, *Yeah, son, right . . . but lay off my eight-track tapes. And my 45s—leave 'em alone!* But when I left the house he messed with them again."

Michelle "Red" Wheeler "My mama had this 'Ring My Bell' [record]. It was another one that he just scratched up so terribly, my mama was just totally upset about it. It was one of her good old ones. Anita Ward, Marvin Gaye. . . . I mean *all* of her old records."

Ida Mae (as told to Michael Hall) "It was something that came natural to that kid. I'm proud of that kid. I wasn't proud of him messing up my albums!"

Larry B "In junior high is where we invented the name DJ Screw. That 'DJ Screw' came when we was all sittin' around one day after school, and that's when we decided to really create a clique—create names and stuff, you know. And Shorty Mac said it. Screw was over there messin' with the tables. He started messin' with the tape, and stoppin' the tape with his lil thing. And he said, *Man, who you think you is, DJ Screw?*"

Shorty Mac "Records he didn't like, he would take a screw and be scratchin' 'em up. So one day he was doin' it and I said, *Man, who you think you is—DJ Screw or somethin'?* And he started laughin'. He said, *But I like that.* So he really just kept it, and ran with that name."

DJ Screw (as told to Daika Bray) "Like records I didn't like, I thought was bullshit, I'd take a screw off of it. Anything, I'd scratch the record up. They'd come to me, *Man, nigga, who you think you is? DJ Screw or something?* That kinda stuck to me."

Larry B "And that just clicked, and it rolled from then. It's legendary now! It's funny. I had a binder. It was a red binder you could keep, you know, paper in—notebook paper in—and notes and stuff. And signed on my notebook—you know how you get your pen, you keep goin' over it, you keep goin' over it, and you make it thicker and thicker? It said DJ SCREW."

THE HANDS

One of Red's friends dated a guy from La Grange named David Harrison. He was a DJ and played gigs throughout the Hill Country and the state, spinning hip-hop records under the name D.W. Sound. Around the time Robert Earl started going by DJ Screw, D.W. Sound was living in Smithville, and he had all of the new vinyl with him—including exactly what Screw and his friends were trying to hear.

D.W. Sound "Pretty much that's all I played was hip-hop. Funk, R&B, hip-hop, all of that. Whatever was current at the time, I was playin' it, because I wanted the country to have whatever they had in the city. There was nowhere to buy records in the country. I'd make that drive—like every two weeks I'd make that drive to Houston. I used to go to Soundwaves off of South Main. In Houston I was playin' just lil hole-in-the-walls, so to speak. Purple Shadow, Last Chance. In Smithville I played West End Park, Texas Lounge, and then in La Grange we had Circle T, Club Mahogany, Cozy Corner . . . I mean I played the whole country. I played Weimar—Jungle Hut, Club 90. Giddings . . . I played everywhere in the country."

Screw crossed paths early on with another turntable enthusiast, Smith-ville native Daryal Butts, who graduated high school there in 1975 and then went into the US Air Force as a teenager. He was stationed in Europe, passing through Spain, Germany, and Lajes Airfield in the Azores, off the coast of Portugal, picking up records at every base.

Daryal Butts "When you're overseas, you don't spend much money. But one thing I would buy each month was some albums. I would go to the PX and buy albums, so I had a few records when I got back home, and then once I got home I started buyin' a lot of 45s. I had bought a lot of albums overseas. That's when I got exposed to really great stereo equipment. I saw some Bose 901s and man—I had never heard this sound come out of a speaker like that! It was like unbelievable. So I said, *I'ma start buyin' some of this stuff, man!* It was so much cheaper through the Army and Navy Exchange that you could buy really good stereo equipment really cheap. When I got ready to PCS [Permanent Change of Station] away from the Azores, I had all that stuff shipped home. That was probably the first time people in Smithville got to see that type of stereo equipment."

Butts returned to Texas in the summer of 1980, enrolling at the University of Texas in Austin, where he studied computer science. Four years later, he was back in Smithville, working the night shift at the Colorado River Authority's Fayette Power Project, a coal-fired power plant in La Grange. He brought his equipment with him.

Larry B "He was a lot older than us. He lived down the street when Screw moved down, when his mother finally got her new house. They had moved down the street from him, and he would give Screw music, you know, beats. And he'll let us hear some of *his* stuff. He had some nice music, but it was weird. He was just in his own world. But he had a whole *lot* of music. He would lend Screw that little old turntable back then. It ain't have no weight to it—you'd have to put pennies and stuff on top of the needle."

Daryal Butts "Robert was a young kid who would come over my house and he would play on the turntables, and play with the cassette decks and the reel-to-reels, and he would . . . you know, I had a turntable that had a strobe light on it, and he would drag his finger on that strobe light and change the strobe speed. I didn't know what he was doin', but he had the headphones on and stuff, and he'd be goin' to work on it."

Charles Oliver (brother, as told to Reggie "Bird" Oliver) "Really, man, I don't remember seein' nobody *teach* him. It was just every day on the tables."

Shorty Mac "He learned everything—he didn't play no instruments in school. The only two people who played instruments in school was me and Larry. Both of us played the trombone."

Daryal Butts "I can't take *any* credit for anything he did. I worked in the power plant, and I worked twelve-hour shifts, and so when I would get off, I pretty much was goin' to sleep. I was working nights and I was sleepin' during the day, and he would come over and ask, *Can I get on your stereo equipment?* And I'd say, *Go ahead.* So he would put on the headphones. The stereo equipment was in the living room. My mom would be at work, I would be asleep, so he would have the house pretty much to himself."

Screw picked up on music anywhere he could hear it. He played around with all of his mother's LPs and 45s, and whoever would loan him theirs. He was recording songs off the radio—mostly stuff from New York—onto the few cassette tapes he owned. Slick Rick and Doug E. Fresh with "La Di Da Di," Whodini with "Freaks Come Out at Night." And then there were the tapes that D.W. Sound brought back with him from Houston.

Larry B "What really kicked us off—Screw said, *Man, you gotta hear these dudes, man, outta Houston.* It was Wickett Crickett, and Lester 'Sir' Pace, and some more artists—Jazzie Redd. They'd come on, and I would hear them freestyle, oh man it *done* something! We got to writin' like crazy. I remember some of the flows! Wickett Crickett say, 'I'm a MC finest' . . . It's kinda like that D.O.C., where he say, 'You call me your highness.' He was just goin' on and on, and I'm listenin', and I'm like, *Man! I like that!*

Me and Shorty Mac started writin' *strong* after that. Screw didn't write back then. He was just into the music. You know, *mixing*. Mixing the turntables."

Screw put every record he could to work on his mother's turntable at home, and eventually started borrowing Butts's gear and connecting the parts. He also got to see D.W. Sound do his thing *live*, and in fact would come to his gigs early enough for a chance to get his hands on a real set of turntables and a mixer, a request the older DJ obliged.

D.W. Sound "That was at the Texas Lounge. He knew his way around. I wouldn't let him do it if he didn't know his way around. I checked him out. He knew what he was doing, because I think [he] had a little something set up at home that he was playin' around with. He was workin' with what he had! Just think if he had what we have now."

Z FORCE CREW

Shorty Mac, Larry B, and DJ Screw had been close before they got into music, but now the three of them were starting to develop their creative selves. They walked up and down the streets playing their tapes. They talked about rap in school. They talked about it outside of school. They weren't just fans of hip-hop, they wanted to be a part of the music.

ACT (cousin) "It was him and Shorty Mac and Larry Bates, they had a lil crew together, and they used to call theyself the Z Force Crew. They put them letters over shirts and spray-paint the shit out of 'em and make they own lil shirts and shit back then. That's when we was walkin' around with jam boxes and shit."

Larry B "Z Force Crew. ZFC. We got to jammin' back in the days through the jam boxes. Everybody was goin' to the flea market and get the newest jam box. Screw had got this one—it was a *nice* jam box I called a Lasonic. Chromed-out, you know. Really nice. And workin', hustlin', get the batteries, you know, put the strap on it, and we would walk around, and I remember he used to blast that Run-DMC. He used to *jam* Run-DMC.

I forget what song but one of his favorite songs was that 'We Are Who-dini.' He used to jam that one."

ACT "They were dancin' back then. A *lot* of dancin' goin' on. That was like the *real* rap era, before all this hip-hop, hip-hippety-hop shit. You know, you could tell a *story* about rap and shit like that. It was artists. It wasn't just rappers. Anybody could rap, put words together, but you know, to make hip-hop—a real hip-hop song—you gotta have some kinda *meanin'* behind it. And that's what it used to be, man. Cardboard boxes gettin' put out in the neighborhood and backspinnin' and tryin' new shit that you seen on *Breakin'*."

Larry B "Screw just doin' it, messin' with them turntables. Back then you would get some bricks or something, stack it up, put stuff across, set the tables up. And we would get a snake light at night and wrap it up with a shoestring or like a fishing yarn or somethin', you know, string, and we would tie it up to the ceiling and we would get that snake light and twirl it, twirl it, twirl it one way, and then it would just start goin' around like a DJ light. And he'd do his own Mastermix. And we would be in there for a couple of hours until his mother told us we needed to cut it down or stop or whatever."

With the overlapping schedules of the multiple jobs she worked to support her two children, Ida Mae started posting a note on the door saying what time Screw's friends could come into the house. If they showed up before the time on the note, they had to turn around.

Shorty Mac "I can't tell you every job she had, but I know at one time she was workin' two or three jobs. And that's how they got that house. She had that house built. One of them had to be at night, 'cuz at night when we were at his house, and she wasn't there, and we was *there* 'til like . . . sometimes we'd be there at . . . twelve, thirteen years old, we were up there 'til two, three in the mornin'. With the *music* playin'! Right now I can't even tell you how she done that, man. That's why she put that note on the door sayin' we couldn't come over to her house until after twelve o'clock."

Screw was extending his whole understanding of music through every record he could get his hands on, and he soaked all of them up. Shorty Mac borrowed his sister's copy of "Rumors" by Timex Social Club, and Screw mixed it with his own. Screw also liked to mix in Dana Dane's "Nightmares," a 1985 Profile Records twelve-inch that Z Force made a part of their repertoire when they got in the door of Smithville nightspot West End Park to perform for last call.

Larry B "The last time the lady flipped the lights for the place to close? She'd just give us the last fifteen minutes, and we would take it and run with it. And we had the out-of-towners—who seen the haters, plexin' and all that back then—but they were standin' up at the front rows, runnin' up there to see us do our thing! We done dance contests—like I say, Screw was sharp with the dancin' and all that."

Shorty Mac "He already knew what different stuff was. Like I went to go get a keyboard for Christmas one day and he went with me and my daddy, and Screw was like, *Man, get* this *one. I can make beats offa this one.* I was like, *Huh?* And he was like, *Man, it got all the drums.* He knew *everything.* I was lost! I guess that would go back to the sounds that he was hearin' off the drum set. That dude was a genius in his own way."

THE NEXT EPISODE

Robert Earl Davis Sr. wasn't out of the picture, even if the family was getting on without him in Smithville. But Screw's dad legally needed to pay child support, and that wasn't happening. So on a late summer morning in 1986, he drove his truck up from Houston and rolled in to Smithville around breakfast time to see Ida Mae about the issue. She had coffee for him in the kitchen, and Red was there with Robert's baby granddaughter, Shimeka, but he wouldn't be staying long.

Later that morning, Shorty Mac knocked on the door. The note that was usually posted saying what time he and Larry could come over was missing.

Ida Mae opened the door and Mac asked to see Screw.

"Honey, his daddy came and got him and took him to Houston."

3. Smithville to Houston 1986

Two hours—Smithville to Houston, Texas—if you stop for a meal along the way. Truckers know all the good spots, and so did Screw. He'd made a lot of trips back and forth to the city over the years. But the farther his dad drove them away from the country, the heavier this particular trip out of town became for Screw. He was leaving behind all of his friends in Smithville, and plenty of cousins. And Z Force Crew, who were both. Of course he was going to miss Shorty Mac and Larry B, but also D.W. Sound and Daryal Butts, each of whom opened a new channel for him into the world of music—on his instrument of choice. On the drive they passed through La Grange, where Butts worked and where D.W. played in the clubs, and where D.W. had told Screw about the records that made people go wild on the dance floor. There was excitement for Screw going to the big city. He couldn't know then he'd left Smithville for good.

But the change of scenery went way deeper than music. The last several years had been all about the women in his life—his mother, his grandmother, his older sister, and his niece Shimeka, who was only six months old when he left. Suddenly disconnected from them all when he left in that truck, he wasn't going to be growing up under the same roof as them anymore, or even in the same city. And he had only *just* become Uncle Earl.

His mother did want him to have a father figure, but Screw couldn't have known what that was going to be like. For his first few months in Houston, they stayed at his dad's girlfriend Patricia's house, where Screw shared a room with her two sons. The older brother, Russell, had just graduated high school then and was getting ready to go to college for business at Texas Southern University. During his time living there, Screw kept his headphones on and didn't say much, but Russell had been around Screw's dad enough by then to get to know him.

Russell Washington "I always liked Mr. Robert. My mother only dated two guys that I really liked, but Mr. Robert was always cool to me. He was like my stepdad. But he was *actually* an old player! I think she had met him at bingo. My mom played bingo real heavy, and Mr. Robert played bingo real heavy! He shot pool, he played dice, he was just out hustlin', and my mom—I thought they were a terrible match honestly, because you can't have the same vice as your mate. My mother is a gambler, and *he* was! I was like, *Where they get that money?*"

SOUTHSIDE

Not long after Screw's arrival in Houston, Robert and Patricia split up (and in an early example for Screw of how everyone in town was connected, he would end up working with Russell's record label years later). They moved out of her house and closer to where Robert worked, between Highway 288 and the Gulf Freeway, way over near Hobby Airport. Smithville covers about four square miles. Greater Houston is nearly ten thousand, and by 1986 it had surpassed Detroit and Philadelphia to become the fourth-largest city in the country. There was a lot of space to get used to, and it was a fraught moment for moving to a big city in the United States. The era of crack cocaine was in full swing, and socioeconomic conditions in the city combined with the imbalance created by the drug hit the city's poorest neighborhods the hardest. The oil bust of early 1986 sent Houston into a recession, and its population growth had slowed right along with the economy. The job market was buoyed in part by medicine and NASA, but this was also the same year the space shuttle *Challenger* disaster happened, so a dark cloud still very much hung over Space City.

On other fronts, Houston was in better shape. The Rockets and University of Houston alum Akeem Olajuwon made the NBA Finals, and José Cruz and Billy Hatcher nearly took the Astros to the World Series for the first time. The Texas Medical Center had received an influx of cash and was building up along Main Street in the area southwest of Hermann Park, and the city's spirits had been lifted somewhat when French electronic musician Jean-Michel Jarre's *Rendez-vous Houston* concert drew over a million people in and around downtown to watch the fireworks and light show and see saxophonist Kirk Whalum (formerly of TSU's Ocean of Soul marching band) play on "The Last Rendez-vous" in place of astronaut Ron McNair, who was killed aboard the *Challenger*.

So a lot of things were happening in Houston that year, including in Screw's part of town along the South Loop. Just off 610 on South Main was Carrington's—Carro's—the already legendary billiards bar and nightclub where you could hear DJs throwing down whether you were partying or just shooting pool. And plenty of those DJs bought their records and tapes just a couple of blocks away at Soundwaves, right around the corner from the storied Rhinestone Wrangler nightclub. The Astrodome was just on the other side of Kirby Drive, with the amusement park AstroWorld across the freeway, always shining, morning or night. Not far away was King's Flea Market, Ray Barnett's Cinder Club, MacGregor Park, King Leo's, and Blast Records & Tapes. Screw couldn't see it all—he wouldn't even have known where to look—but an entire culture was blooming all around him in Houston.

By the time fifteen-year-old Robert Earl Davis Jr. rolled in to town with his father in the summer of 1986, they were already calling him DJ Screw back home, but he was still unknown in the big city. In the handful of years since his family had left Houston for the country, hip-hop had convincingly broken through to the mainstream, and local scenes were developing far outside of New York—even in the Bayou City. In fact, Houston had plenty on the fire—Screw knew that from the radio tapes he'd heard back in Smithville—but now he was going to *be* there, and it was right when a juggernaut of young local artists were making a shift out of the clubs and into making records. A scene that had been building for years was coming into its own, and Screw arrived just in time to hear it.

NIGHT PEOPLE

Depending on how you start the clock—that is, unless you go back to The Last Poets, Gil Scott-Heron, Melvin Van Peebles, or Pigmeat Markham—rap music started coming out on vinyl in 1979. The first records recognized as hip-hop (Fatback Band's "King Tim III," Sugarhill Gang's "Rapper's Delight") weren't truly representative of the genre because so much of what was going on in New York (Cold Crush Brothers, Grandmaster Flash and the Furious Five) was still happening in the clubs. In Houston, a lot of what passed for hip-hop on the radio was really R&B. The clubs were how the music was going to reach the people.

MC Wickett Crickett "Most clubs wasn't *clubs* back in the '70s—all them were 'gyp joints.' They was cafes. They cafes was considered clubs. They didn't know about clubs. They didn't really know nothin' about big club scenes down here until they seen that shit in New York. Down here it was just cafes, because this was like a cowboy area. You know, everybody would be like *go western*. You wore cowboy hats, you went to the parade downtown, you could wear your little guns and stuff . . . I mean, it was a cowboy area in the beginning. They was proud of it."

Tommie Langston (Stickhorse Records) "Although it came around '79, '80, hip-hop was not big in Houston at all. We sold a lot of R&B—and when I say R&B I really do mean rhythm and blues as opposed to just the word 'R&B.' Rhythm and blues with *blues*. And this was really even prior to zydeco becoming a big thing in the greater Houston area. This was in the early stages of *that*, and hip-hop was really just taking a footing, because I remember a heck of a lot of customers—they had a definite *hatred* for hip-hop at that time. Quite a few customers who came to it had a big hatred for it, didn't wanna hear anything about, *That hippity-hop stuff, or whatever you call it.*"

Screw had arrived during the battle rap era, when young Houstonians were rapping against each other in the streets and the hallways of their schools, working their way up to the clubs. Rap battles were the first place they got to feel hip-hop in a communal setting, where the energy of the music could come to life. Black music, Black voices, Black stories, making Black history in the process. So much of the hip-hop experience then was wrapped up in the stories of New York and Los Angeles, but in Houston, they had something to say, and the stage was set for that to happen long before hip-hop.

Ray Barnett's clubs had been the hottest places in town for Houston's Black nightclub-going clientele since the late '60s. There was the Cinder Club, Baby Grand, Big Apple New York, Fantasia 5000, Screamin' Eagle, and eventually Club New Jack / Midnight Hour (which would be where Barnett and Screw connected). DJs were playing all kinds of music in his clubs, but mostly they were the place to *be*. By the time hip-hop came around, Barnett had been in business for over a decade, coming up alongside radio personality and KCOH DJ Skipper Lee Frazier, who was managing Archie Bell & the Drells and produced their 1968 hit "Tighten Up." Barnett and Frazier's era was taking off as Don Robey's Duke-Peacock empire came to a close. And though they were in different branches of the industry, with Robey releasing records and Barnett running nightclubs (though his partner, a young Kansas City native named Charles Bush, would go on to produce a number of records), they were equally instrumental in the development of Houston's musical legacy. Barnett started his enterprise in the late '60s, taking on Bush as a protégé (even sending him to business school), moving through trends in Houston nightlife with clubs all over lower Third Ward that became seminal gathering spots through the decades, no doubt influenced by Robey's Bronze Peacock Dinner Club era.

MC Wickett Crickett "Ray Barnett already had a stack of clubs that catered to the older people. The club scene been goin' on down here since they used to have the old Majestic Theatre. That's how far back they had clubs jumpin'. He had clubs when people were still goin' to the drive-in. Ray Barnett is the original godfather of Houston. He had at least ten different custom-made cars that I seen him in. You know, he had after hours, he was at all of the Rockets games. All of the original Rockets— Bobby Joe Reid and Allen Leavell and all them—they used to be at his spot around the '70s. That's when Ray Barnett was the main star. He had all the bread—he just didn't know how to keep his books. Charles Bush kept his books."

Darryl Scott "Ray Barnett was up and down OST [Old Spanish Trail], which was known as the Houston Strip. That's where *all* of the clubs were. And in all of the clubs they had a theme behind it, and that was all behind Ray Barnett's brilliant thinkin', man. He was a *genius*, but then for some folks they thought he was crazy. They didn't understand Ray Barnett, and the reason they didn't understand him is because he was actually—he was a walking enigma, is what he was. He spoke in codes, he spoke metaphorically. If you didn't understand those codes and those riddles and how he spoke metaphorically, you would miss what he was tryin' to say to you. You would have to be a thinkin' person to pick up on what he was *talkin'* about when he would say some of the things that he would *say*, and that's where that old sayin' comes from, *If you swing, you gon' ride.*"

On the Northside in the early 1980s it was a bearded white boy originally from Chicago named Steve Fournier who was flooding Houston's cow-boy-boot-filled dance floors with hip-hop. His family moved to Houston when he was a kid in the late '60s, and a decade later he was spinning funk records in the clubs, trying to slip in as much rap as he could. The club owners at Strut's Disco up near Aldine weren't hip, but Fournier charged forward enthusiastically, with "Catch the Beat" by Bronx rapper T-Ski Valley (who came up as an MC alongside hip-hop's originator DJ Kool Herc) and Kurtis Blow's "The Breaks" emerging as early favorites. In fact, Fournier liked "The Breaks" so much he ended up bringing the rapper to Strut's for Houston's first rap concert.

Kurtis Blow "What I remember is back in those days, Houston was a hick city. It was *Texas*! When you thought of Texas, you thought of the cowboy hats, and horses and steers, and all of that—farmland, chickens. But it had some urban qualities to it! I remember playing Strut's in 1980. It was packed, sold out. It's hard to explain the energy and vibe and spirit around the club, and around Houston, but the energy seemed as if it were an urban town. During that time, my whole thing was crowd response, and I was a *master* at call-and-response. My show—my live performances—would live or *die* if the crowd was not participating. When I'm like, *Say* HO! and they say, HO! If it's maybe about twenty-five people and there are five hundred people there, that's not cool. But the energy of Houston, I just remember the crowd being very, very loud, and havin' 1,200, 1,500 people: *Everybody scream!* You could hear that miles away. That was one of the things that stood out about Houston. They were always ready to party."

In 1981, things at Strut's came to an end, and Fournier went right to the next spot. A businessman from Louisiana had been driving around Houston, checking the parking lots of nightclubs to see who was pulling in the people. He owned a club called Boneshakers in the Rapides Parish city of Alexandria, and he wanted to open one in Houston. He was no fan of rap music, but he saw Fournier pack the place at Strut's and knew he was doing something right.

Fournier was on board, and he brought his crowd with him. Boneshakers was even bigger than Strut's, and he was allowed to play more hip-hop in his sets there. Club owners didn't understand rap and were slow to get behind it, so funk and dance records were still the foundation, but folks in Houston wanted to hear *everything*, and they were about to start hearing something from their own hometown.

MacGREGOR PARK

Darryl Scott grew up on Blodgett, near the area of Third Ward known as the Bottom. In the early '70s, his mother would take him to a record store that sold liquor (or a liquor store that sold records) called Obina's, where he would be allowed to purchase one album and four singles each week. The allowance had him soon amassing a collection that ran the range of funk, soul, R&B, disco, and anything that appeared for sale in that shop. He didn't know what some of the records even were—he just bought and played them. That was how he learned.

In middle school in the late '70s, Scott started making pause tapes, punching the buttons on his tape recorder with the timing and pressure to get the tape to stall exactly where he wanted it. If he released the record button in one deck at the same time as the play button in the other deck—or the needle on the turntable from which he was about to record—then there was no skip in the beat. You can believe a young

Darryl Scott got that part down. Then he'd mix in the next song, on beat, like he was counting for all of the moments between when he paused the tape and cued up the next song—wherever it was coming from—radio, vinyl, or another tape. He made his first mixtape on a bulky eight-track tape in elementary school. Scott pulled in sounds from everywhere, and made the relationship of turntables and tape central to his sound.

He got a job spinning at OST Skate World before he was even in high school, working with a guy named Disco Harold, who came from Ana-huac, Texas, and wasn't a DJ or necessarily into disco but *did* rent out gear, like the turntables Darryl already knew how to use. That got Darryl closer to the equipment, and in high school he started selling his mix-tapes, painstakingly running them off all night long one by one onto Memorex and JVC cassettes.

Those tapes sold. People bought them from him in school, they bought them out of his car, in the park, at the car wash, the barbershop, or anywhere in town they found him. Neither his DJ sets nor his tapes were exclusively rap—Scott trafficked in heavy funk and dance party tracks—but folks associated him with hip-hop because he adopted it right away, seamlessly blending the new genre into his own mixes. That was the first place a lot of Houstonians ever heard hip-hop. Before Scott was finished with high school, he was already being courted by local club owners—including Ray Barnett.

Darryl Scott "All of the club owners had a price war with me because they knew wherever I went, that's where the crowd was goin'. Finally it got to a point that when they feel like the crowd came and *they* got 'em there, and that they can start talkin' to me kinda crazy. And then I'd leave! I'd take off a couple of weeks. That would be the first in weeks I was just free for a minute. Then I'll pop up somewhere else. It didn't matter. Wherever I popped up—I don't care if it was a hole-in-the-wall, terrible parking, whatever the case may be—*boomf!* There they come. They're just *there*, and it almost shut 'em down, and so they'd end up rasslin' and beggin' and goin' back and forth, fightin' over who's gon' get me, until finally they'll be like, *We can't pay you anymore.* Well, *Hey, I can't do it anymore. I have to move on.* And then I move on to the next, and they end up closin' down. After the skating rink closed down, Ray thought he had me! He's like, *I got him now! He can't go nowhere!* Like, *Maan, I got the whole* city! *Whatchu talkin' about?*"

By the time he graduated from Third Ward's Yates High School in 1982, his mixtape hustle had grown lucrative. What had started as Scott running off tapes for classmates had turned into a cycle of demand that far exceeded what he could produce. Scott was still in the clubs, as was his protégé Walter D, but his mixtapes were getting so hot that he couldn't satisfy demand. He would make a new mix, run off dozens of them on a good night, and they'd sell out so fast he'd often have people offering him double for his tapes—a deal he was all too happy to accommodate. Scott was also hauling a big sound system out to MacGregor Park every Sunday, drawing a caravan of cars to the Southside park.

In the summer of 1984, Scott was spinning at a club called the Plaza Room in a small strip mall in South Park, the primarily Black Southside neighborhood full of World War II–themed streets that got its name from its location south of MacGregor Park. The Plaza Room gig was short-lived, but for Scott's career it was a major breakthrough because that shopping center at 4977 MLK soon had an empty store available.

So in late 1984, a few doors down from where he'd been deejaying, Scott opened his own record shop, Blast Records & Tapes. Of course he would sell new releases, but he also knew that the main attraction to his shop was going to be those mixtapes. D. Scott Blasts were the currency, both a doorway into and a building block of the culture in mid-'80s Houston, and folks were inspired. A young Black man had opened his own business right down the street from where he grew up, and he was able to do so from spinning records and making tapes for the people of Houston. Rap was real.

More proof of that arrived in 1985 with "MacGregor Park," a seven-inch single by an artist who called himself the L.A. Rapper but whom everybody knew as the South Park Rapper. Robert Harlan was from South Park, so it was no surprise that the first hip-hop song *about* Houston referenced the big park to its north: "MacGregor Park / Is where I got to be / MacGregor Park / My car, my freak, and me / MacGregor Park / There ain't *no* time to waste / MacGregor Park / 'Cuz on Sundays it's the place!" Old-school vocal phrasing, fat beats and wailing guitars, electronic dog barks. And on the cover, there he was, mustache and striped sunglasses, the first visual representation of Houston hip-hop on the cover of a record, cartoon-drawn in blue with white clouds floating through a yellow sky. Houston rap music was on the shelves.

There were a few records out in H-Town before that. The earliest by all accounts was a seven-inch cut in 1981 by a couple of New Yorkers, Colin Bucknor and Robert Harkness, who were attending Texas Southern University. They called themselves Brother's Disco, and the single was called "Thumpin." That was the outlier in a scene where the clubs were always full, but local hip-hop wouldn't come alive again on wax until 1984, when Fourth Ward's Jazzie Redd recorded a single with Steve Cummings's funk band Chance, and the veteran Houston club MC Captain Jack released his theme song "Jack It Up," an electro-infused twelve-inch party single that is part of Jack's rich legacy as a relentless promoter of the art form. In 1985, SDR Records, which had put out "MacGregor Park," released a twelve-inch called "Space City Rock" from the Royal Style Force, and Mel Owens of the Houston funk group Perfect Timin' dropped a single called "Don't Stand (Me Up)" that sounded like it could have been recorded in New York. There was no Houston sound yet, but the voices were out there.

HOUSTON RAP ATTACK

In 1986, folks had other ways to hear hip-hop in Houston. On Saturday mornings, if Screw got up early enough, he could tune his radio to 90.9 FM and pick up KTSU out of Texas Southern University in Third Ward. It started as a jazz station in 1972 but by the early '80s was broadcasting Houston's first all-hip-hop radio show, featuring a group of young musically minded folks who would go on to do their own work in the genre of hip-hop and beyond.

Lester Pace went to high school at M. B. Smiley on the Northside, where he was rapping in a group with Thelton Polk (who called himself Sir Rap-A-Lot), and a couple of other guys, Anthony Watson and Melvin Dewalt. The group was called CC Gang. Thelton would go on to become one of the original Ghetto Boys, but Lester's voice stuck out for another reason.

Lester "Sir" Pace "At the end part of my junior year, this lady heard me doin' the morning announcements and thought I should be a DJ on the radio. She knew this lady named Pam Collins over at KTSU. Pam had the show called *Kidz Jamm*, and they would allow young people and kids in high school to come and operate the radio station on Saturdays from ten to two. So on Saturdays, I got off work at McDonald's and I'd go over there and we kids ran the radio station! Stacy Porter, Charles Porter, Michael Mitchell—there was a lot of kids there runnin' the radio station. At that time, the music they was playin' was R&B. They didn't play no rap music. But I was rappin', so I was into rap music! I had the opportunity to be behind the board and play more music, so I start playin' the rap music, and Pam, who was the program director, called me on the phone and kinda chewed me out and told me, *Quit playin' that rap music!* And you know, nobody wanna get into it with Pam, so I'll play a couple of R&B songs and then I'll put another rap song on. So we had this one show that came on—like, we were on from ten to two—so at twelve o'clock we had a show called *Be Yourself*, which was a talk show for kids from twelve to one where we talk about different subjects. So we just kept havin' this debate about the kids wantin' to hear more rap music, so we took a tally to see if they wanted more rap music or more R&B, and that time the votes came back and people said, *More rap music!* And Pam let me go with it. *Kidz Jamm*—it was already born, but that was the birth of *real* hip-hop bein' on the radio in Houston."

Screw knew Lester's voice, and the other voices on the show, too, because it was tapes of *Kidz Jamm* that his sister's friend D.W. Sound had brought back to the country from Houston years earlier. Lester "Sir" Pace and Walter D were some of the first DJs from Houston that Screw ever heard mixing, and the voices of Jazzie Redd, O.G. Style, and MC Wickett Crickett were the first voices he would have heard freestyling. Now he could hear them live on the radio, and the whole city was listening along with him.

Lester "Sir" Pace "One Saturday I forgot to hit the button for the record to be played at 45 and it started off at 33, and it was slowed down. So, when it went on the air, I couldn't stop it! We just kinda let it play, right?

It was by accident, but the next time, when we sped it up and started playin' it, we had so many people calling saying, *Man! Play 'Fresh Is the Word' again slowed down! We want it slowed down!* So anytime we would play that record, it was always played at slow pace."

In the clubs, Darryl Scott made the same oversight and went ahead and left his turntable spinning on 33⅓ rpm, too. The crowd ate it up. For Houston, nothing quite stuck like that song at that speed in that era. Scott would later mix slowed-down versions of Mantronix's "Fresh Is the Word" and "White Horse" by the Danish electronic duo Laid Back onto what became his best-known mixtape, 33½.

As *Kidz Jamm* was getting its footing, Steve Fournier's tenure at Bone-shakers was coming to an end when he was approached about turning an empty Southside dance hall into a moneymaking nightclub. A local businessman offered Fournier full reign of a former honky-tonk in the shadow of the Astrodome called Rhinestone Wrangler, and the DJ readily accepted, bringing with him fellow DJ RP Cola and promoter Big Steve (not to be confused with the late rapper of the same name). Fournier had the owner replace the mirrored walls with drywall and put a railing around the in-the-round-style dance floor, and Rhinestone Wrangler was born anew as Houston's first all-rap nightclub. The owner let them do as they wished, kept the lights on, and made his money. The place was packed every night.

On Sundays, Fournier held the Rap Attack Contest, and the first local names began to emerge: Romeo Poet, Willie D, Royal Flush (Rick Royal, Albee, Class-C, Sergio, Cowboy, Tricky-T), Born 2wice. James Prince was watching, and the roots of Rap-A-Lot Records were forming in Fifth Ward. The early Ghetto Boys, even if they weren't all battle rapping, were in the clubs, too. Bushwick Bill was a dancer then. DJ Ready Red was out in the clubs. Lots of East Coast transplants became rappers in Houston. Ricky Royal was one of them. Prince Johnny C was another. Everybody came through the Rhinestone.

For the Rap Attack, Fournier was the MC, and RP would spin instrumentals for the rappers while Big Steve would watch out for people cussing, and the winner would come away with a hundred bucks. The skill levels of the rappers either grew exponentially every week or they were crushed and never came back. Careers were established and obliviated on that dance floor. The money came with winning the Rap Attack Contest, but the real street prestige came *afterward*, from winning the ranking, or cap rapping contest, at the end of the night. One repeat offender was Fifth Ward's own Willie D, the future Geto Boy and voice of the South whose influence can still be heard in rap today. Fournier watched him win that contest thirteen weeks in a row. Styles were born, respect was earned. Pretenders fell off and found other paths. Battle rapping was the boot camp for Houston's original crop of rappers, and the way the crowd was immersed in the experience influenced Houston culture going forward.

THE MEADOWS

After Screw's dad and his girlfriend had broken up, he and Screw moved to just south of Fuqua near Monroe Boulevard. On a map, the neighborhood is technically called Skyscraper Shadows, but everybody in Screw's orbit called it Gulf Meadows because of the north-south street running parallel to Telephone Road. Screw went to South Houston for the eighth grade, and they lived in a one-story brick house of their own on Gulfwood Lane, where he had plenty of space to set up his gear.

Larry B "We kept in contact with Screw. Really, the first year he was in Houston, he was just doin' his thing. His daddy was pushin' him to go to finish school, to get a job, be responsible, but *nothin'* overpowered his mind but that music. His daddy used to tell him, *Boy, that music is not gonna ever get you nothin'. You should leave that music alone, that ol' stuff y'all listenin' to.* He would talk bad to him, too. Screw would have his face down, but he wouldn't let it discourage him."

Shorty Mac "Like, you hang around other people, but they not the same people like Larry and Screw was. I don't think I even got *close* to nobody else like that. Like, we *cool*, but me and Larry—me, Larry, and Screw—we've never had an argument, we never had a fight with each other. We never bumped heads, and that's what I be tellin' my son. I said, *I don't know about y'all, but for me—if you get into with somebody, then that's not your best friend, to me. Because your best friend—y'all might get into a* *whole bunch of trouble together, but they gonna be there with you, and y'all both gonna get in that trouble, or y'all both not gonna get in trouble. One of y'all gonna talk e'rebody out of it.* Like, *Naw, let's not do that.* Like, that's how it *was.* Like, if we was gonna get in trouble . . . all three of us would be walkin' around, and we might just go next door, knockin' on people door and takin' off runnin'. And back then everybody had tin roofs, so if we didn't wanna do that, e'rebody pick up rocks and we hit your tin roof and take out runnin'. Like, either we all was doin' it or we all *wasn't.* But that's why I say Screw shoulda ran track. He didn't run in Smithville, and that's probably one of the things he was better at. Screw could beat me runnin' by at least fifteen yards."

Big Bubb "I know he ran track at the middle school he went to out there. I think it was just called South Houston. He ran track. Yeah, Screw used to run track! Screw faster'na motherfucker."

Al-D (friend from high school) "I said, *You wanna race?* He said, *Al, you can't fuck with me.* And me, myself, I was point guard in basketball, real athletic, runnin' every day and shit like that, so I said, *I'ma smoke this lil dude, man.* Say man, Screw *smoked* me, man. I could not fucking believe. That lil short motherfucker—when I tell you he smoked me, this lil motherfucker *Jesse Owened* my motherfuckin' ass. He was *gone!*"

By 1988, Screw was spending more time spinning records than he was running track, and that was when he started meeting folks who lived in Quail Meadows, a two-story apartment complex a couple of miles up Telephone Road. The surrounding area was a middle-class neighborhood of one-story houses built in the '50s and '60s, flanked by open prairie land and air traffic, with Quail Meadows off to the side. But the complex was very much the center of its own universe, with hundreds of units stretching three full city blocks, and the residents of that complex were some of the first people in Houston Screw connected with over music. One of them was a guy named Toe, who would later be the first person to buy a tape from Screw.

Toe (neighbor, Quail Meadows) "I went to Screw house in Gulf Meadows before. My homeboy Johnny Durio lived across the street from him, and we went in there and went and looked at his DJ equipment and stuff like that, and you know, he had a lil Mickey Mouse turntable with one of the old-school turntables, somethin' like that. So that was like his setup at the time. That was my first time meetin' him."

Bernard Barnes (neighbor, Quail Meadows) "He was perfectin' his craft really. I used to DJ myself, and then a buddy of mine, you know, he turned me on to him. He was a DJ also, so he said, *Man, we need to go check this guy out.* So we went over off of Coastway, and his equipment was like—how could you do this on this type of equipment? It wasn't professional—it was like real just . . . just a turntable, he had like nickels and change all over the arms, keep it from jumpin'. You know—he was just smart! He had all kinda old amps and one big eighteen-inch woofer in there. It was a little crazy. You'd see all the guts of the equipment and everything, but he was ahead of his time! You'd watch him just like, wow—*this dude is amazing!* So after I got to dealin' with him and, you know, he teach me this and that, I'm like, *Man, look—you can have some of my stuff.* Because my stuff was a little better. It wasn't professional or nothin', but I was like, *You can have my stuff, my records, and I'll just come over here when I wanna do a lil somethin'.*"

GHETTO BOYS! GETO BOYS!

After Screw got to Houston, the Rhinestone Wrangler on Murworth eventually ran its course, moving north to West Parker Road, near Acres Homes. The new club had a few names—Ultimate Rhinestone Wrangler, Rhinestone Wrangler II, and even Rhinestone Rangler—but plenty of folks just kept calling it the Rhinestone. In 1988, a number of touring acts came to play there—Ice-T, De La Soul, Big Daddy Kane, Stetsasonic, Public Enemy, and N.W.A among them—and the crowds overflowed like they had before. Steve Fournier was still promoting at the new spot, having started up his Rap Pool of America to service DJs around the country with hip-hop records. Captain Jack took his crowd to a club called the Bends. Darryl Scott kept making his way through clubs all over town and holding it down at Blast, issuing classic Houston mixtapes like *D. Scott*

Blast 19½ and *8 on the Double*. Going into the '90s there was *still* nothing hotter than a D. Scott tape.

Meanwhile, the new Rhinestone served as a sort of home base for Rap-A-Lot. The scene that had developed in the original Southside club had gone to wax, with the Ghetto Boys, Raheem, and Royal Flush all releasing records by 1988. Raheem was signed to a major, but almost every other hip-hop record in Houston was coming out on Rap-A-Lot. The label was the brainchild of Fifth Ward's James Prince, who owned a used-car lot on Nineteenth and North Shepherd in the Heights and started the label because of a pledge he made to his younger brother Thelton (Sir Rap-A-Lot, from the early group with Lester "Sir" Pace) and a couple of his high school classmates that if they graduated, he would produce and release a record for them. Prince made good on the deal, and thus was born the Ghetto Boys, whose primary MC's name was swept out from under him when Lil' J (Prince) took it for the label instead. Sir Rap-A-Lot became K-9, the label became Rap-A-Lot Records, and Lil' J's first release was the Ghetto Boys twelve-inch "Car Freak," in 1987, produced by Mikki Bleu (or Johnnie Boy), who had written and produced countless funk, R&B, and proto-rap records for artists all over Houston.

In the years following, the group's lineup evolved, with members including Sire Jukebox, Prince Johnny C, Raheem, Grand Wizard DJ Ready Red, and Bushwick Bill. By 1989, the group would drop everybody but Bushwick and Ready Red, taking on Willie D and South Acres' own DJ Akshen (who soon after joining became known as Scarface) to complete a lineup that was more geared to where hip-hop was going nationally. Rick Rubin got involved. The name changed from Ghetto Boys to Geto Boys, and the things they were talking about in those songs were about to get a lot darker, with one theme being the shift between the hustles of the drug trade and label ownership—as was evident in Scarface's relationship with his first label and his new home at Rap-A-Lot.

Lil' Troy (Short Stop Records) "I *had* money. That's why I wasn't worried about when Lil' James came and asked me about he wanted Scarface to be the new Geto Boy. I was makin' so much money in the streets, it didn't make a difference! I let him have Scarface, and he told me he'd do something for me later in life or we'll make somethin' happen together.

It never came to be, but I didn't care 'cuz I was movin' so much work. Rappin' wasn't makin' no money right then at the time. We was just doin' that as a hobby."

Crack cocaine had appeared on Houston streets as early as 1981. By the late '80s, it had produced such a level of panic in the city that the local Fox channel created a stand-alone news program called *City Under Siege* (an early predecessor and inspiration for the TV show *Cops*), the title of which became a Geto Boys song a few years later. When Scarface rapped, "Born in the ghetto as a street thug / At age sixteen I started sellin' cheap drugs / Ecstasy will cost you three / A year later I robbed a dope house and stole a ki," he made it known that the landscape was changing.

While Screw's life was still unfolding—his new living arrangements, the absence of his father when he was away driving trucks, new schools, new friends, new neighborhoods—something else had been simmering in the streets. Like many American cities in the late 1980s, Houston was weathering changes to its inner-city communities. It was the last of his generation's innocence. Crack was the catalyst for an awakening of what was going on in the neighborhoods, and it was coming alive in the music. A new era of gangsta rap was about to explode, and Screw's ears were tuned to what it was going to sound like.

4. 10201
1989

Robert Sr. was still driving for the same company he'd been working at since Screw was a kid, maintaining a base right near his Southside employer all the while. As long as he was on the road for a living, Robert didn't waste time with a long commute, and that's how he and Screw ended up moving a mile up the road from Gulf Meadows into the big complex at 10201 Telephone Road. A hundred cars line the back fence that separates Quail Meadows from the streets behind it, and that was a line between two worlds. Screw and his dad had been living in a one-story brick house in Gulf Meadows. In Quail Meadows, they were in a small apartment, together, in close proximity to a few people they knew and hundreds more they didn't. Screw's half brother Charles's mother, Christine, stayed with them for a spell, but mostly for Screw it was about him meeting a lot of new people.

Screw started ninth grade in 1987 at Sterling High School in South Park, and for one of his classes he had a teacher named Coach Bull. One day in his class a skinny kid with a big mouth named Albert Driver showed up and *immediately* got Screw into trouble with him. Everybody remembers Screw being pretty quiet in school, but Driver was the opposite, with a live personality he was destined to turn into something. To that end, he called himself Al-D, and Screw started calling Al-D his little brother.

Al-D "We kept gettin' kicked out the fuckin' classes because I had him laughin' in the class. I was drawin' pictures of my cousin and shit, and man, Screw wouldn't shut up because I was crackin' jokes and he was tryin' to hold his breath and shit. His face was all fat and the teacher would look at him and he had tears rollin' down his eyes."

Some of Screw's fellow students were then on their way to becoming artists. K-Rino (Eric Kaiser), Point Blank (Reginald Gilliland), and Klondike Kat (Andre Parish)—all of whom would go on to form the Southside rap collective South Park Coalition—were at Sterling. The battle-rap era of the Rhinestone had passed, but they were all still battling in the hallways of their high schools. Others were starting to DJ, at house parties, the roller rink, or at the dances at St. Francis. Everybody went to AstroWorld. There was also another turntablist at Sterling, Andrew Hatton, who went by DJ Chill.

DJ Chill "I met him through Al-D, because I had wanted to learn how to scratch. But I was already doin' like little parties, so whatever party that I was doin', I incorporated him into it. I had the skating rink on the southwest side when I was probably like about sixteen, but I'm doin' house parties and school parties like Sterling, Hartman Middle School, Attucks . . . whenever somebody had a party after a game or something. Because I had more equipment than he did. Once we came together as a team, we shared the majority of everything."

K-Rino (as told to Jason Culberson for *Screwville*) "I think I was in like the eleventh grade when Screw was in the ninth. We was at Sterling and he was DJ Screw from the first day I met him. That's what he always called himself, just messin' around on the tables like a normal DJ. He wasn't even slowin' it down or nothin' like that back then. We used to battle rap in the corners and hallways and he would be one of the people that'll be in the crowd, just checkin' it out, and he used to always just be like showin' me love and just like, you know, givin' me props or whatever. And we just got cool, you know, because he was that kind of dude. He was cool, laid back, humble dude."

It was Al-D who would have the most immediate musical impact. He and Screw were friends from the moment they met, but it was music that turned that connection into a bond. He started coming over to the apartment at Quail Meadows, and while DJ Screw worked at the turntables and made mixtapes, Al-D Tha Lion practiced his craft as a rapper alongside him, working on songs together. At first, they called themselves Criminal Alliance. Def Rock and Sexy Chocolate were the other guys who eventually joined them, and later the group would become known as Hard, Black, and Untouchable.

Al-D "We used to catch the yellow bus out to Quail Meadows so we could do our music. If not, shit, I was walkin' eight, nine, ten miles to get to him. I *walked* to him. I would walk from South Park all the way to fuckin' Quail Meadows. Quail Meadows. Apartment 100, man. I used to walk all this way from this area *all* the way over there just to do music, man. Just to do music, and go to sleep up under the turntables. He taught me everything I know. See, when we started out here, he had *one* turntable. A Technic, man, and it wasn't even a 1200. It was raggedy as hell. He didn't have nothing but one speaker. So I started takin' Mom's equipment and shit. She just started noticin' speakers and shit started comin' up missin', mixers and shit. And she was like, *Where's the fuckin'... where's my fuckin' music goin'?*"

3-4 ACTION

The first crew in Houston to form around DJ Screw was based at Quail Meadows. There was Toe, Bernard Barnes, T-Road, Jade Caballero, Ray Holmes III, Jay Questo, Mike Henry, Freddie McFly, Gabriel Scott, Brock, and K. Venable (Back Doe), whose nearby Honeycomb Hideout house was another gathering spot. The larger group was called 10201 ("ten-two-oh-one"), or 10201 Young Gunz, and there was a smaller crew within that called 3-4 Action—which included Nate "Poppy" Ellis and his cousin Frank Popa Watts. Bernard, Big Chance, and Back Doe would later record as 10201, releasing a song called "I Love These Streets." Collectively, all of them formed Screw's earliest support network in Houston.

Al-D "The guys that was around him from the beginning, man, they was gangsters. They was not playin' no games, man. That's what Screw had around him. It was past music, man. It was no battlin' on a microphone or music and shit like that. Nobody wanted to talk shit because the people that was around him would hammer you, man!"

Frank Popa Watts "Poppy brought everybody together. He brought everybody from the North to the Southside every year to do them shows, and it was *big*, you know what I'm sayin'? And Poppy done it single-handedly. Poppy had the juice! That's my cousin, but Poppy got the juice on the Southside! Poppy brought everybody together with Screw. Poppy is the glue. Like right now Poppy can do somethin' and call everybody and everybody gonna come from the North to the South. Poppy brought everybody together. I'm talkin' 'bout that block party every year. Everybody perform and then everybody came through. I don't know how he still do it but Poppy got somethin' in him . . . man, Poppy got some type of formula! He just know how to—everybody just gravitate towards Poppy, man."

Big Bubb "All of them niggas over there done took Screw in with open arms. After a while, *e'rebody* over there would ride for him. When he went over there, he had a group of soldiers that embraced him. They all came for Screw. Especially when he had his own apartment downstairs? Aw, man, it was the spot to come to, to get away, to make a tape, to just chill out, know'm sayin'? And they all embraced him, and I love that. I seen that he was in good hands over there. You know, as far as *caring*, aside from his kinfolk. He used to lace me up on different shit. There wasn't no way he could tell me about everythang that went on over there, but he'll tell me about certain shit, and I'd be like, *God damn, for real for real?*"

Al-D "There was two cops named Best and Brooks. White guys. Best kicked one of Pop-pop's teeth out of his mouth. When you would see that cop, he used to have a key ring with gold teeth on his fuckin' key ring. Yeah, man! He was a motherfucker. Everybody knew Best and Brooks. If you were in the southeast side or South Park, you knew Best and Brooks.

Two badass fuckin' cops. They used to *whoop your motherfuckin' ass*, and they *stayed* in Quail Meadows bustin' dudes."

Knock (Herschelwood Hardheadz) "The police *stayed* over there! You know, Poppy and them was doin' they thang over there. They had it fired up over there. They was makin' a lot of money over there! They had all the slabs and stuff over there. You know, Quail Meadows used to be a known lil spot. So, when Screw came from out of town and came right there, he came to a boomin' spot, which was a good thing for him because he was able to meet somebody who was connected to the streets. If he just would have went to a regular apartment complex, he pro'ly wouldn't have got on or met as many people as he met right then. By him goin' to Quail Meadows, and hookin' up with Poppy and all them—like I say, we was just claimin' the Southside then. We all had our own neighborhoods we was claimin', but you know, that's when that Southside-Northside beef was goin' on, so pretty much e'rebody on the Southside was connected with each other. He slid right in."

Robert Earl Davis Sr. (as told to Michael Hall) "When I'd leave home, I wouldn't worry about him bein' on the street. I knew he'd be in his room playin' his music, making his tapes."

Big Bubb "My dad and Screw daddy were brothers. There was a bunch of uncles, and all of 'em came with a pool game. But Uncle Robert carried the meanest stick of all them. He was e'rebody's favorite uncle."

Al-D "Pops always treated me like a son. I been callin' him Pops since the day that we first got together. He didn't like nobody else around, I can tell you that. But he knew that me and Screw was inseparable, you know what I'm sayin'?"

Toe "His old man was pretty cool, though. His old man used to work. He didn't give us too much problems. You know, we wanted to be outside anyway. At Quail Meadows, we wanted to see what was goin' on, so we'd go to Screw house and maybe shoot some dice, somethin' like that for a little bit in the kitchen. But you know, Screw daddy used to shoot dice, too. So you know, his Daddy come in and he see us shootin' dice, he'll shake up his dice and start shootin'. He'll hit you, too! He'll make you be like . . . he used to hit a little *too* hard, to where you don't even wanna face Screw daddy. He knew somethin' slick. You could tell. We stopped puttin' our money out in front of him so he would start leavin' us alone."

Al-D "I'll never forget—I walked all the way to Quail Meadows, man. I had eight hundred and somethin' dollars on me, and I went over there, and Screw say, *Let's get on these dice.* He say, *Man, Al, I'm tellin' you—I love you, you my bro. But man, gamblin' is gamblin'. If you lose, you lose.* He took eight hundred dollars from me, bro. Screw got me for eight hundred fuckin' dollars. He taught me a motherfuckin' *lesson.* I never played dice again after that. He taught me not to fuck with him on the fuckin' dice!"

Nikki Williams "When I first met Screw, he was at his dad's house, and his dad was drivin' trucks at night. Screw literally—there would be times when Screw didn't have food to eat."

Ms. Patricia (Al-D's mother) "I know that Screw was a lot of times left alone in that apartment. His daddy was truck driver and he worked and stuff like that, and he was kinda left a lot of times like . . . without *food*! And I used to come home—when I used to stay somewhere else—I used to come home and in my refrigerator . . . *Who ate up all this food? Where is this food goin'? Who y'all havin' over?* Come to find out *he* was goin' in my refrigerator. I used to make gumbo, a lot of gumbo, and I said, *Oh no. I'm gonna find out who's coming over here in the daytime, eatin' up all this food.* Come to find out Al would get him a bag, a sack or whatever, and just fill it up with food, put it on his back and walk to wherever Screw was in them apartments!"

Screw was held back in ninth grade and then dropped out of Sterling in March of 1990, before the end of his tenth-grade year. He got a job sacking groceries at Rice Food Market just down Telephone Road, where his friend Keith Venable worked, too, and they both learned how to make money cutting hair. And of course, there was the deejaying. With his father away on the road a lot of the time, Screw had plenty of time alone in the apartment to practice.

AI-D "He was hustlin' a little bit and he had a connect at the store where he knew this chick inside of there, and that's where he got his groceries and shit. She'd let him go through the line and shit and get his groceries for free. Had a big-ass box of chicken to last the whole week. I was takin' gumbo from the house. Mama had to wrestle me off. I was takin' big pickle jars of gumbo out the house. That's how we were survivin' back then! Sugar with the rice and sugar on the corn. Man, pork chops and chicken. That's all it was! That's all we had. We was at Sterling with free lunch cards, you know what I'm sayin'? It go *that* deep. Free lunch cards! Ridin' the bus from school back to the house, I'm talkin' 'bout when we go home I catch the bus right there to Quail Meadows with it to get on the music."

WHITE INSIDES

Whatever money came into Screw's hands, he spent it at the record stores. Of course there was Darryl Scott's Blast Records & Tapes, but he also got rides to Soundwaves on South Main and to the one over by the airport, too, and if he followed Main Street far enough north, there was a Soundwaves at Westheimer and Montrose. Serious Sounds wasn't open yet, but Big O Records was, there was Gil's Records & Tapes on Almeda, and of course, Stickhorse on Cullen Boulevard, which had been around longer than all of those.

Tommie Langston "He was a customer coming in purchasing records, as a DJ. He would come in quite often, and from time to time we would have bins full of a whole lot of cutouts and a lot of other type records in there and, you know, he would wanna spend hours and hours of goin' through that stuff. And anything that we got in new, he would wanna go through it and grab what he could use as far as his DJ work, and be able to do that. This was early in his deejaying career."

Screw was making mixtapes mostly for people he knew, but an expanding record collection meant those tapes were evolving along with his musical knowledge. Screw was growing up—folks always change when they leave their hometown—but he never lost touch with home for long. Back in Smithville, Red showed up at the high school one day to give Shorty Mac a new phone number for Screw.

Shorty Mac "I called him and he told me that he wanted me to come up there. I waited until after I graduated and I came up there that summer and he was in Quail Meadows. I went up there and I chilled, spent the day with him and we actually made a tape! But it wasn't slowed down. We just done like we used to do when we was kids."

Tyrone (Herschelwood) "By him goin' over there, my homeboy Toe, they used to be out there grindin', you know, runnin' around the whole Quail Meadows and shit, so we used to be over there, you know, just blowin' and kickin', you know what I'm sayin', lettin' a nigga grind and shit. Just so happened that nigga had moved over there. You know how you be runnin' around apartments, but *now* when you runnin' around them hos, you hear some scratchin'! Nigga got the door open and playin' music, so shit . . . you like, *Well fuck it! We gon' start postin' up right here!* So niggas just start postin' up by wherever that nigga playin' that music!"

Toe "The first tapes, he started with the funk. That 'Jamaica Funk,' some of that Earth, Wind & Fire, some 'Computer Love.' A lot of the old funk, whether it was Roger Troutman or Funkadelic, George Clinton, anything with that type of funk back then. 'Sugar Free' in the sun, all that type of stuff—funk, R&B. So he introduced us to a lot of that stuff that people sampled—or started samplin', like if he would have been a producer, he would have been findin' a lot of those samples and stuff like that. He used to start with a lot of R&B funk that a lot of the rap artists end up samplin' later on, even after Screw put 'em on Screw tapes."

The first tape Screw sold to Toe in 1990 was called "White Insides," referring to custom leather car interiors. Every tape might not have had a name on it before that, but every tape had a name on it after that, even if it was Screw himself who just made it up as he wrote it. He put his phone number on there, and also started writing FOOL in the top right corner in a nod to the crew S.A. Fools. When word got out that you could buy a custom mixtape right there in apartment 100, people started making lists of the songs they wanted to hear, and when he got too many of those lists, Screw started stacking them in a shoebox.

Toe "Him and Poppy end up gettin' close, and Poppy the first one I end up listenin' to a Screw tape with. We was at Poppy house, chillin', listenin' to music and stuff, and you know Screw had came on the mic and had said somethin' to him. You know, they used to play about each other mamas and stuff like that, so he was like, he was tellin' Poppy, *This is a story about Grace.* Poppy mom named Grace. There was that 2 Live Crew song, 'One and one / We're havin' some fun,' and they just had me *laughin'!* We probably was . . . what, sixteen, seventeen?"

Ray Holmes III (Quail Meadows) "I was in middle school, and I remember my buddy John Jenkins—he's no longer with us—RIP. He was the one that really around me knew Screw best. He was the one that basically was like, *Hey look, it's these new tapes—they's DJ tapes. Mixtapes people are listenin' to, like, cats listenin' to around the hood, man, you know?* And I was like, *Man, what are you talkin' about?* And he just kinda like slowed down, like he was tryin' to kinda explain it to me. You know, when you first tell somebody somethin' about the concept of slowin' music down, everybody's kinda like, *Huh? What?* You know what I'm sayin'? But that is what everybody that *we* knew in our little pocket, in our own little Quail Meadows, Telephone Road, 10201 section, what the *older* cats was listenin' to. And so that's how I kinda came into it. See, Screw was the DJ at the neighborhood skate rink. That's when I first seen him. You know, all my homeboys like, *That's Screw there!* He was the DJ on Sundays at the neighborhood skatin' rink."

ALMEDA

Screw had been playing house parties with his cousin Big Bubb and DJ Chill, but he was still yet to get a *job* spinning records. The story goes that MC Wickett Crickett got Screw his first DJ gig, which is likely, considering how many artists the legendary MC gave an early break. But Screw's first consistent gig spinning records happened when he was seventeen years old, after he met Ronnie Spencer, a fellow DJ and a singer who spun at the skate rink near the South Belt.

Ronnie Spencer "Almeda Skate Rink. It was called 'the Rink,' and I played a lot of music and deejayed there. After a while I turned it over to Screw. He took over and I started in my music career."

King Bo (Gulf Meadows) "Back at the skatin' rink, you know, that was when we was all gettin' off the porch, you hear me? So when it got later into the '90s, man, we was all buck wild. E'rebody spirit changed, you feel me? After all the drugs, everything changed. The music changed with the mind. You still like today these guys with the lil tempo, beat tempo and all that. There wasn't no beat tempo! It was in his head!"

Chris Cooley (cousin) "I remember goin' to the skatin' rink, walkin' with him, carryin' a box full of records, girls coming up to us, complaining about the slow music. All the guys loved it. Women finally caught on."

Big Bubb "Screw would take one of them old songs and mix it with an instrumental and get to scratchin', or he might just play an instrumental where he just scratchin', the whole party—e'rebody be on the floor. And then Screw knew how to *groove* shit that *kept* 'em on the floor. See, I could brang 'em to the floor. They'll pro'ly dance one or two songs if I play two *good* ones back to back, but Screw could play two *old* motherfuckers and have them out there sweatin' and shit, you feel me? He was always special. He had a different ear than most. His thought pattern was different."

Heat Houston (10201) "I was only in the seventh grade when he first started goin' up there. So, we would stand at the DJ booth because the skating rink—the reason why it was so popular for youths was because it would be a skating rink until . . . well, the doors opened at like seven on a Friday, Saturday night, and we would skate 'em about *nine,* and then about nine o'clock, man, Screw would turn off the regular skatin' music, you know, bounce, skate, roll, all that kinda stuff. And he'd actually go into a club *DJ* mode, and all the kids would take their roller skates off, and we would run out to the floor—and it was a dance floor! They would convert the roller-skating rink into a dance floor, man. And Screw would be up there in the booth, doin' his records, and at that time he had one turntable and two cassette decks, you know what I'm sayin'? He was *workin'* that up in there, man. And we were jamming. We were like twelve, thirteen. Screw was probably seventeen. But *that's* where his inspiration dawned on me, man. In that booth, just sittin' there just watchin' him, just admirin' him. Because my grandfather was a big-time DJ in Bryan–College Station, Texas, and so it was in my blood. But when I met Screw, he took it to another level."

IMG/NATION

Almeda Skating Rink put Screw out there. People were paying attention to the sounds he was making, and they got out there and danced—or skated. These were his first real experiences rocking a crowd, beyond the house parties. His tapes were reaching folks, too, taking his music somewhere he couldn't actually be himself—especially considering he was spending the bulk of his time in the apartment, working on the turntables. But in 1990, the first people to have him work on a recording project came from inside the house, as it were—from Sterling High School. In the midst of all the battle rappers there at the school were a couple of artists from South Park, Julian Washington and Shawn Austin, who had formed a group called Legion of Doom.

Initially, L.O.D. went by the names DJ Ice Cream and Trouble House, but as Ice Cream transitioned over into an MC, renaming himself Great Black Shark, they started looking for someone else to take over duties on the wheels. Legion of Doom went through a few prospective turntablists before they got connected with a local businessman and music aficionado named Charles Washington, who had a lot of ambition for promoting local music.

Charles Washington "Back then records were basically the MCs and the DJ, but the DJ was the main part of the show. We didn't know anything about the music business as far as how to put this company together, so all we was concentratin' on was goin' into a studio, and puttin' some songs together. But we knew we needed a DJ, and once we started doin' live shows, you know. A friend of mine, he was like, *I know a DJ. He's pretty good, too.* I said, *Okay, well, who is he?* He said, *His name is DJ Screw.* I called Screw and told him what the deal was, that I had a group and we needed a DJ. He was like, *Well, come and see me.* That was at 10201, Quail Meadows, in apartment 100 at the time. I walk in the door, you know, his system was right there by the door, and I look at it, he got one beat-up turntable and one halfway decent, and his mixer didn't look too good at all, but as he started doin' his thang, I'm like, *Okay, he's good with it!* Actually, Al told me that the speakers he had was Al's mama's speakers. That's what Al told me, that those were his *mama's* speakers that he hijacked. So that's how I basically ran into Screw, how we hooked up, and *why* we hooked up. The name of the group at the time was L.O.D.—Legion of Doom—and then we had switched it to IMG/Nation when Screw became involved with it."

Trouble House (IMG/Nation) "He had the records, and we would listen to the records and get samples off of there once we got in the studio with Screw. He mixed in a bunch of songs from artists we listened to back then in a song called 'Tribute to Our Idols.' Mainly Ice-T."

Splitting time between a couple of different studios, Screw ended up doing the cuts on about a half dozen songs for IMG/Nation. And though they met with some labels—including Lil' Troy's Short Stop Records—nothing was released at the time. But Great Black Shark had plenty of equipment—including an Alesis drum machine and a Roland TR-808 drum machine. When Screw started working with the group, he had access to both that gear and their collective experience to add into his learning process, which by then included sampling and the art of tapping—flipping the crossfader open and closed with his fingers to go from one record to another with a quickness.

Great Black Shark (IMG/Nation) "Tapping was something we got from the New York guys, because it wasn't common there, or big, but it's something that we liked, so we incorporated the tappin', double break. Tap, you only hear the first beat. Doubling, you'll hear four or five beats and you'll hear those same four or five beats *again*."

Trouble House "He didn't have the slowed-down music then, but he knew all the DJ tricks. He had a hole at the bottom of one of his tennis shoes! He would do all this behind the back and leg and put his foot on the record and man it was *cold*! He was a cold lil dude!"

BLAST

At Almeda, Ronnie Spencer introduced Screw and Darryl Scott. The younger DJ had spent some time in Blast Records & Tapes, but they had never officially met. Scott made it a priority to be a positive force in the lives of the young people who came in there, and he mentored many of them not just with respect to music but to whatever was going on in their lives. The three of them skated together at Almeda that day, and after that Screw was a more regular sight at Blast.

DJ Cipher (Blast employee) "Stickhorse at that time was more a place you'd go in, you'd buy your music, and you out. Darryl's shop was more of a place to where everybody was hangin' out—*all* fuckin' day, 'cuz everything was in that little center. You had the barbershop down the sidewalk, and of course all the big-timers came through there because he not only sold music, he also sold snuff and tobacco products. For me and my friends, that plaza was a place to hang out and skate in the parking lot. That was the hangout."

Screw knew Scott's late-'80s tape 33½, on which he slowed down Laid Back and Mantronix, and *8 on the Double*, where he was doubling (or tapping). He might have even heard Lester "Sir" Pace dropping 45s down to 33 on *Kidz Jamm* in that same era. Slowing down records was not something new. Eight hours away in Monterrey, Mexico, a new movement called *cumbia rebajada* was then in its formative stage. Colombian cumbia records were popular in Monterrey, and Gabriel "Sonido" Dueñez— having discovered his own city's thirst for down-tempo music—was slowing down records at parties. Screw's tapes were making their way around Houston before Sonido started releasing tapes in 1992, but a thousand miles away across the Gulf of Mexico, slow tapes had been in the streets of South Florida for a decade. Miami is known for its bass, but predating Luther Campbell and 2 Live Crew and even the legendary Florida DJ crew Jam Pony Express (who were slowing down their music as well), there was Disco Dave, making slowed recordings of his own in the late 1970s. He called them drag tapes.

Disco Dave "A lot of people focus on Miami as far as bass, but it was more the DJs, and built around cars. And me playin' around with music, I'd start slowin' certain tracks, where you extend the bass a little bit. I played around a lot with time delays and stuff like that, and it made a big difference on the bass. So I didn't slow it down 'em the music was just like . . . pretty distorted. It's just that it really gave the bass—it enhanced the bass a hell of a lot. And I had been doin' that for quite some time. I know that Screw had been doin' what they call choppin' and screwin'. I didn't do choppin', but I had been slowin' down records like since '79. I was just doin' it with pitch, and even with 45s to 33, it was just like I was workin' more off of the pitch, playin' around with pitch. Like at first it was more by *hand*, it was my hand slowin' it down, slowin' down parts of the track, and then I was like no—actually, this whole thing sounds real like that! I was slowin' it down with the added effect of a time delay, so the space would double up sometimes and triple up sometimes. And it gave it an effect all on its own. It sounded much larger, much bigger, and the guys liked it in their cars. In the cars it sounded tremendously big. The cars sound like, sound a *hall* as opposed to a small, confined space. Now the space is *huge*. And the bass would sound monstrous, and that's how we really got that whole, 'City of Bass' thing."

There is no one truth as to *why* Screw started slowing records down, or exactly when—though his cousin Big Bubb was there for one of the earliest instances. There are lots of stories, and lots of influences. The only sure thing is that it was *Screw* who took his mixes in that direction through experimentation. He was using the pitch control, he was letting his finger drag against the wheel of the turntable, he was on his way to figuring out how to slow it down in the tape deck, and he was getting more and more of a feel for the pace of records and how different songs would blend together. Slowing things down opened up his ears, and he wasn't the only one.

Lil' Rick (DSD1) "Michael Price was a neighborhood nigga, man. He was just a hood nigga who had a passion for deejayin', you know what I mean? Michael Price was a gangsta, man. A gangsta on them turntables. Street nigga like a motherfucker."

A party DJ from Third Ward, Michael Price was also an enthusiast of slowed-down music, only through another route. He did drop the pitch on the records he played at parties, but vinyl wasn't even really his thing. Price was into cassettes, which meant going about things differently when he was inspired to slow the music down. And the modification he came up with had him calling what *he* was doing "screwing" the music, too.

Darryl Scott "Michael used to come up there and he started workin' out with me, and with him workin' out with me, he would always buy the lil mixtapes. Same thing, Screw used to buy the mixtapes, take 'em home to study, try to figure out what I was doin' and would give me a call every once in a while and try to figure out, *How do you do this? How did you do that?* But it wasn't until—and there's still a lot of controversy behind this, but Michael and them was out and they was on the cut—that was the story where the batteries had went down and they was listenin' to one of my mixtapes, and I only had about three songs that were screwed, and from that point I didn't . . . that wasn't one of my things, that I wanted to screw *everything*. I just, you know, slowed down a couple of things as a favor for a couple of people. But when they was out there on Calumet and the batteries went down, everything started soundin' good, and then they was all smoked out, and that's when Mike decided he wanted to come up with the idea of just screwin' *everything*."

Mike-D (Southside Playaz) "Mike started deejayin' and he start doin' house parties, and when we was 'bout fifteen, sixteen, his signature would be slowin' the party down. Darryl Scott—he had talked about how we used to come over there and see Mike there with the radio or whatever—that's true, but he was already doin' it with them parties. He would take the song and he would slow it down at the party. That was his signature, so when you all fucked up it be soundin' weird, know what I mean? What he did—you could slow the record down from 45 to 33 or whatever, the knob on the side that you could turn it down—it wouldn't be as slow as a Screw tape, but you know, the record player, the turntable slow. The pitch would be all the way down. That would be his signature, so he was the first one slowin' it up. We didn't even notice what he was doin'. That's Michael Price sound."

Darryl Scott "He had the radio that had a screw in it that would slow the motor down. He would turn that screw in that motor to slow the motor down, to screw everything with it bein' plugged in. Not just batteries. And when he would grind it down a little bit further, he'd turn that screw in a little bit further. And that's where the term 'screw' came from. But people look at me like I'm crazy when I'm talkin' about the term 'screw.' It was created *by* him. Him and Screw were friends with each other, but that's when he was sayin' they wanna screw everything. Like, what are you talkin' about, you wanna screw everything? And he said, *The way it was when I had that screw in that radio that would slow everything down. When you tried to show me how to* slow *it down.* And I did, I tried to show him how to slow it down with the voltage regulator that was on there. It slowed it down but it didn't slow it down to, you know, *his* pace. They wanted it down *slower* than that. So instead of a sixteenth, it was eight. They wanted it at a sixteenth, but all I could do was slow it down to an eighth. And that was based on the little CD players that I had and then also the lil four-track that I had. I would slow it down with that. And when I slowed it down like that, *that* wasn't slow enough for 'em!"

GULFGATE

December 26, 1990—On the day after Christmas, Screw is arrested for the first time in his life. Al-D and his brother Marvin "Bird" Driver took him out that night to show him how to hotwire a car, and Screw was the one who ended up in jail. It was a big shock for Screw, even if he wasn't completely staying out of trouble himself.

Lil' Sock (producer, DSD1) "Screw, he was still doin' *bad* when he was in Quail Meadows! Quail Meadows was the come-up spot. He was a DJ at the Almeda Skatin' Rink, you know, he was young, man! Screw was cuttin' hair, sellin' weed, and deejayin' when I met him. He was cuttin' hair, sellin' lil dime bags of weed, and deejayin'."

Shorty Mac "Me, him, and Larry, we all went to jail the same week. We was in different places, though. I went to jail in La Grange, Screw went to jail in Houston, and Larry went to jail in Smithville, and they was all different kinda charges. I got caught with some dope. Him and a potnah was stealin' cars, and they got caught by a security guard."

Al-D "He didn't do it. My brother did. My brother Bird bust the window to the car and stuck a screwdriver in the neck and was crankin' the car, and the fuckin' security guard came. Everybody started runnin', but he caught Screw. I was gonna shoot the security guard that day. He had Screw, man. Me and Screw and my brother was *together* when Screw went to jail for the first time. He had never been in trouble. Screw just wanted to see my brother crank a fuckin' car. We wasn't into auto theft, but my brother and them was, and Screw wanted to see how. We were at Gulfgate Mall at the cinema—it's not there anymore, the movie theater— and then you had a bridge that crosses over the freeway to Gulfgate Mall. Screw, that's where he went to jail at, at that fuckin' theater, behind the theater where all the cars are parked. We walked there and my brother just hit the window—*bam!* He was fast. Screw wanted to see how fast he used to crank a car in like six seconds. It took him six seconds to be *takin' off* in your car. He'll fall through the window and already be at the dash, jump in, gone! And when he did that, the security guard had already been lookin' at us and followin' us."

In court, Screw pleaded guilty to burglary of a motor vehicle and was convicted of a third-degree felony and sentenced to three months. He was released after serving sixty days, and following that he put all of himself into his work. That's when the music changed.

SCREW TAPES

March 8, 1991—After Screw gets out, Shorty Mac drives down from Waco to visit him during spring break of his first year in college. By then, Screw was loaded up on cheap gear from RadioShack and making it work for him, eventually purchasing a four-track recorder with a pitch-control function and rigging up a rudimentary microphone so he could talk over what he was recording. That added a new dimension. Screw was making some beats, he had a couple of different recording projects under his belt, and now he was starting to make a different kind of tape.

Shorty Mac "I rode down to Houston and that's when he gave me *3-N-Da Morning*, in '91. He gave me *3-N-Da Morning*, to where I'm on my way back home—and we didn't have cell phones—all we had were beepers. I'm playin' the tape and I was like, *Man, I think he gave me a bad tape.* So when I got home, I called him, and he start laughin'. He say, *Aw, that's supposed to sound like that.* I said, *Oh, okay!* Then I put it back in, and then I said, *Alright, I see what you're sayin'.*"

DJ Screw (as told to Bilal Allah) "In the crib mixing, you know, getting high. When you smoke weed, you don't really be doing a whole lot of ripping and running. I started messing with the pitch adjusters on the turntables and slowed it all the way down. I thought the music sounded better like that. It stuck with me, because you smoking weed listening to music, you can't bob your head to nothing fast."

Bernard Barnes "Poppy would invite some of the real well-known guys in South Park, *Come get you a tape made. Y'all get y'all tape made.* And they see what's goin' on, and they go back to the neighborhood with that tape. *Man, who's that?* . . . *Well, that's Screw over there in Quail Meadows got this goin' on.* My other potnah Toe, you know, Toe knew a lot of people in Third Ward, Yellowstone and all that, and he would invite them over, *Get you a tape made.* And it just started blossoming from there."

Al-D "It was a bunch of dope dealers, a bunch of hustlers pushin' Screw's music in their fuckin' cars. When Screw started slowin' the music down, them niggas was jammin' that shit. All of them had bangers, slabs with swangers and candy paint, comin' down. They were the first ones. Everybody say, *What the fuck are they jammin'?* All these white cars with white insides. That is owed to them."

Bernard Barnes "It started happenin' in apartment 100. He wanted us to talk on the mic because early in the game when he started gettin' out, people were dubbin' his tapes and sayin' *they* did it. So he'd be like, *Man, if I'm bringin' in a song or somethin', you know, just speak on it. Speak on there. Say somethin' on the tape. You know, say it's a Screw tape or whatnot.* To protect his material."

Toe "Since he knew us, you know he would like just say stuff like, *I bet y'all ain't high right now! Whatch'all think?* You know, like, *What up, Toe? What up Fool, what up D, what up Poppy?* We was his friends, so that's where the whole, *Lemme talk to 'em,* came from. Darryl Scott wasn't talkin' to people. He wasn't talkin' to you while he was ridin' with you, so that was the whole thing that made Screw . . . he would talk to you while you was in the car with him. That was what was so special. Some people at first, you know, they kinda didn't understand it or whatever. Like, *Who is this talkin'?* . . . *Well, you know, that's my homeboy Screw.* It was different. Nobody had ever heard that. So that was a whole thing that he started, was talkin' to his friends while they ridin' listenin' to his tape, you know?"

Ray Holmes III "He would come on and he would be like, *Man, y'all ain't gettin' high!* It was just like little certain little things you could see him sayin' around to his potnahs that's in the room while he's doin' these tapes, man. At the time, I was just gettin' to high school, and I was really just kinda gettin' my hands on some of these tapes. But it was a whole different vibe back then, man. Before he met up with the S.U.C., Screw was already known amongst a certain group of street cats as that DJ that you wanted while you was comin' down in your slab, chillin', whatever— you would have a Screw tape in there."

Lil' Sock "Lil' T took me over there to see Toe. They was fresh from TYC [Texas Youth Commission, juvenile corrections]. Screw had just now crunk up the movement. And it wasn't . . . everybody didn't know nothin' about Screw. We actually promoted Screw, *Listen to this tape!* Me and Lil' T and this guy Tyrone from Herschelwood."

Duke (Herschelwood Hardheadz) "I grew up listening to Darryl Scott. I never met him but I've been in his shop and bought tapes, and like that same guy that I was tellin' you was fuckin' with Screw . . . Tyrone, he met Darryl Scott and that was his boy. That's how OG—he older than us and shit. That's what the world need to hear. That nigga—he the *beginning* beginning."

Tyrone "I met [Screw] through my homeboy Toe when he had just moved over there. That nigga was just deejayin' but didn't nobody know that nigga. He was just a nigga that was in some apartments, but that nigga was grindin', and that nigga was just a music player and a nigga start just standin' in front of that nigga house, you know, listenin' to the music and shit, you know, trappin' in front of that nigga house. He'd be grindin' back then. Nigga wasn't makin' no tapes. He was just a DJ. That nigga was just a nigga that moved to Quail Meadows and was playin' music. You know, niggas would be grindin' back there."

Tyrone puts forth for the record that *he* was the one who got Screw to up the price of his mixtapes. Tyrone bet Screw that people would buy the tapes for ten dollars and said he would bring people over there himself to buy them if he would get half the cost of every tape. When Tyrone brought Quincy [QDOGG] over there, and Quincy bought ten cassettes, Screw handed over fifty dollars to Tyrone. But that was the only time. From there, Screw moved on, as people started coming in from all over to buy his tapes, and Tyrone admits he's still mad about it.

Tyrone "I'm supposed to be rich off that nigga! I get half of every tape he ever sold from the time I'm talkin' about until now! You know how many tapes that nigga done sold?"

Knock (Herschelwood Hardheadz) "When Tyrone tellin' the story, you got to know who he is, too. Like, if his *mama* owe him five dollars, he gonna go crazy and not speak to her for life. And that's him for real."

Toe "Tyrone had a lot to do, too, with Screw makin' you know, whenever he pushed the lil . . . and make it go *rrrrrrr*. You know, how you—he was playin' like this, *rrrrrrr*, 'Chk-chicken rice.' So, Tyrone got a lot to do with him doin' a lot of *that*. You know, he wanted him to do a *lot* of that on his tape, you know what I mean? He was like hands-on, wanna keep on bringin' it back and choppin'. He got Screw on doin' a lot of that stuff because that's what he liked, so you know, he had a lot to do with it."

DJ Chill "The scratches he was doin' were fantastic and different, the techniques that he used were real sharp and exciting, and the timing of the scratches was unbelievable. When I say that to people, they really don't understand the energy that I put into sayin' that. He'd put you on another scratchin' level when it came down to deejayin'. When I started learnin' how to count beats, mix, I used to have a metronome. But he had an internal clock. I had to be *taught* to count beats. He already had the beats inside him. To count the beats? He had that inside of him already. He *knew* it."

Al-D "Screw had a little bitty old drum machine that had a kick drum and a snare, and there was no extended bass. It wasn't like an 808. But what Screw would do was he would scratch the bass. He would take a record and he would scratch the 808 bass in, then stop it, and the beat would go, he would scratch the 808 bass in, and then he would stop it. That's what Screw used to do. He scratched the bass off the fuckin' album. He was one creative motherfucker, man."

Toe "And he always knew how to catch it at the bass part a lot of times, too, to where it's like *double* the bass. He would catch it right at the bass part and tap it at the bass. Some people didn't know how to—you know, they'd just start tryin' tappin' and all that stuff, and you know, they wouldn't do it when *he* did it, and that's when you could tell it wasn't right because it wasn't him. He knew exactly where to make it go twice at."

Ronnie Spencer "A lot of people didn't like the analog sound on vinyl, and the fuzz on the needle, but that's what *created* the sound. That's what the beautiful part of it was, if the needle scratched, we *loved* it, because people know we are really in there. We doin' it *live*. He didn't stop. He let it keep missin', and he'll start talkin', and he'll tell you, *Yeah, this shit is live in here right now. We on the air. We don't stop just because it scratched—I'ma fuck it up some more!* And he'd scratch some more until the needle jumped to another track, and then he'd blend that. And that was the beauty of it. You don't get no needle fuzz, and it ain't gonna scratch and skip over the record like a needle will. And you still have control of it. That's why a lot of the guys are like, *I don't like that, I don't feel it, because it's not the way Screw did it. I don't hear no fuzz, I don't hear no analog sound. I don't hear him fuckin' it up, talkin' on it like* they *did it.* Because it was *real*."

TELEPHONE LOVE

April 22, 1991—Houston radio station KFMK, which debuted in the late '60s as the progressive rock station "Mother Radio," abruptly changes its call sign. The channel had switched musical styles over the years—rock, Christian rock, adult contemporary—before finally changing to a format that would lead it into playing hip-hop. The call signal at 97.9 FM became KBXX, "The Box," and one of its first employees was DJ Chill. He and Screw were still sharing equipment and picking up gigs together, but The Box opened up a new line of communication because when he was at the station, Chill was usually the one who answered the phone. So when folks called up looking for a DJ to hire for a party—which wasn't at all a service that the station then provided—he took the liberty of booking the gig himself, bringing Screw along to work with him.

DJ Chill "We started gettin' more parties because I would answer the phone and people would call up to the radio station and then they would say, *Hey you got a DJ to do my party?* And I would get the party! I'd get the parties, then me and Screw would go out and do the party together."

The mixtapes were getting Screw's name out there. The parties he played with Chill—plenty of homes, schools, sporting events, or random spots via The Box—were another way folks heard about him, and the skating rink was an obvious outlet for a certain age group. But it was once Screw got into the clubs that his game changed. Going into the summer, Screw was spinning with Chill at a club off Griggs and MLK called 808. Later, that place would become Infinity, as Soca Village would become Boomerang after that, and Screw was at the beginning of a run of gigs that would see him spinning at all of them, getting more exposure as a club DJ even as he focused harder on his tapes. All of it put him at the crest of the wave of what was next in Houston, as Screw would decide what was next for him.

REBEL RAP FAMILY

July 1, 1991—Geto Boys release "Mind Playing Tricks on Me," the first single from We Can't Be Stopped, which would fast turn into their break-through album. Kicking off the first track, "Rebel Rap Family," was the group's mainstay DJ Ready Red, who says in part, "A band of musical assassins, headquartered out of Houston, Texas / Will soon unleash a wrath upon the ghettos of the world." The lines could hardly have been more prophetic, but it was about a lot more than just the Geto Boys.

Ready Red quit the group before the album's release, to be replaced by DJ Domo, but his opening declaration had proven correct. "Assassins" referred to an older song, one that connected the old Ghetto Boys to the newer Geto Boys in that different lineups had recorded it—the first with Ready Red, Jukebox, and Prince Johnny C in 1988, and then another version by the now superstar lineup of Scarface, Willie D, and Bushwick Bill. Both the album and "Mind Playing Tricks" spent months on the charts, with the single going gold before year's end. By the spring of 1992, We Can't Be Stopped would be certified as the first platinum album by a Houston rap artist.

The seeds for the movement that burst with We Can't Be Stopped had been planted years before when Raheem dropped his debut, Royal Flush released their first album, and then Born 2wice (a.k.a. B-2 Omega) dropped his single "Child 4 Freestyle" in 1990, the same year that Choice issued her debut on Rap-A-Lot and Memphis transplant Jhiame Brad-shaw out of Acres Homes dropped "Doesn't This Love (Feel Good 2 U)" on his own label. Convicts released their album the next year, O.G. Style's debut finally arrived, and Dope E and the Terrorists were preparing their first album. Ricky Royal and his group Royal Flush kept on with a sophomore effort, *976-DOPE*, which included their biggest hit, "I Never Made 20," a biographical reflection on the turmoil of the crack era and its toll on families.

Outside of Rap-A-Lot, the South Park Coalition was coming together, Tony Draper was putting together the Suave House label, and Steven Caldwell and his Perrion imprint would soon release the first record by a Louisiana rapper named E.S.G. The Northside/Southside group Street Military was about to release records with both Keith Babin at Jeriod Records and Beatbox, the label started by former Houston Oilers cornerback Richard Johnson. Over in Third Ward the group A.N.M. (Anti Nigga Machine) was dropping their first album, *Let the Message Rize*. That group featured a young Mike-D, whose future would involve DJ Screw, even if he was then on his way *out* of the industry.

Mike-D "The rap business wasn't too intriguing for me. I mean, I finished out the course of the record, but after that it wasn't no more records for me. I wasn't worried about that no more. I went back to hustlin', and then that's when Lil' Troy had end up goin' to jail, so that kinda put a stint on everything, too. Because that was back when Troy did his first bid, so you know, with the head gone the body just was lost. Everybody end up doin' they own thing. And that's when Screw dropped."

KINGS

Pimp C and Bun B of the Port Arthur, Texas, group Underground Kingz (UGK) walked into King's Flea Market in South Park one afternoon in 1991 and saw a sign posted by someone looking for a record to produce. They were both living in Houston by that time, and just happened to have a record they wanted to make, so they went into BigTyme Recordz, where they were greeted by Russell Washington, who quickly realized the talent that had fallen into his hands and drew up an agreement with them. BigTyme was in the process of expanding from a record store into a label, and UGK became its first release.

It was a crucial juncture for another reason, too. Southwest Wholesale was a record subdistribution company opened in San Antonio in 1976 by Robert Guillerman and Richard Powers. They started out warehousing 45 rpm seven-inch records, but as that era faded along with the disco craze, Guillerman moved to Houston. That was in 1981, when the whole country scene was about to go *Urban Cowboy*. He opened a branch of Southwest Wholesale in town, and throughout the 1980s the company grew a successful distribution business servicing Houston-area record stores.

Robert Guillerman "In the early '90s, we closed the San Antonio branch and we just had our accounts payable office there. And we were down here in Houston and we were doin' real well. We were a pure one stop until 1991. And then the first record we really started with was 'Tell Me Something Good,' by UGK."

By late '91, Screw was spinning at Club New Jack, one of Ray Barnett's Southside spots, with Charles Washington promoting the Thursday night gig. Screw had more money to spend on records, and was selling some mixtapes, but that also brought attention to the apartment he lived in, which at first meant changing units at Quail Meadows before eventually getting kicked out of the complex altogether—along with his dad. So just as his story was moving into another chapter, along came the group that would change things for him, and he for them. UGK's "Tell Me Something Good" was released as a twelve-inch single and as the opening track on their debut album, *Too Hard to Swallow*, and their story was about to become entangled with Screw's.

Bun B "He would come in and consign his mixtapes at the store. I got to know him through that, and he was deejayin' over at Club New Jack, and so I would go over there at different times. So when we got the test press vinyl for 'Tell Me Something Good,' that was the first place I took it to. I took it to Club New Jack, and I took it *to* Screw. So Screw was the first person to ever play UGK."

Charles Washington "Next thing you know, everybody—I mean, it only held like . . . the fire code was like 130, but *we* packed about 250 to 300 people would be on the *inside* of the club, and when he played it, wow—the crowd just went *crazy*. And so then when the song finished, they had wanted him to play it *again*! So he played it again, and then once he played it three times, back to back to back, that's how I knew it was a hit, that's how Russell knew it was a hit, and that's how *Screw* knew it was a hit."

Bun B (writing in *Houstonia* magazine) "Then, a couple months after our EP dropped, he brought me one of his new tapes. It was completely different. This mixtape played at half speed—almost. And there was a guy, just some random guy, shouting people out at the end. He wasn't shouting out fellow rappers, but homies from the hood. I'd never heard anything like it before."

5. Broadway
1992

The roar of jet engines ripping through the clouds overhead got louder for Screw and his dad when they moved from the south side of Hobby Airport to the north, into a newer complex just past the end of one of the runways. Foot traffic had brought unwanted attention from Quail Meadows management and the police, and Robert Sr. wanted them out of that orbit, especially wanting to get his son away from a couple of cops in particular. So he found them a two-bedroom apartment three miles up the road in a place called Broadway Square, with a fence and trees all over the grounds and a swimming pool right outside, even if Screw was never going to go in it (he didn't know how to swim). Pops wanted them starting off cool at Broadway, so things got stricter. There would be fewer people allowed to come by, so Screw would have to become more selective. At Broadway, DJ Screw still sold his tapes, but it wasn't as easy to get the list to him.

King Bo "When he was over there on Broadway, they was tryin' to get away from the heat, you know what I mean? So, over in Broadway, there wasn't a lot of traffic over there. He was tryin' to kinda clean up."

Will-Lean (Botany Boys) "He stayed in the back, and his window was right there before you would get to they porch, so we used to knock on his window, and he would come to the window, he would say something like, *Man, my daddy got company,* or he'd be like, *Shit, y'all come on in.* But sometimes you'd page him—you know, your house phone wasn't on, you had to go to a pay phone. It was like a bunch of poppin' up. There wasn't no cell phones. Back then we had beepers. You couldn't charge 'em up in the wall. If your battery went dead, you had to go and get you another AA battery."

The area they moved to was called Glenbrook Valley, but it was really part of a super-neighborhood that encompassed Golfcrest, Bellfort, and Reveille—forming the easternmost boundary of the cluster of mostly Black and Hispanic communities known as the Southside. When Screw lived at Quail Meadows, the traffic circulated around him, all the time. The pathways to him had narrowed, but he had found a new home base.

Al-D "Dot's. By Gulfgate. Screw loved them damn steaks in there. He *loved* them steaks, man. He used to *love* them fuckin' steaks, man. Dot's, Hartz, and Frank's was the top three that Robert fucked with. Frank's Grill would serve breakfast at three o'clock. They cook it right there in front of you. It was right by Southway Manor. I was just in Southway in the little apartment complex right there."

Broadway Square also marked a turning point for Screw because of a reconnection with a young lady he'd met at the apartment in Quail Meadows. Nikki Williams was the cousin of Charles Washington, who managed both IMG/Nation and a group called Triple Threat. Washington's specialty was connecting people, and while he was running around promoting Screw, he and his sister Monique both ended up helping Screw make a connection that went way deeper than music.

Nikki (as told to Jason Culberson) "When we first met, I was sixteen and he was seventeen, and we met on Telephone Road in that apartment. My cousin Charles was managing him and Triple Threat, with Al-D, and I was sixteen, and I swear, from that day, I was like, *We gonna be friends.* I was convinced *friends.* That's what I said at first. It was not until I was twenty that we met again, and that was actually at Charles house, and they were getting ready to go to the radio station and do an interview, and it was him and Al-D, and my cousin Charles and my cousin Monique, and we were all there and I was over there for the weekend visitin'. They lived in South Park. And we exchanged numbers—he was really, really shy, though!"

Charles Washington "My lil sister introduced them at my mother's house. Screw and I had went to Soundwaves on a Tuesday—that's when new music dropped in those days. We decided we wanted home-cooked food instead of our usual—Popeye's five-piece special, legs and thighs. As we were eating our plates at Mama's, my lil sis and Nik-Nak, as I called her, pulled up. My lil sis introduced the two and they were inseparable."

Nikki (as told to Jason Culberson) "My cousin is who encouraged us to exchange numbers, because I was polishin' my nails and he walked in and I was like, *Oh, he cute!* He was a little bright for me! I wasn't used to that! I was like, *He cute!* My cousin's like, *That's DJ Screw!* And I was like, *Yeah, I remember. I remember him.* And I promise—the day that we exchanged numbers, it was like we was in an instant relationship. We didn't date, we didn't do nothin'. We was just in a relationship. It was from then on, just . . . I can't even explain it without getting teary-eyed because this was somebody that really became my friend first. Like, he was my friend, and I could talk to Screw about anything. And we could . . . music—because I had a love for music, he had a love for music—we just became instant friends. It's really hard, because when I started livin' with him, he was livin' with his dad, and my mom was like, *You need to go back to school! You're stayin' with some dude, and I don't even know who he is!* Soon as she met him: *This my son! . . . Wait a minute—you don't even know who he is, remember?* But it was instant. It was instantaneous. I can't even . . . I don't know. I can't explain it, because you can put some relationships into words, but I can't do that with him. Because it was different. It was authentic, it was genuine."

TRIPLE THREAT

Screw's first actual release also involved Charles Washington. It was with the record label Jam Down, and Screw was making beats for a group called Triple Threat—Mikey and Lil' Red, from east of Houston. The label's founder, a Caribbean immigrant named Patrick Lewis who came to Houston in the 1980s, was working with Washington to get a few things off the ground. It wasn't an artist deal—Screw wasn't actually part of the group—but rather a production arrangement. His services were in demand.

Patrick Lewis (Jam Down Records) "I got introduced to Screw from Charles Washington, and then we came together and with the microphone in the restroom, we recorded off of I-10 in a mechanic's shop. The guy let us use his restroom as a vocal booth back in those days, and then we went to a little studio and did the rest."

Al-D "Triple Threat from Baytown. Mikey and Red. Mexican guy and Black guy. Lil' Red. Screw made all those beats for that album. They had a song called 'Woop Em' In.' Screw fuckin' *mashed* on that beat!"

DJ Chill "He got an ASR-10. They used to practice in my dad's garage. My dad had a welding shop, warehouse off of Telephone Road, and they went there to practice."

Big DeMo (Long Drive) "I was in Pickwick Music, and the guys knew me in the store 'cuz they know I'm comin' to buy every rap record there is. And the guy say, *I don't know who these guys are but they from Houston.* I said, *Well lemme have it!* I didn't care who they are or what they say—if they're from Houston, I'm supportin' 'em. So I bought it, and I had that little tape, *Man, there's some alright little music on there.* I can remember it bein' a little mini-hit, you know? And unbeknownst to me, that DJ was Screw. And I remember hearin' him say, *Screw this, Screw that,* but it never dawned on to me that it was *my* Screw! And when I met Screw [he said], *You know, I do a little bit of producin', too, with this here group Triple Threat.* I say, *Well I got that! I bought that record without even hearin' it man, 'cuz they said they were from Houston! That's you, huh?!* He said, *Yeah, that's me they talkin' 'bout, Screw.* I said, *Yeah, man, I got that record!* I said, *Man, put that on my Screw tape. I got that!* So, he was producin' back then, but there wasn't too many people knew he was producin'."

Triple Threat's *Young and Explicit* was released on cassette in 1992. Screw made the beats for all of the songs, "Woop Em' In," "Gang Related," "Hard-Core Life," and the title track, with a credit in the liner notes as producer. There were a number of early Screw tapes floating around Texas and Louisiana by that point, with Screw's own handwriting on the label, but *Young and Explicit* was the first official release on which DJ Screw's name appeared.

SMOKE ONE / SMOKE TWO

DJ Chill and Screw had been sharing two good turntables between them, working as MC and DJ, with Chill on the mic and Screw on the tables. They were putting in hours, and as the gigs multiplied, so did the haul. As was always the case, the money Screw was making was going back into buying more records, and sometimes gear. Turntables, mixer, recording devices. Chill had a car, so he and Screw could get where they needed to go, and they played everywhere from the gymnasium of Gregory-Lincoln High School in Fourth Ward to clubs like Soca Village (later Boomerang), and 808 (later Infinity). Screw had also started spinning at Ray Barnett's after-hours spot Midnight Hour (formerly Club New Jack) in South Park at Scott and Old Spanish Trail.

Toe "Midnight Hour's a bit more gutter, and a little bit more *hood*. Little pool table, you know, a lil hole-in-the-wall. Kinda small, but the music was good, they had some good dranks, and around that time, you know, it was . . . it was a gangster spot pretty much. It was a G spot. It was cool, man, and he got to play whatever he wanted to play. That's when people started really comin' just to listen to Screw—at Midnight Hour. They were just goin' there because Screw was there."

Playing in clubs and getting paid was on another level for Screw, and it brought him into other Houston orbits because the people who were hearing him, seeing him, and meeting him in the clubs were connected. And so DJ Screw's name started to move around Houston—and for different opportunities. The group Convicts was Big Mike from South Park and Mr. 3-2 from Hiram Clarke, different areas of town doing business with one another, both of them doing business with James Prince.

Mr. 3-2 (as told to Polow's Mob TV) "We was lookin' for a DJ, so we went to go meet him at Club Boomerang and see what he had goin' on, and he was slowin' down music. All DJs used them 1200s back in the day, and he was throwin' 33⅓ and was slowin' it down even slower to slow it down, to really hear the words in the songs and get the meanin' and understandin' of the song. So that's where slowed-up music really came about, it's just really slowin' down a song so you can actually hear the words in the song, and hear what's goin' on and get a understanding of the thang."

The Convicts' hiring of DJ Screw never did materialize, as their career instead took them to Los Angeles to work with Dr. Dre's Death Row Records (Houston rap fans with their ears to the ground say they could hear 3-2's influence in Snoop Doggy Dogg's inflection). But the Rap-A-Lot connection was kinetic, as evidenced when Scarface of the Geto Boys released "Let Me Roll" in the summer of 1993.

Scarface (as told to Insanul Ahmed for *Complex*) "When I said, 'Jammin' to a tape my homie had made / Growin' up in the hood being mixed with Face.' That was DJ Screw back then. I was talking about DJ Screw."

Screw soon indirectly crossed paths with Rap-A-Lot again, when another young group with a completely different thing going on came looking for his skills. Odd Squad was Devin the Dude, Jugg Mugg, and Rob Quest. All three of them wrote, rapped, and produced, with Carlos "DJ Styles" Garza working with them on production. When they were looking for added leverage on the turntables, Devin's cousin introduced him to Charles Washington, who connected Odd Squad with DJ Screw. They booked studio time with a student producer Devin knew from the Art Institute of Houston, and the night before their planned early morning session, Screw paid a visit to Rob Quest's house in Third Ward.

Devin the Dude "We told him to come a day before to pick up the vibe

and get a plan. So he came over there and we just vibed. We was smokin'
and chillin', just coolin', havin' a cool time. He stayed about four or five
hours. That night, man, we were just *obliviated*. We fucked up, and we
passed out around about one o'clock, and we was out of it! Until we
heard a *bangin'* at the window at like seven forty-five! At the window
in Rob's room, there was a BAM! BAM! BAM! We like, *What the fuck?
Who is that?* Because nobody didn't just like knock on the window like
that! So we was gettin' shit together, *Man, hold up—make sure it's not
the police. Hide the weed.* And we looked out, and it was Screw! And he
was like, *Man, it's seven forty-five, man, what we gonna do? We gotta go!
The damn studio's at eight o'clock, right? Let's go!* We was lookin' at each
other like, *Man, what the fuck? This nigga here . . .* But he ready to do the
cuts! He got his albums, he like, *I'm ready, man! All the songs we talked
about for all the cuts, I got 'em. I got the records right here. Let's go!* He
was juiced up."

Rob Quest "I had never seen a DJ that would come with his gear. He had
his mixer, he had his turntable, he had his crate of records. He's about to
do a gig! We were like, *What the fuck? Where you goin'?* He was like, *Y'all
said you're gonna need a DJ. I'm ready. Wake up.*"

Devin the Dude "He was ready. It wasn't gonna take him nothin'. All he
needed to know was what songs we was wantin'. He got the albums
that he chose that'll fit what we talkin' about, like for instance, 'Runnin'
the Streets of H-Town'—I remember he had a record that was screechin'
tires that he got on an album, and he cut that up! Like, we runnin' the
streets of H-Town and he was like screechin' out on him, hittin' every
part of town, every time we talk about a different part of town or goin'
somewhere, he'll throw that cut in like we're peelin' off to go to that
particular side of town."

Jugg Mugg "He didn't actually cut on the Odd Squad's album. He cut on
the demo tapes that we sent out to the CEOs at record companies, and
we put one bio in Crazy C's hand and he put it in Lil' J [James Prince]
hand, and that's how we got on Rap-A-Lot. I just barely had knew him,
but I just knew he was a hell of a DJ, 'cuz he was *cuttin'*, man! 'Runnin'

the Streets of H-Town,' he was scratchin' that Rick James—he was cuttin' that shit and that shit was *hot!* His cuttin' on the demo tape got us our record deal."

Devin the Dude "On 'Runnin' the Streets of H-Town,' he was talkin'! He did the intro, actually. He say, *What's up, man, y'all got the beer? We was* like, *Yeah! . . . Man, y'all got the weed? . . . Yeah, man! . . . Shiiit, well let's roll, then!* You know what I'm sayin'? He would say all that. He had a nice intro on every song where he talked and we talkin' before the song started. He starts cuttin', and it was goin' *down,* man!"

Rob Quest "He really had DJ skills. He can scratch, but mix like for *real* for real. Like somebody you put up against somebody on the East Coast. He had cutting skills—scratching, transforming, crab, and all that kind of stuff. He was doing it. Real professional."

Devin the Dude "He was amped, and *that* made me think about it . . . man, there's people who believe in us *probably* a little bit more than we believe in ourselves! And when we let people down, we're not only letting *ourselves* down, but we're probably missing opportunity because we're gettin' so fucked up and not thinkin' about what we should, you know what I'm sayin'. *Ethically,* studio-wise, he made it kinda clear to me, you know, *It's not just for you. It's not just for your sake.* If you're doin' it and people appreciate it, and you want it to be heard, you got be adamant about gettin' your shit, gettin' up, goin' and gettin' it, goin' in the studio and makin' the best out of the opportunities that you have. Because they're not always there. The people that line up at certain times are there for a reason, so do your best when it's time to put shit together collectively. So he kinda instilled that early stage that I was like, well, *I'll never sleep on a studio session again!*"

Playing in the clubs, Screw brought the same records he made his tapes with, but the responsibility was different. The DJ gigs compelled him to be more professional, because the truth was Screw was *proud* of his craft, and he wanted to feel so when taking it out into the world. He had worked enough DJ gigs by then to sharpen his skills, and radio seemed like a natural progression. Everybody around him thought that. Chill got him a meeting with KBXX.

DJ Chill "The person that was over the mixers at The Box, his name was Reg-N-Effect, and he was a badass DJ. He was cold. But that's who was over the DJs at the time, for mix shows. When Screw came up to the radio station to get a job, once he start changin' the wires for the back, they was like, *Whoa! What are you doin'?* You couldn't *do* that. That's why they have a switch on the mixer to where you could do a reverse. They didn't *have* it at first! What he was doin', nobody was doin' that *I* know—that was doin' it backwards. And when he went to do that part, they was like, *Naw, you ain't gettin' ready to do that.* So that was a 'no' when it came to him gettin' the job, too. That was the deal breaker. Dude was extremely serious about what he wanted to do. He might not ever say much, but you could tell by his actions."

SOUTHSIDE CONNECTION

Screw shook off not getting the job. There had been people around him helping to shape his musical growth going all the way back to Shorty Mac. But it was while he was at Broadway and the music brought new people to him that the mix of personalities and styles would begin to line themselves up in front of him—coming from all different places, not necessarily knowing each other—and sort themselves into a musical energy around Screw. On a drive with Al-D, ACT, and Shorty Mac, he told them he wanted to call it the Screwed Up Click.

Stick 1, so called because he towered over everybody else, was from the Orleans Apartments in South Park's Dead End, and despite not keeping out of trouble himself, his steady demeanor had him maturing into a big-brother role around Screw as he got to know him. The Botany Boys from Cloverland were coming around, and they were *definitely* getting into trouble. The Louisiana rapper E.S.G. started making regular trips to Houston and met Screw at Broadway. Corey Blount from South Park came through with the cars and the clothes and was the inspiration for the whole style of the Southside.

Lil' Keke (as told to Douglas Doneson for *Vice*) "He [Corey Blount] had a house on the corner of Martin Luther King, his mama house. This is a known statement on our side of town; there is nobody that drives down that street, and don't look to the right. He always kept something in the driveway for you. That's why Corey Blount is the S.L.A.B. King. Corey Blount was the dude with the Suburban, the Lexus, and the drop Eldorado."

Blount was all but inseparable from another South Park style icon—the rapper Fat Pat. Patrick Hawkins and his older brother John "Big Hawk" Hawkins were from Kennedy Heights Apartments, in Dead End. They were both big and full of bravado, and while Hawk, the eldest, was more low-key in his delivery, Pat was probably the most complete artist of any of them at the time: charismatic, flamboyant, full of noise, and, as Lil' Keke calls him, "jiggy," bevoiced with booming, bassy pipes that devoured all of the oxygen in the room. Attention immediately turned to Fat Pat anywhere he went. The word is *throwed*. Fat Pat was everything great about Houston, Texas, and Screw could see that right away.

Man Poo "Fat Pat gonna have everybody laughin', you know, he could dance, he'd be like, *I'm a big ol' nigga, but I can dance!* Fat Pat really thought that he could *dance*. That big ol' nigga really had some *moves*, man. For real! He was just fun to be around, man. A nigga could have a bad day, man, he'd come around, he just gonna shake you out of whatever kind of hole you in. You kinda down that day? Man, he gonna put a smile on your face."

Big Swift (producer, as told to Donnie Houston) "He was kinda arrogant at first! I'm like, this motherfucker arrogant as hell! He wanna sing, he wanna rap, he want everybody to do what he say first. But then I was like, damn, nigga got *creativity*."

Mike-D "When you hear that *Maan, hold up!* and *Maan, know what I'm talkin' about?* That's Pat. That's Pat! And really, to be honest with you, Pat was makin' fun of this guy named Lil' T! That's a guy from *my* neighborhood, Terrence, you feel what I'm sayin'? He was the same way as Blount, ridin' all them cars, Jags. Scott, Sock, and T—they part of it. Screwed Up Click deeper than just the rappers. This was a whole *movement*, so you can't speak on this without talkin' about the real street niggas that put this shit together, you know, all the way back from Baytown. So Pat used to just make fun of T—that's how he got his slang, you know, just like, *Maan!* He used to just be makin' fun of T, but he kind of incorporated it into his talk, and then when he started puttin' it on the tapes, everybody start pickin' it up, pickin' the slangwich up."

Some of the people Screw was meeting in '92 and '93 he was actually going to connect with further down the line, like Big Moe. Knock, Duke, Archie Lee, Lil' Keke from Herschelwood (once Keke and Pat met, a chemistry was forged on the spot). There were the Botany Boys, who were deeper than just C-Note, Will-Lean, D-Red, and B.G. Gator (there was also Pappy, Dez, Lil' 3rd, Head). The love that Screw showed to the people around him was *keeping* those people in his circle. Charles Washington was still promoting him everywhere. Al-D was ever present. DJ Chill was getting them club work. Michael Price was tooling with his tapes, and he and Screw got more and more into what they were doing in slowing music down. But now newer people were starting to come around, and they weren't just there to buy tapes. They were artists in waiting, and for many of them, Screw unlocked the thing that allowed them to step through that threshold and work on their music.

Quincy "QDOGG" Evans "He was just messin' with music all the time. He was makin' tapes, but didn't nobody know about him! I heard about him because of my cousin had a tape, and he put it on. I was like, *Man, that boy jammin'! Who is that? . . . Man, that's Screw. . . . Screw? Man, bring me over there so I can make me a tape.* You know, make my own tape. And when I got over there, man, I was like, *Man, this dude is real.* He had all the albums I ever wanted! Because, you know, I used to make tapes, too, when I was little, listenin' to Darryl Scott, so I had all the albums. But this guy had albums that I *didn't* have! You know, the vinyl albums, I mean, maybe three of each! Goin' over there, at his house, and his dad used to be . . . his dad was cool, though! His dad was cool. We probably was over there probably smokin' some paper squares. And long as he ain't doin' nothin' bad or in trouble with nothin', his old man was cool about it. There wasn't nobody recordin' freestyles. You could get on there—you know, he'll say something, you know, TAPE BY DJ SCREW. But wasn't nobody even goin' over there! Because it was his dad's."

Lil' Keke "Screw used to get his hair cut by my barber. My barber named Steve, and before . . . well, we had already got turned on to Screw. First time I heard Screw, I wasn't really turned on to it. I didn't really understand. So I was like, *I don't really like it.* I didn't really like it, because it was my first time hearin' it, and I was like, *Why it so slow? The radio broke?* I ain't understand. So it started to grow on us a little bit, just a little bit."

C-Note (Botany Boys) "I actually met Screw through my OG potnah QDOGG, Quincy. One of Scarface best friends. Yeah Quincy'n them were ridin' around jammin' it in they slab, and I wanted to jam it in my slab, so I asked him to take me over there one day. And I actually met Screw and got my first dub, and then from there by the time I got my next dub, that's when I asked him about freestylin' on it."

Once Fat Pat heard about that, he had to get on a Screw tape. C-Note of Botany Boys was the first to do a whole freestyle on a tape, but it was Pat who would forge the tone of the Screw tape freestyle with his command of the vibe, through his boisterous freestyles full of the vocabulary that made Houston slang so rich, in the process bringing a transcendent swagger to the S.U.C. right from the beginning.

Big Hawk (Fat Pat's brother, as told to Presidential Records) "People was runnin' up to me, *Man, your brother is cold, man!* I was like, *Man, my brother can't rap!* Man, they put the tape on—the tape was goin' slow, so it really made him sound like ten times better than what he would have been at a regular speed, man. And when he done that, bro, it was like we was outta that room, like we just got up and was hypnotized by Screw music. We was just like, *Man! We gotta do this here.* So the next day, my brother take *me* over there to meet Screw! I go meet Screw, he stayin' over there at Broadway, mane. Screw old man answered the door, Pat already had warned me, *Man, Screw old man, he kinda be trippin' some-times,* so we be over there kinda nervous at the door. Screw come to the door, man, just *boom!* Cool. It was like the first time we met, that was it right there. We had built our relationship right there, man. So I go to Screw house, I get down and go to flowin' myself."

Meshah Hawkins (activist, widow of Big Hawk) "If Hawk was doin' something, Pat was gonna do it. That's the type of relationship they had growin' up. As brothers, they were just very, very close. And so when Pat heard C-Note rap on a Screw tape—and I think they credit C-Note with bein' the first person to freestyle on a Screw tape—so when Pat heard C-Note freestyle, it was over with! Pat was like, *Man, I'm goin' over there!* And he went right over there, I believe it was the *next day.* And, you know, started . . . I don't know how the conversation went down, what went on between them, but he freestyled at Screw house that day, that very next day, and so then after that, he came home with the copy of that. Once Hawk heard that, it was over with! Hawk was like, *Aw man, I can do that too!* You know, they always competin' as brothers. *Man, I could do that! I could do that!* So that's how both of them got inspired to go over and start rappin' and everything."

Will-Lean "Scarface was in South Acres. Cloverland is right there, so it's just like one big neighborhood divided by streets. Anyway Face had got a Screw tape, and he gave it to a lil homie named QDOGG. His real name Quincy Evans. Quincy gave the tape to Courtney 'cuz he ain't like it, 'cuz it was slowed down. This was like '91. And he gave it to C-Note, to Courtney. So he liked it, like, *Man!* Screw was all on that West Coast. That's what we used to listen to—Ice Cube and all that, that West Coast, the C-Bo and Spice 1. And Screw had his number on there, so shit, we beeped that boy! And we went over there, bought some tapes from him and shit. So that's how . . . you know, we were smokin' blunts, we'd go over there, kick it with Screw, and he used to be like, *Ah! Y'all them Botany Boys! I be hearin' about y'all.* So months comes, and we done start freestylin' on tapes."

Pat and Blount were the most visible engines of the culture, but the car customizers of the Southside were its great innovators—candy paint, leather interiors, swangers, elbows, and fifth-wheel trunks that popped open to reveal messages in neon lights. People had been refurbishing old cars ("slabs") with custom insides and spoked "elbow" rims in Houston for years, but in the early '90s it became an art form, and Floyd "R-U-GAME" Clark of Surround by Sound was *the* customizer in Houston.

Charlie Franks (S.A. Fools) "Quincy was the first one with the pop trunk! And then Blount did it. But Floyd . . . this why Blount and Quincy got into it. Because you know Quincy used to be mad 'cuz Blount could do everythang Quincy do. And so, Blount wanted the pop trunk *before* Quincy, but Floyd wouldn't give it to him. He say, *Naw, I got to give it to Quincy.* And he gave it to Quincy."

Head (Botany Boys) "Quincy—if you had a slapback, Q gonna run you down, swang in front of you, hit them brakes, and pop that trunk in your face! You can't *do* that! But it wasn't motorized at first, so we used to be followin' behind him and he gotta get out and close it. But I remember when he motorized, though! He gonna *wave* the trunk—and that's where that came from, makin' a trunk *wave*."

Ray Holmes III "It kinda seemed like around that '92 time, the tapes started changing. Same gray Screw tapes, but then he started gettin' these *flows* on the tapes. Well, people didn't mind, you know what I'm sayin'? You high, listenin' to it, but it would get to a point to where if you knew what a Screw tape *was*, you ask the question—where's all the music, and why are these people flowin' on the tape? That was the main question you would ask. And it wasn't in no disrespect, but it would just be like . . . *The Screw tapes changin' now? What's up with the flows?* Because we didn't—I didn't know some of the people at first, but as time got on and it caught on and everybody kinda started diggin' the vibe, there was more flows put on the tape, and he just became more popular. Like that's one of the things I'll say the S.U.C. did for Screw—they made him like *über*-popular. They made him popular with people that he probably never would have came in contact with before."

DJ Screw (as told to Desmond Lewis) "A couple of my potnahs out the neighborhood like Fat Pat and my brother Al-D, C-Note, Pokey, E.S.G., know'm sayin', a couple of the neighborhood kids came through and just . . . know'm sayin', I got 'em on the mic one day. Then they heard they voice on tape behind some music, and they kinda liked it. And the people around us kinda liked it, and *felt* it, 'cuz what we was talkin' about stuff that was goin' on around our neighborhood. Basically everybody in H-Town could relate to that, and that's when people kinda jumped on it, 'cuz they was understandin' what we was talkin' about 'cuz everything we was talkin' about, they see us do it every day."

C-Note "When we first started, we weren't drinkin' syrup. We were smokin' paper squares and drinkin' forty ounces, stuff like that. When we first made the Screw tapes, it was at his dad apartment on Broadway— we would have to actually wait 'em his dad would leave—because his daddy was strict. He didn't want all these niggas in his house. So we had to play it cool. And as soon as he left, we crunked that music up!"

Stick 1 "I went over and we went through some lil thangs, wrote my lil list down for the tape I wanted, and comin' from out of there, he called me a few days later and told me I can come pick up my tape. And it just so happened, man—I was always a big tennis shoe guy, and it so happened I was at the mall when he called me, so I just kinda surprised him and said, *Hey man—what size tennis shoes you wear?* I mean, I pro'ly been knowin' the guy personally about a week, but like you say, it was a legitimate connection, and they had some black and blue Streetball Adidas was kinda hot at the time, and I grabbed him a pair while I was at the store. So when I came in to get my tape, he was like, *Yeah, man, I got your tape right here.* I say, *Hey, man, I appreciate ya, man. I got somethin' for you.* He was like, *Huh?* I say, *Yeah, man.* Pulled out the tennis shoes. And he pulled 'em out, put 'em on top of the box, and it was almost like . . . you know, bein' at his dad house pro'ly—me not knowin' the whole situation—[Screw's dad] pro'ly was like, *You know, you got traffic comin' in my house, these guys . . . you know, I'm not really likin' this.* You know what I mean? Man, he put the shoe on top of the box and said, *See, Dad— this* can *be real.* And I looked up and I was like, *Wow.* They just looked at one another. He actually pulled the shoe out, put it on top of the box, and said, *See, Dad—this can go somewhere*. And they kinda looked at each other . . . and I knew that was *their* moment, so I let them lock in. And Dad went back to doin' what he was doin', and we went to the back room to get the tape. It was somethin' where Screw was tryin' to actually let his dad know, *Trust me, Dad. I know this might not seem right, but this gon' go somewhere*. But from that time on, man, anytime a fresh pair of tennis shoes came out, I bought him a pair. Jordans, whatever. It was either ten and a half or eleven. Yeah—Robert Earl had some feet on him!"

Koldjak (a.k.a. Runn G, Dead End Records) "Screw came in at the right time. I'm talkin' about when he come in, it was almost like a transition period, because Darryl Scott ain't really playin' the music that we really listenin' to. He strictly old school. Not takin' nothin' from Darryl Scott, but Screw had the sound! Screw had the sound of the streets, and he had the sound of the street before the streets knew that was the sound we *wanted*."

MICHAEL PRICE
August 17, 1993—On an otherwise quiet late-summer night in southwest Houston, Michael Price, the young party DJ alongside whom Screw was working toward a slower sound, is murdered outside of an apartment complex where he was shooting dice. Price left the game with some money, somebody followed him outside, and he never made it home.

Lil Rick "They was playin' dice, man, and Mike was winnin' or whatever, and then Mike was out of bounds where he was gamblin' at, you know. He was *with* somebody that was from that neck of the woods, but you know, back then . . . if you not where you supposed to be at, that doesn't mean they gonna respect you like you respect your own neighborhood, you know what I mean? Just so happens, shit—he was winnin' on dice that night and then somebody went down on him that was down on they dick I guess. You know, made that decision to go rob and kill my nigga. I'm quite sure if they would have just pulled a gun on him and robbed him, Mike would have *gave* that shit to 'em. Cuz like I said before, Mike was a street nigga. Mike was a hustler. Mike knew how to get money from all four corners of the board. Gamblin'. . . that was just *one* of his hustles."

A young visionary was gone, and his sound was lost. If Michael Price left behind any mixtapes, slowed down the way he did at those parties in Third Ward, none have surfaced. Darryl Scott was left without a protégé, Screw without a contemporary, and Houston never got to hear what a movement built between them would have produced—which included, possibly, one in a series of recordings that would become Screw's masterwork.

Mike-D "From what *Mike* told me, he helped with the first 3 *'N the Mornin'*. Because not a lot of tapes had came out, because people had personal tapes back then. The tapes wasn't for the public consumption until later. He wouldn't sell you a personal tape. I'm sure with Mike, it wasn't no sellin' him no tape. They would just hook up and mix some dope music up. I've never heard a Michael Price and DJ Screw tape, officially."

Lil' Rick "Mike was the first one I actually heard slow a record *down*, you know? And then when we get over here with Screw, he was not just slowin' 'em down—Screw was slowin' 'em down and brangin' other songs in *with* it, while the song's beat still playin', but the lyrics for the old song still playin', and the beat for the new song was startin' to come in!"

Mike-D "They were definitely collaborating from day one. I know they did a lot of music together because of the fact that Screw had one turntable and Mike had one turntable so they would . . . you know, when they'd come together that made 'em have *two*. That's because we didn't have a lot of money back then. You try to make do with what you got. So yeah, they did a lot of collaboratin'. Chill was around then, too."

DJ Chill "I met Price because I was deejayin' parties, and sooner or later we had to come across each other. I'm from South Park, he was from Third Ward, so we had to come across sooner or later. We hung out quite a bit before he got killed. He was on the rise because he was in

Third Ward, so he was closer to Darryl Scott than we were. I know that the distance don't sound too far, but as a young man, Third Ward and South Park was a little bit of a distance! But that boy—he was on the rise, though."

6. The Wood Room
1994

At the end of 1993, Screw moved out of the apartment he shared with his father and rented a 1,300-square-foot house on the Southside off of Reveille, under the 610 Loop just south of Gulfgate Mall. The neighborhood of Golfcrest was three miles north of Broadway Square, still well inside the roar of the airport and the Gulf Freeway a few blocks away. Aside from that, it was a pretty quiet middle-class area, like plenty of other Southside neighborhoods. Nikki had been staying with him at Broadway Square already, so they made the move together to a one-story wood-frame house on Greenstone Street.

Nikki "Corey Blount had his slab, his Cadillac Seville. Corey and Fat Pat helped us move—in that car. In that Cadillac. I mean his car was *beautiful*. It was so pretty. They put Screw's records in that car and helped us move! Our clothes was just like one car. He took better care of his music than he did our things. I'd say, *Screw, where are my shoes?* He'd say, *I don't know.* I'd say, *Where are your records?* He'd say, *Oh, they're in such and such.* He *knew* where his records were."

For the first time in his life, Screw was no longer living under the roof of his parents. More immediately, since he wasn't under his *dad's* roof, he wasn't bound by his rules, his schedule, or his mood. There were no curfews, no turning the music down—no turning the music *off* if he didn't want to—and no job to wake him up in the morning. Because of that, Screw had the freedom to stretch into an entirely new relationship with time. His mixtape income had allowed him to rent an entire house, so that's where he was going to work, and he wanted to work in the middle of the night.

The house had two bedrooms, one bathroom, a small kitchen, and a living room with big windows looking out to the street. It was built in 1951, on a corner lot with a driveway to one side and a tiny covered porch in front. There was plenty of lawn, but Screw would no more be hanging out in the grass there than he was in the swimming pool at Broadway. Even with the garage around the back—where he would eventually install a pool table—the house on Greenstone was all about the wood room.

It's not a proper name, per se, but that's how everyone describes it. It was a one-hundred-square-foot room with wood-paneled walls that would have been a second bedroom were it not for Screw's equipment. His turntables were waist high against the wall, with the opening to the hallway on his left. He would hang Al-D and C-Bo posters on the wall in front of him, and when Bun B came by and gave him a UGK test pressing, he hung that up, too. Post office mail tubs and crates full of records dominated the floor behind him. His filing system looked random to everyone else, but Screw could locate any record in the room within seconds—both copies. The people sitting on those crates marveled at how he went directly for the vinyl he needed and retrieved it faster than they could get out of the way.

Screw had created a space to work. The wood room was the stage for recording the broadcast—a live setting, even if folks would all hear it at different times. That was the magic. On certain nights, some kind of incredible, untapped energy would materialize inside of that room. The wood room gave them permission to be themselves—seen, heard, and understood not as rappers, but as people. The Screwed Up Click was about a lot more than just rappers.

On a musical level, Screw was already digging deep, cutting into the beats, chopping between two copies of the same record on the turntables, one playing a little bit behind the other, flickering back and forth between them with the fader, running back vocals and getting the rhythm to step on itself. He gave it stride, made it dance. Screw didn't invent the techniques, but he combined them into his own tool, to exploit what *he* was hearing. He didn't just accent what was there, but cut into it and imposed his own rhythmic bounce in a way that made it a dependent part of the song from there on out. One can never hear it the same again. There is no such word as "unscrewed."

The Greenstone era was the emergence of new structures in what Screw was doing, all of it live. On all but the early regular-speed tapes, the music was slowed down—"screwed." Eventually, the songs were "chopped," too, in the rhythmic flourishes Screw imprinted on a piece of music by flipping between copies of the same record spinning at different points, so "chopped and screwed." At Greenstone, the other parts of a Screw tape started to emerge. Screw didn't write song titles on the tapes, but on later annotated versions of his recordings, Screw working at the turntables would become "Screw on the Tables" or "A Screw Mix." No talking, just scratching and chopping for however long Screw got lost in it. Then there were free moments, "Shout-Outs," which were also often called an "Intro" or "Outro," usually with Screw himself talking. There were also "Skits," and then there were the "Freestyles."

People had been doing shout-outs on Screw tapes since Quail Meadows, but at Greenstone, they had time to draw it out. Now Screw had folks freestyling off the top of their heads into his microphone, everything going straight to tape, in the moment. The name Screwed Up Click was already floating around, but it was at Greenstone where the voices of the S.U.C. would start to really come together around him. Everything was a product of Screw as the main conductor, lightning rods all around him bringing energy together under his roof. Screw was laid back, but he was serious about how everybody acted in his home.

Tyrone "There pro'ly been some niggas from two different places that wanted to kill each other, but if they fuck around and end up in Screw house them niggas got cool! They coulda been enemies like they wanted to be, but nobody knew it, because when they made it to *that* nigga house, the beef was squashed!"

Knock "Screw was the reason that a lot of neighborhoods got together. He really brung the Southside together. If you from the Southside and you fuck with him, you Screwed Up Click. When we used to go do our shows, everybody from every other neighborhood would come to everybody show. Because you know, you meet up with Screw, you got somebody from every neighborhood damn near in there, and you want somebody from another neighborhood, shit—you call 'em in there! And you just fired up. He gonna lock that gate on you, and he ain't gonna let you out 'til in the mornin'."

The house on Greenstone started off as a place *away* from everything, removed from what was going on in South Park, Yellowstone, Cloverland, South Acres, Herschelwood, Dead End. But once people started coming over, a new atmosphere came alive, and Screw's house became a hub of its own. Screw tapes evolved into something more transactional. Personal tapes were now the master for a dub, and DJ Screw would start to make—and sell—a lot more tapes.

SWANGIN' AND BANGIN'

February 1, 1994—E.S.G. releases his first album, *Ocean of Funk*, on Steven Caldwell's South Park–based Perrion Records. Cedric Hill is a native of Bogalusa, Louisiana (about an hour north of New Orleans), who was coming back and forth to Houston in the early '90s, calling himself E.S.G. (Everyday Street Gangsta). They knew him all over Louisiana because he made himself seen and heard in the clubs out there, taking the mic and rapping anywhere he could. At college in Lafayette, he met a young producer from Houston whom everybody there called "Solo."

Sean "Solo" Jemison "He was rappin', but he was the first guy I ever seen loop—you know how they would splice cassette tapes? He was loopin' beats like that and rappin' to 'em. We were goin' to talent shows in these little clubs in Louisiana, and he would win 'em easily by just freestylin', just lookin' around the room and blowin' people away. He was gifted with that shit. He was doin' that way back then."

Louisiana would always be his home, but E.S.G. was drawn to the big city of Houston, and started releasing records there in 1992. That was when he met Screw and gave him a copy of his first twelve-inch, "If It Ain't One Thing It's Another." In early 1994, E.S.G. came by the house on Greenstone with something new for Screw to hear.

E.S.G. "I went back with an actual record—a single of 'Swangin' and Bangin'" that I had got pressed up and was like, *Look—this is my song I was tellin' you about.* So he put it on the tape! Man, by the Kappa Beach time, when everybody just go to the beach? I was like, *Damn! Every car playin' my song!* He had put it on the tape. And so by now, Screw music—it was just like drinkin' water. No matter who dropped—no matter if it was Ice Cube or R&B, whether it was Brandy, Mary J. Blige—it became in the hood, a regular statement that like, *Oh, what's-his-name just dropped? I'ma wait 'em Screw screw it.* It just became a normal way of everyday livin' was to listen to a Screw tape."

E had a reputation for long-winded, unyielding freestyle sessions that could go for the entire side of a tape. When he had an audience, he connected with them and drew his narrative from what was happening all around him in real time. It was perfect for Screw tapes. And once he did start working with Screw, who slowed everything down to where *he* wanted to hear it, that raspy voice took on a new tone.

Big DeMo "I went to Screw house and we was just chillin' and he was like, *E.S.G. on his way through. He fittin' to do a tape.* They came through and . . . man, I already knew how good this guy was. Everybody used to just flow on the end of a Screw tape. You know, one freestyle song right at the end. And this tape here, this was the first tape that I know of, of anybody jus' doin' the *whole tape.* I think he had three or four guys with him, and on each song, just about every song, one of 'em fell off until it was all E.S.G., which didn't take long. See, you can hear his flow tapes and you would just say, *Yeah, this guy pretty good,* but he flow so good that it sound like it could be written down. Because he's *that* good at it. And to see him do it live and to know he not writin' it down is just incredible. I mean, he has an uncanny skill that I've seen few MCs possess."

Charlie Franks "When I first met E.S.G., it was when he come down here from Louisiana. E.S.G. rapped from like eleven o'clock that night 'til seven o'clock that mornin'. I went to sleep, woke up, and E.S.G. was *still* rappin'! Man, that motherfucker there the freestyle king. I don't think anybody can outrap that motherfucker. He'll just rap about anything. We had a block party down on Mykawa. The system cut off, that boy goin'! System came back on, he *still* goin'!"

Warren Lee (Scarface's brother) "We had this club called Jamaica Jamaica. It was one of our longest-running clubs, and this night in the club was Treach [Naughty by Nature] and his brother Diesel in there, E.S.G., Face, and me. I think at this time Marcus Love is the DJ at 'Maica. And I just made him go on there, *Man, put instrumentals on, man*. And I mean E.S.G. went to the name, *I'm here with Treach*, and everything he got on, then go to that man over there, everything he got on, Face, everything he got on—that's when you knew that he was the truth, man."

Head "We comin' down Selinsky. The police comin' *up* Selinsky. We ridin' with Will-Lean. Will had his lil Beamer back then. E.S.G. in the back seat. I don't know *what* made this cop trip, but Will look in the rearview and man, the law *right* behind us."

E.S.G. "Niggas in Louisiana went to school, but when I moved here, I was like, *These niggas don't go to school!* In Louisiana, your grandmother or your mama would beat your ass if you didn't go to school. But when I moved to Houston I used to see niggas that's fifteen and sixteen in slabs ridin' candy paint and not goin' to fuckin' school! We some young niggas ridin' around, and Will-Lean had just got a BMW and put the rims on it, and he barely could see over the fuckin' dashboard, over the steering wheel. And here we are in a $70,000 car. I'm sixteen, he sixteen, that nigga's fifteen, and we ridin'. So the police look at us like—it's a Black cop—was like, *What the fuck?* He pulled us over, *Nigga? What the fuck y'all* *doin' in that car? I know this car is stolen.* That nigga hit the lights on us so fast. We like, *Man, we rappin'!* That officer was like, *Y'all ain't rappin'.* I said, *We rappin' for real! . . . Okay, if you're a rapper, rap.*"

Head "Will was like, *Man, look, we goin' to the studio, me and my potnahs. This E.S.G. the rapper.* So E was like, *Yeah, I'm E.S.G.! I'm a rapper.* And the cop was like, *Oh, you rap?* And then E start freestylin' the second the man asked him do he rap."

E.S.G. "'Well look officer / it's three o'clock / you done pulled us over on Scott block / what you think about the car? / No, we really, really bought it,' and he just was like, *Gon' the fuck away. Man, y'all are some rappers! Go on back to y'all business.*"

Head "He freestylin', and man this what fucked the dude up—he say, 'Man, we ain't tryin' to waste time / we just tryin' to get where we goin' / Officer A. Hines.' I'm talkin' about *freestylin'*, read that man badge, and put it in there! Dude was just like, *Man, y'all go on!*"

Terence "Big T" Prejean was more singer than rapper, but it was a freestyle session that brought him out of his shell at an early instance of the famed Los Magnificos Car Show. Founded in 1982 by Joel and Helen Carmona, the car show over the years grew into an important annual event in Houston hip-hop culture, with live performances, rows of booths with local merch, and lots of appearances from Houston artists. During Screw's era, its home was in the Astrodome complex at the nearby Astrohall convention center, and that was where Big T found himself standing in a circle with E.S.G. on a Sunday evening.

Big T (as told to Stric Hustle TV) "Everybody was there, Keke, Lil' O, the whole Botany Boys clique—I'm talkin' about everybody from Dez, Head, you know, both of them boys done a lil time . . . but anyway, man, they was all freestylin' at the end of the car show. Screw had his booth set up, so Screw doin' his thang. So, them cats got to doin' what they do, like they do at Screw house. They was passin' the mic around. So Keke get it, Fat Pat get it, Pokey get it—well by me *hangin'* around E.S.G. and them like on a daily basis—E.S.G. was hangin' with the lil clique I was messin' with, right? So, they passed E the mic and I happen to be right there. I'm vibin', feelin' good, drankin', smokin'. I told that nigga, I said, *Man, gimme that mic, man.* 'Cuz them niggas was passin' that around. I said, *Man, gimme that mic, man.* You know, havin' fun. So I'm right there by his side when he gave me the mic, and I done my thang, just off the top of the dome, like we do. Like I say, I came out with that smokin', [*sings*] 'When I'm smokin'! / I said I'm *smokin'* with E now / and when I'm rollin' / said I'm rollin' on them '83s now!' I say, 'I got no love for them player haters / and boy I wear them gators / when I go out to the club I got a fat dub / everything's tight 'cuz I'm sittin' on white / when I'm smokin'! / said I'm smokin' with E now, yeah yeah.' And when I passed that mic, them boys said, *Whooo! That boy T a fool!* That nigga E.S.G. say, *Man, let's go to the studio and record that* right *now. Not tomorrow*—right *now.* That nigga say, *Let's go. It's over with.* Broke the mic, man. And that was my first shout-out. I give it up to that nigga, man, I'll never stop. Day one, man."

HERSCHELWOOD

Herschelwood isn't an official neighborhood—it's a street between South Park and Sunnyside—but plenty of spots on the Southside can't be found on a map and are very real places with real histories, especially when it comes to rap music. Herschelwood Street runs northeast to southwest through a residential area just on the other side of 610 from Yellowstone. The guys who grew up there and walked those streets knew the whole area as Herschelwood, and a group of four of them were rappers—Lil' Keke, Duke, Knock, and Archie Lee—who came together to call themselves Herschelwood Hardheadz.

Knock "Back then we used to wear our hats with our neighborhoods on 'em. Like Botany'll have they Botany Bigshots on they hats—first we had Herschelwood Moneymakers, and then we had Herschelwood Hardheadz. It was South Acres, they call theyself S.A. Fools. You had Yellowstone, you had Third Ward, you had Dead End, D.E.A. Sunnyside, Southbank, Wayside, you know . . . man, everybody had they names on they hats, and then once Screw came along, we was able to rep our neighborhoods on Screw tapes."

Lil' Keke "Freestylin' was already a mainstay. It was already somethin' to do. So we used to have our *own* Screw house, where we practicin' before we get here—if we ever *gonna* get here. So, I was already warmed up and ready to go by the time the first time I got to Screw house."

Duke "We was just in the neighborhood. We grew up together and fucked around in them neighborhoods and shit. And as far as the rap, we was just ridin' around. That's how we do it, we just ride around with the freestyle. That form of freestyle, we was ridin' around and doin' that shit in the cars and standin' out on the corners and shit, fuckin' around like that. And then we realized Screw was over there and he would let you come make a tape, so we end up just goin' over there, to do it like that."

Lil' Keke "My barber had a good relationship with him, so by the first time I met him, the Screw house, it was '94, '93, or somethin' like that. I didn't get to go to Quail Meadows. I knew a friend of mine that was goin' to Quail Meadows named Tyrone. If you let Tyrone tell it, he the one turned *everybody* on to Screw, to hear him tell it. He think him and Screw should be partners in this game or somethin'. But he had really turned us on to the slow tapes, and like I said, by the time I got to meet Screw, the phenomenon—it wasn't as big yet, but goin' to his house had already became somethin'. And my barber Steve was under a lot of pressure to get people over there, so when Screw used to come get his hair cut—I'm talkin' about when haircuts was two dollars—that was my first time meetin' him, *at* Steve house, when he was over there gettin' a haircut. And just like everybody else, I was beggin' to go over there. You know, he wasn't really payin' attention. My first time goin' to his house, that's when I went—with Steve, with the barber. And that was the first tape that I recorded. Steve used to get to go because of his relationship from cuttin' his hair."

In February of 1994, only a few months after they had moved in, Nikki was in the kitchen when Screw opened the door and a bunch of big voices poured into the house. These were the Hardheadz, who then had drama swirling around them because of the murder of somebody from South Acres by someone from Herschelwood, which none of them had anything to do with but nonetheless carried the association. So of course during one of their earliest Screw tape freestyles, the subject came up, and plenty of people heard the tape.

Stick 1 "There was somethin' about them. I said, *Go tell them youngstas right there I need to connect with 'em.* Because what I saw was, this gon' cause a problem. This tape gonna cause a problem. These youngstas, they wild. You know, maybe if I can get in between this, we can kinda mend it a little bit. So I told Bird, and Bird got word to 'em. I pulled up on them youngstas by myself, man, in my car, and they was all over there in the streets, all hangin' out. I pulled up over there, *What's happenin', mane? I hear this and that. I heard about this, I heard y'all tape, man. Lemme tell you somethin', man—I feel like you youngstas real. I feel like y'all got nuts, man, y'all legit, man. But you gotta know how to go about this stuff.* And from *there*, man, me and Keke got cool, man."

Koldjak "When Keke and them said they were goin' to Screw house and they wanted a tape, they wanted to rap against Pat! And that meetin' was so epic that Stick *befriended* Keke. A real genuine friendship was formed from Stick fuckin' with Keke like that. So next thing you know, Keke around! Man, Keke *family!*"

Lil' Keke "In my neighborhood, I was already the *guy.* So basically, by the time I got ready to get to Screw house, I was well prepared. Like I knew one thing: when I get over here, it's over. And when I got over there, it was *over.* I'm talkin' about the first day that I went over there I took Screw ass by storm, and from *that* moment, he was after me, Screw. When I was in the neighborhood, before I got to Screw I was always reminded that Pat is the man, and Pat got the freestyle trophy from High Rollers. When I first *met* Fat Pat I was about seventeen! He's about twenty-two. He's about five years older than me, so it was a *very* nervous experience, because he was more experienced than me with it. But man, from that moment, me and him took the complete lead. Everybody had a

Screw career, man, but me and him took the lead, and it changed everything. It started a scene where every tape was gettin' bigger and bigger."

WELCOME TO THE GHETTO

Robert Lee Green Jr. was born on July 2, 1970, in Bryan, Texas. When
he was a youngster, his family picked up and moved to California, and
Green ended up going to high school in Hayward, near Oakland, where
in the mid-'80s he started rapping under the name Spice 1. He told folks
it was an acronym for "sex, pistols, indo, cash, and entertainment," and
his lyrics delivered on that.

When he was sixteen years old, he recorded a song with local Bay-area
hero (and by then already world-famous rapper) Too $hort, and then
came back through Texas carrying a stack of records with his name on
them. Spice still had family in Bryan–College Station, and none of them
could believe he'd grown up and made a record with Too $hort. His
self-titled debut album broke through in 1992 with the single "Welcome
to the Ghetto," which would find its way onto many a Screw tape over
the years (as did the S.O.S. Band's 1984 song that it sampled, "No One's
Gonna Love You"). DJ Screw was known to be a fan, so when Spice 1
returned to Texas in 1994, his cousin Demond in Houston had someone
for him to meet.

Spice 1 "He was like, *Man, there's this dude named DJ Screw, and he be takin' your songs, and he slow 'em down, and people ride around here listenin'
to him all day. Your music slowed all the way down like this.* I'm like, *Man,
lemme hear it!* So he played it for me and I was like, *Damn, that's crazy!*
He was like, *Let's go to his house.* I was like, *We can go over there?* So we
went over there and shit, and this was like way back in the day. I was
like twenty, twenty-one."

DJ Screw (writing in *Platinum* magazine) "Everybody that came to Houston wanted to meet me. Spice 1 came by the house. It shocked me, 'cuz
I ain't know he was comin'. I was makin' a tape at the time, and heard
a knock on my door. I look up, it was my partner that stayed in Quail
Meadows, he was kin to Spice 1. It was a trip. So, Spice 1 came in. We

kicked it and everythang. He spent the night at my house, we just basically hung out."

Nikki "I was in the bedroom folding laundry when Spice 1 got a phone call. He came in there to take it and just laid right across the bed like it was his house! He was at home. He was relaxed."

The tape they made that night, *The Meadows*, was a tribute to Quail Meadows, where Screw and Demond had met. Bernard Barnes, whom Screw had known since he lived at 10201 Telephone Road, was there, too. For the occasion, Screw didn't shy away from local flavor, mixing in UGK, 8Ball & MJG, and a couple by Street Military. Since an artist from Cali was in the house, of course he laid down some West Coast, but really he mixed together a cross section of hip-hop from all over, with selections from Ice Cube, Snoop and Nate Dogg, MC Eiht, Da Brat, and MC Lyte, ending the first side with a Spice 1 track. But it was the beginning of the second side that would echo through Houston from that night on: a national artist freestyling on a Screw tape.

Man Poo "That nigga Spice 1, he just did his thang that night. He was high, full of that oil, just the vibe in there that night was just so *right*, man. Spice 1—just bein' a fan of Spice 1—and he actually in Screw house! Then he takes the mic and freestyles, man! He ripped that motherfucker up! We just couldn't believe that he was in Screw house flowin' that night. It's goin' down! We pourin' up, Screw got the Big Red goin', we got the Sprite goin', aw man, we got the squares goin', sittin' on that crate, man—you know Screw had crates in there. He ain't have no chairs in that motherfucker. You had to sit on a crate, where he kept his wax, his records at. Screw on them tables, Spice 1 had his eyes closed while he was freestylin'. He was feelin' good! He was full of that lean! Back then, it was Barre. It wasn't Actavis, none of that shit. It was 'Barre Baby,' the real potent stuff."

Spice 1 "He was sippin' on some drank, some syrup, and I asked him what it was. I brought a little bud, and you know, and we switched it up. He's like, *Oh! What's this? . . . Oh, this what we smoke in the town, in the Bay.*

I'm like, *What's that?* And he like, *That's what we drink. We been drinkin' out here, man. It's called syrup.* So we switched up! I rolled a blunt and I started drinkin'—I *kilt* that shit! I was like, *This shit is good as hell! What the fuck is this?* It had Jolly Ranchers in it and shit with all the ice. Next thing you know I was snorin', wakin' up, they smokin'. But we actually were able to record after that. He was just sittin' up in a room full of smoke, pourin' up some drank with his shirt off and shit, you know, 'cuz it was hot as hell. I was just like, trippin', you know, after he gave me that shit and I drank it. I like was, *Damn, that's what these motherfuckers out here drinkin'?"*

THE DRANK MAN

When the Botany Boys released their five-song EP *Smokin N' Lean' N* on Big Shot Records in 1995, it was the first official release by a group that was part of the Screwed Up Click. Also of note was that the "leanin'" referred to on the title of the Botany Boys EP brought something else into the light that had mostly been referenced on underground Screw tapes.

Will-Lean "We didn't start drinkin' syrup until like mid-'94. A lot of people think Screw slowed his music down because we drank syrup. Wrong! We was drinkin' OEs, forties, and he was chop, chop, tap and tappin'. This was years before drank."

Marijuana was the elixir of choice in the city's hip-hop scenes, but recreational codeine-promethazine cough syrup had been a thing in Houston for decades. More folks got turned on to it when rappers started talking about it on Screw tapes, and then doctors around town began to get loose with prescriptions, and as the tapes gained popularity, so did the drug.

It's called "syrup," "lean," "oil," "drank," or "barre." People in Houston do not call it "sizzurp," and even though Big Moe would later record a song called "Purple Stuff," folks don't really call it that either. The way it's prepared depends on who's mixing, but most folks pour a couple of ounces of codeine-promethazine over ice into a white Styrofoam cup, topped off with sweet soda—Sprite, Big Red, Sunkist, or whatever's around. Some throw in a Jolly Rancher, some say it already tastes like one. There are different qualities of syrup, depending on the manufacturer, but most say Barre was the best, and in 1990s Houston, you could get the best.

Big Moe (from "Sippin Codine") "I sip codeine / it makes a Southside playa lean / stackin' green / steady stackin' green, steady sippin' codeine / Screwed Up Click / representin' dat H-Town and with it / it's goin' down / representin' dat Southside of dat H-Town / it's Big Moe / I never been a hoe, sippin' on a potent fo'."

Key-C "One thing about Big Moe—he *big*, but he gonna stay fresh. So he get in the car, man, this dude pulled out a pint of Barre. Ain't *nobody* have no Barre. We had some drank, but it wasn't Barre. We had URL. United Research Laboratories. They had switched up the brand. They was movin' too much. What's that . . . the FDA? They kept switchin' the brand. You had Rugby, you had Barre. Barre was the one that really, really is nasty. The best is Phenergan. The *old* brand. Now *that* tastes nasty. That's the one where your mama goes in the refrigerator, they give you that cough medicine—blah! It'll knock your ass out and you'll feel better the next day. That's Phenergan. Came in a glass bottle. Barre came in glass bottles, too, for a long time."

Once Screw moved to Greenstone, people started bringing around drank. Pat Lemon brought drank. There was Dave from Fourth Ward—and if somebody was talking about "Dave" on a Screw tape, they were always talking about Fourth Ward Dave—he brought drank. And of course over the years there would be any number of people who started bringing syrup over as an offering to get a recording session with Screw. Lemon was *the* drank man, though.

Tyrone "He was the drank man! Really his wife was the backbone, but he the one really started that drank, really, as far as hittin' the scene. I mean it been out here, but as far as hittin' the scene on the Southside, really? Bein' the man with it? Oh, that was the first nigga to be the *man* with it, where it's unlimited—beyond gallons. As many as you wanted, and as many people wanted it! Shit, that nigga there, he was the man for that."

Reggie "Bird" Oliver "He was a drank man like none other. I know a lot of other people showed up, but they didn't do it like him. He had all the cases and gallons. Me and Pat Lemon, he was like a brother to me. That's why they rapped about him. Gotta pop the trunk for Pat Lemon! Him and Screw was in the same category, as far as giving. They didn't care about nothing. When we go out to eat, same thing with Pat Lemon. He would not let me spend my money. He would be mad! Seriously, *real* mad if I tried to pay for something. Lemon, Screw—there was a lot of guys that didn't want to see me get into drugs. I sold marijuana, and they were like, *Man, Bird!* What Pat Lemon would do, he'd say, *How much you got?* I'd tell him. He'd say, *Give me all of it.* He wouldn't even smoke it. If I had a pound, whatever I had, he going to buy all of it just because he didn't want to see me having to go deal with different customers."

Man Poo "My cousin Pat was just a people type of guy. Everybody just loved him. He gon' pull up and gonna pour up, and people ain't have to have no money or nothin'. He just wanted everybody to be happy, man. *Hey, man, get you a cup. Run and get you a soda.* As far as rappin' and all of that, my cousin didn't do none of that. He done talked more shit than anything. But everybody fell in love with my cousin, man. He just a people's person. His experience was just beautiful. He just wanted to put a smile on people's faces, have everybody laughin'. You don't owe him nothin'. Just be present."

Pat and Dave had plenty of people looking forward to their visits, and one of them was the aforementioned Kenneth "Big Moe" Moore. Moe had a hefty frame that he put to work playing football at Yates. He rapped, too, but he was really in his wheelhouse when he was singing, and his soulful crooning came along at just the right time to stand out in a group of rappers. The girls went crazy every time he put his powerful lungs to work. To Moe, drank was something to rap *and* sing about.

Big Moe (as told to Matt Sonzala for *Down-South*) "I had a cousin who deejayed every Thursday at this club where I was a bouncer. DJ Screw started working there also and we used to hang out with him, help him bring his boxes in and stuff like that. So one day he brought me a tape and he let me hear a demo of his album that was going to come out nationwide. I was playing an instrumental from the tape and started singing and rapping some lyrics I made up and he heard me singing and said, *I'm going to take care of you if you hop on the album.* So I hopped on the album and the album did real good and everybody wanted know who was that dude singing? That's how I got through—that song on DJ Screw's album *3 'N the Mornin'* called 'Sippin on Codine.'"

The mix of the drug and the music wasn't a given for everybody, but Moe was one of many talking about it on Screw tapes. His high school classmate George Perry Floyd—Big Floyd (not to be confused with Big Floyd of South Acres, the slab pioneer)—only appeared on a handful of tapes, but he didn't shy away from talking about drank either. Floyd was born in North Carolina and eventually ended up in Houston, where he came up in Third Ward around Mike-D, Man Poo, Bird, and a younger artist named Cal Wayne. Floyd and Wayne lived in a one-story housing project called Cuney Homes, named after the trailblazing Galveston politician Norris Wright Cuney, who was born into slavery, freed, educated, and then rose to leadership in an era in which Black people were becoming empowered in Texas politics, before his death in 1898. Floyd's own story would have a tremendous impact on US history years later, but in 1996 he was an unknown voice on the mic at Screw's house, delivering his lines right into the rhythmic pockets Screw was hammering out of the music, and showing love to other artists from the S.U.C.

Man Poo "I'd see him in the streets, *Man! That's a bad motherfucker, man, you and Yuda did!* He used to always call Screw 'Yuda.' Everybody'd be 'Screw Yuda,' but Floyd used to just call him 'Yuda.' He used to say, *Man, Yuda never let me down on none of your tapes. You never let me down!* Everything I'd do at Screw's, he always got it."

Big Floyd (from "Cocktails") "Young nigga just like to let the dollas fold / let 'em all fold / yeah, I'm talkin' green / talkin' 'bout my hood sippin' codeine / that's the barre / you can call it syrup / I'm a young nigga like to smoke a lot of herb / watch me go fly on the plane / call Mary Jane / me and the Screw Zoo / got the fame on my name 'cuz I'm real / tryin' to go grill / jumpin' out of jail / on the real / stayin' dyne / true Southsider / watch me crawl low on my motherfuckin' spider / welcome to the ghetto / it's Third Ward, Texas / boys choppin' blades on they motherfuckin' Lexus / boys rollin' butter / some comin' white / it's that Big Floyd / throwin' Tre in the night."

SCREW THE WORLD

The tapes were getting out there. The biggest metropolis in Texas and the fourth-largest city in the United States was sending its youth off to college and the military elsewhere in the state, in the country, and around the world, and they took their Screw tapes with them. The state capital of Austin didn't have a rap scene that rivaled Houston's, but it was still the *livest* city in Texas—whatever one's definition of that may be—and there were myriad cultural connections drawing Screw there, where he'd first seen *Breakin'* a decade earlier. Austin is a cross section of cultures just like Houston, and plenty of people move there from the Bayou City, so of course they were down with Screw music—and it was Screw's oldest collaborator who brought the noise to them.

Shorty Mac "I think when I first brought a Screw tape *to* Austin was in like '92. And it was called *3-N-Da Morning*, and everybody used to think that my tape deck was messed up. I used to tell 'em, *Naw, that's the way the tape goes!* So then I put some music in my car, and I used to just ride around and bump these tapes, and I would go see him, and every time I would go up there he would give me a different tape to listen to. But then he eventually got me to start sellin' tapes. I was out here hustlin', so he kept tellin' me, *Man, the only thing you gonna do is do* time *if you keep doin' what you doin'.* I came back and he gave me a box full of Screw tapes. He said, *It's gonna take you about six months, but I want you to go down there and start pumpin' these tapes.* And I'm lookin' at it—I'm still on my other trip, but I'm lookin' at it. So I said, *Alright, I'm gonna see what it'll do.*"

Larry B "Shorty Mac was runnin'. He was Screw runner! He was doin'— he was runnin' them tapes for Screw. Austin, San Antonio, all around!"

Shorty Mac "By the time they had the first concert—it was Keke, Moe, Screw, and I think Point Blank was there. And Keke was standin' outside, a Suburban passed by jammin' *Straight Wreckin'*. He said, *Screw! They jammin' Screw in Austin?* We got on the inside of the club, the club was jam packed! It was all they wanted to hear! It just turnt—it went to a whole 'nother level. I'm talkin' 'bout they was ridin' Daytons in Austin. Them Screw tapes hit down there, they started tradin' in the Daytons for swangers, and they start tryin' to fix they cars up. They wanted candy cars and this and that. By the middle of '95, I would come to Houston every two days, pickin' up boxes of tapes, bringing 'em back down here to Austin to sell 'em and shit. It just jumped off that quick."

This was the year Screw finally got some ink, especially outside of Houston. New York hip-hop magazine *The Source* ran a one-page article on Screw, titled "Have You Been Screwed Lately?" Writer Cheryl Smith interviewed him for the piece, and in her lede she wrote, "23-year-old Houston native DJ Screw is taking the hip-hop underground by storm. Often imitated, but never duplicated, his mixed 'Screw' tapes have sparked personal requests from heads overseas as well as in the U.S.—from New York City to Los Angeles, and from Atlanta to Alaska."

DJ Screw (as told to Cheryl Smith) "It's only a Screw tape if I DJ Screw it. You'll know it is me because in addition to slowing the songs down and mixing and scratching them, I also give shouts-out to my boys and to all the hoods in Houston."

That same month, Screw also got some column inches in the magazine *Rap Pages*, where he was interviewed by writer Bilal Allah for an article entitled "DJ Screw: Givin' It to Ya Slow." Photographer Ben Tecumseh DeSoto, a longtime *Houston Chronicle* contributor who documented Houston's punk scene in the early 1980s, was tapped to shoot photos of Screw for the piece. He visited Screw at Greenstone one afternoon and took pictures of him going through records and working at the turntables. He also got some shots of Screw passing off tapes through the gate, and a few for which he reluctantly posed, but it was his time spent in the wood room with Screw that would produce his most iconic photos.

Ben Tecumseh DeSoto "He had three thousand albums easily that he worked with, and so these samples are coming out of this huge, deep collection. He became an authority and he had this huge inventory of music in his space. I mean he had it at his fingertips so he could roll from bin to bin, from room to room, pull out pieces and pull 'em together and work. He was literally living in that space. He was very laid-back. He was living in a complete richness of culture, from the fade on his head to his connection to the outside world about doin' the tapes. And it was like this *trip*! As we were there, people rolled up and he handed off a tape. Some money came through the gate with the main lock, and the door opened up and you'd pass him a twenty and the tapes would come out."

SO REAL

One hundred miles east of Houston, between Beaumont and the Gulf of Mexico, is the refinery town of Port Arthur, Texas. That's where Pimp C and Bun B grew up, and where they formed UGK before relocating to Houston in the early '90s. For the last song on their 1994 album, *Super Tight*, they employed the services of a hometown producer named Dorie Dorsey, who attended high school with Pimp C and went by the name DJ DMD. His family had just then opened a record store in PA called Music World Records & Tapes, which he was helping manage. So DMD was already connected to what was going on musically in the area, but the shop also made clear to him there was music on the streets you couldn't get in a record store.

DJ DMD "One of the reasons that I got involved in bein' part of the Screw movement was because of the impact that it had in Port Arthur. In 1994, 1995, you could not drive down Port Arthur, Texas, streets without hearin' a Screw tape bein' bumped. It was everywhere! It was Fat Pat rappin' over a Jermaine Dupri beat, it was Lil' Keke rappin' over a Ice Cube beat. But I didn't know where it was comin' from. It just popped up everywhere. At the time, I was a DJ in the local club scene. But I didn't *go* nowhere. I was *just* in Port Arthur. So all the influences that *came* to Port Arthur came by way of the streets—came by way of cats goin' out of town, bein' influenced, bringin' they influence from Houston back to

Port Arthur. So I didn't *know* what was goin' on in Houston. I was just deejayin' here in PA. That's all I knew. My family opened a record store, I got the records from all over the country, I *played* the records from all over the country right here. But I didn't *go* out, and I wasn't into the street scene. But my dogs eventually were out there in the streets, and they were some of the people that was in the line at DJ Screw's house buyin' Screw tapes!"

His friends also had their sights set on investing in a record label, and they thought DMD should connect with Screw to build a bridge between the "Golden Triangle" of Port Arthur / Beaumont / Orange and the big city of Houston. Although he says he didn't get it at first, DMD warmed to what he was hearing on the Screw tapes coming in to Port Arthur, and he set out to work on music he thought might fit with what DJ Screw and his crew were doing. Sampling the 1979 Isley Brothers song "Let's Fall in Love," DMD crafted a beat that rode on Ernie Isley's soaring slide guitar work and actually bumped a little faster than the original, but was nonetheless right in the wheelhouse of the vibe Screw tapes put out there. He asked Pimp C to hand off the tape to DJ Screw, which he did. A few days later, Screw called the phone number written on it.

DMD booked them a session at Skip Holman's studio in Katy, Texas, where Pimp C had previously done work. Screw brought Al-D, C-Note, Mike-D, Fat Pat, and Lil' Keke to the session, and the idea was that DMD would record a radio version with Screw and Al-D, and then a Screwed Up Click version with everybody else. Al-D wrote a verse for Screw:

DJ Screw, slowin' shit down
Puttin' in work all over H-Town
See me on the scene, drinkin' codeine
Gat up on my lap 'cuz these haters want my green
Southside for life, that's what I claim
That's what I represent, that's where I hang
Hand on the trigger, pockets gettin' bigger
Screwed Up Click ain't nothin' but real niggas

Screw recorded his part, Al-D followed with his verse, and the regular version was done. Then DMD hit record for Fat Pat, Lil' Keke, C-Note, and Mike-D, who together freestyled for the next two hours, all of it going to tape. DMD would go on to release a Screwed Up Click version of "So Real," which became even more popular than the one that featured Screw rapping. In the process of recording that, he had logged a seemingly endless trove of freestyles. Those recordings, which at the time were unheard by anybody but the artists in the studio, were destined to resurface in Houston's musical future with Keke's 8Ball & MJG–inspired refrain, "Twenty-five lighters on my dresser, yessir."

ALL SCREWED UP

In the summer of 1995, Russell Washington approached Screw about mixing an album to be released on his label BigTyme. This was the same BigTyme Recordz that put out "Tell Me Something Good," the UGK megahit Screw broke in Houston years earlier, and the same Russell Washington whose mother was dating Robert Sr. almost a decade earlier, when Screw first moved to Houston. Their histories had long been intertwined, and now they were meeting in a business capacity, with Charles Washington (no relation to Russell) involved on the business side for Screw.

Russell Washington "I said, *What do you want?* And they said, *Man, we want four hundred bucks and two-point override.* I said, *Bet.* Shook it. Eddie typed it up, and it was off, and I asked them, *How do you need to do it?* And Screw said, *I need everything you wanna use on wax.* And so I called Houston Records and I said, *Okay, I want to do a wax, put my stuff on it, but I don't want the wax. I don't want a thousand of 'em. I just want the test pressing.* So they told me the price on that, and actually the price on that was eight hundred bucks. It was more than Screw wanted to do the record!"

BigTyme provided Screw with the vinyl, and booked recording sessions with engineer Keenan Lyles, a.k.a. Maestro, at his studio, Samplified Digital, in southwest Houston. Maestro had been building an impressive body of work for years by that point, plenty of it with Klondike Kat, the

Terrorists, and K-Rino, whose South Park Coalition movement would be featured heavily on the BigTyme release.

For *All Screwed Up*, Screw mixed together multiple tracks by four different artists. Though UGK had long ago left BigTyme for Jive Records, three of their songs appeared on the album, including Screw's version of the song he broke years before, "Tell Me Something Good," over which he layered "Moments in Love" from the '84 debut album by the English synth-pop group Art of Noise. Rappers Point Blank, PSK-13, and the group 20-2-Life were on the compilation, too, all of them signed to BigTyme.

In fact, though it gets billed as a DJ Screw release, *All Screwed Up* is actually a various-artists compilation with the official title *BigTyme Recordz Vol. II: All Screwed Up*. For the album cover, Russell went to Pen & Pixel, who were already doing the art for every other rap record in Houston, and asked them to create the least expensive thing imaginable. So they took the artwork for 1994's *BigTyme Vol. I: Still Afloat*, drove a screw through the skull, and turned the whole thing green.

Shawn Brauch (Pen & Pixel) "There were two levels of Pen & Pixel customers early on: the mainstream—Suave House, Trinity Garden Cartel, BigTyme Recordz, Rap-A-Lot Records—then quite a few underground labels. DJ Screw's music seems to grow from this underground movement more than the mainstream. I believe this may have been because the larger label had the general consumer market and distribution channels in mind, and they were hesitant to move in unknown territory. However, once 'Screw music' caught traction, they all jumped at the same time. Even to the point that we added the option to offer a 'Screwed' cover at a discount when we were building the main master art and layouts."

Even though Screw wasn't signed to BigTyme as an artist, the label pushed him out there with the same energy as if that were the case, with a publicist named Shakur placing ads in magazines and investing a lot of energy in getting the word out beyond Houston. Screw was selling a lot of tapes on the underground level, but upon its release, sales of *All Screwed Up* lit up the Sam Goody record store chain, so much so that Charles Washington arranged to hold a party for Screw at Club

Boomerang. Charles happened to know that the manager of the Gulfgate Mall store was a Screwhead, and the album had shot to no. 1 locally there, so he had a plaque made up to commemorate Screw's accomplishments and invited the manager to come and present it to him at the club, which he did. *BigTyme Vol. II: All Screwed Up* was the first official release with DJ Screw's name on the cover.

3 'N THE MORNIN'

To know the part that 3 'N the Mornin' played in Screw's life is to understand that it was a series of recordings with variations on that title going as far back as 1991, when Screw passed off a cassette with those words written on it to Shorty Mac. That tape, which Mac took back to Austin with him, was never released, but in 1994 Screw recorded a session at Greenstone that he called *3-N-Da Morning*. The track selection was pretty well split down the middle as far as East Coast and West Coast artists, with songs by Spice 1, Dr. Dre, Too $hort, MC Eiht, N.W.A, and even Houston's own Street Military. His selections also had him digging in the crates, working his way up through the years with Parliament's 1975 dirge "Mothership Connection (Star Child)," LL Cool J's 1985 hit "Rock the Bells," and later closing the whole thing out with Rodney-O & Joe Cooley's 1988 hit "Everlasting Bass," which was a favorite of Screw's when he lived at Quail Meadows.

Two standouts on that early tape would have life on later mixes, maybe because both had left a trail through Houston long before Screw's tapes. One was "White Horse" by the Danish electronic duo Laid Back, which Darryl Scott had put on a tape, and the other was "Sugar Free" by the Queens MC Grand Daddy I.U., the beat of which sampled Taana Gardner's "Heartbeat," a song that itself was sampled the same year it was released (1981) on "Catch the Beat" by T-Ski Valley—a record Steve Fournier was playing nonstop in Houston's earliest hip-hop clubs.

DJ Screw (from *3-N-Da Morning*) "'Sup, Al-D? Little brother from another mother . . . Dennis, Mongoose, what's up? Nik-Nak, she in here, know'm sayin'? What's *up*? In this motherfucker *trippin'*, 'cuz. You know I gotta holler at that boy on that Broadway . . . Y'all niggas quit crankin' them cars. All them boys be crankin', know'm sayin'? Catchin' niggas slippin' *daily*. What's up, Kevin? Smokin' big weed. You know I gotta holler at that boy Will, locked down."

Years later, that particular mixtape would be reissued by Screwed Up Records & Tapes as *Chapter 108: 3-N-Da Morning*. But where Screw really made the footprint of *3 'N the Mornin'* was with Russell Washington in 1996. Technically, *All Screwed Up* was a compilation, but it had done so well with DJ Screw credited just for the remix that Russell felt like Screw should do a record of his own. Screw agreed, so they drew up paperwork and booked another session with Maestro, this time with four turntables. Screw once again flossed together a host of West Coast music—Ice Cube, Spice 1, Too $hort, and plenty of Dr. Dre—but he also looked east, to LL Cool J and "Rock the Bells" and Schoolly D's "Mr. Big Dick." That mix became known as *3 'N the Mornin' Part One*, and it was only called *Part One* because they were forced to do *Part Two*. And they only had to do that because the samples in the original mix could never have been cleared.

Robert Guillerman "Russell brings it in, it's a double CD. We had pre-solicited it. You know, we did like the majors did. We solicited all the record stores. We had a one-sheet, sent it out, we had orders. It was a double CD, *3 'N the Mornin'* volume one and two. And we had preorders for almost forty thousand of both CDs, and then I realized Russell didn't . . . he's got LL Cool J songs on there—I mean it was totally not cool, and I just didn't think we could take a chance with that, so I told Russell he's gotta go back and do another one."

Russell Washington "*3 'N the Mornin'* *One* and *Two* was actually gonna be the record, and at the time when we submitted, we did the one-sheets and submitted it, we had got probably a hundred thousand orders. But what happened was, we hadn't cleared all the samples and the licensing of the songs. After meeting with the legal team, it was just unfeasible to try and do it without clearing it, and it was unfeasible to try and clear it, being such a small company. So, we started workin' and we actually did the whole license deal with all Houston people."

Robert Guillerman "And that was—boy, you talk about hard. Screw was *real* slow. I mean real slow. I mean I've seen Russell cryin' about it, and I'm not kidding. I don't know how long it took, maybe a year to get the version that we put out, and we sold . . . eventually I'd say we sold close to a couple hundred thousand."

Lil' Keke "I remember Screw, when he was tryin' to put it together, it was a lot of problems because, you know, this was when the outside public had started catchin' on. Some of the people that he was Screwin' their music, a lot of people didn't want people to do it on *3 'N the Mornin'*. They was tellin' him—people right in the city—artists right in the city tellin' him, *No. You can't put this on '3 'N the Mornin'.'* I remember this, frankly. Screw had to change that tape a *lot*. That's why it ended up with—back when most of [them] on it, Point Blanks and C-Notes and all that, I remember when he was first puttin' it together we wasn't even actually gonna do a flow. This was Screw, actually his first kind of like record deal. He was really fittin' to get ready to put out—he was gonna put one in the *store*. We hadn't really been in the *stores* like that. He was gonna really get to put one in the store, he was gonna get the autograph signing. This was big, and we all used to be laughin', sayin', *Man, Screw ain't gon' never get that tape done. Man, Screw gonna take forever to do that '3 'N the Mornin'.'* Because, you know, it wasn't that he was just that slow. Screw had his own . . . you was gonna have to show me you was gonna pry him away from them Screw tapes. Screw didn't want no 97.9s, he ain't want none of that. He ain't *need* none of that. Them tapes goin' for ten dollars, it's eight o'clock and that's what it is."

DJ Screw (from *3 'N the Mornin' Part Two*) "Dirty Red. Lil' Courtney. Will. Know'm sayin', Gator. Puttin' it down. Big Dez. Lil' 3rd, Lil' Head, know'm sayin'. Southside. Screwed Up Click. Know'm sayin'. What's up, Lil' Keke? What's *up*?"

Screw finally did finish, and BigTyme released *3 'N the Mornin' Part Two*, having never actually released *Part One*. The way Screw had been working on it, the album was destined to be a classic, and it delivered.

Soundwaves opened at midnight on the day of its release, and couldn't keep the record on their shelves, it sold so fast. Finally they called up Russell, asking about that missing *Part One*, and made him an offer that resulted in a limited local release.

There was one more mix, *3 'N the Mornin' Part Two Remix*, which morphed the two previous versions. Screw kept some of the same artists but changed up the songs, handing the vibe off back and forth between tracks he bent together, finding peaks and valleys from one to another that opened up the music when he finally slowed it down. There was treasure in his taking so long to do it. That was the way of Screw. He kept going.

JUNE 27TH

June 26, 1996—A ninety-degree day in Houston, and since the temperature nears one hundred on the regular, the air outside feels pert near tepid. Houston is always muggy, though, and the humidity in the air meant Screw still would have broken a sweat as he made his way through the parking lot at South Main and Westridge that Wednesday afternoon. But he was going to be standing in the air-conditioned aisles of Soundwaves more than long enough to dry off.

Nikki "We would drive around to different Soundwaves and Screw would hide records in the store and go back in two days and get them. When *The Chronic* came out, Screw had like twelve copies. Some had never been opened."

He took his time going through the stacks, new releases and old. The day before, Brooklyn rapper Jay-Z had dropped his debut album *Reasonable Doubt*. Bone Thugs-N-Harmony were at the top of the charts that summer with "Tha Crossroads." Screw didn't miss a thing. Anybody who took him anywhere knew he moved slow, and shopping for records was his most prolonged investment of time outside of the house. People were giving him records—Lump, DJ Oakcliff, even the record companies themselves—but he was still casting a giant net, and nobody was finding out about music on the web in '96. That was when you took a chance on records, or listened to the people around you. Carlos "DJ Styles" Garza and Russel "The ARE" Gonzalez worked at Soundwaves, and they'd tell him about new records. Eventually, Russel even told him he could order tapes in bulk, when Screw was still buying them in two and four packs.

Screw bought $121.14 worth of records and tapes that June afternoon. A few weeks before, he'd made a tape for DeMo Sherman called *Dancing Candy*. Big DeMo had been the architect of his session, choosing the songs and spearheading the roster. For the music, he asked Screw for Bone Thugs and 2Pac, with local love for 8Ball & MJG, Ronnie Spencer, and Mr. Mike of the group South Circle. For the freestyling, he wanted to bring in a new voice.

Jarvis Lemon had been to Screw's house once before. His cousin Pat Lemon had brought him along when he went there to drop off some drank, and as was the case when the drank man showed up, it became a party. By the end of the night, Jarvis found himself in the wood room with Screw mixing, a dream scenario for the young man. So when he was passed the mic and told to shout out his name, he did so: "Yungstar!"

Yungstar "They was passin' the mic around, and then one of the dudes said, *You want the mic?* He gave me the mic, told me to say somethin'. I thought he was talkin' 'bout freestylin'. I was fittin' to gon' and wreck. I was like, *Hold on, I'm waitin' to catch the beat,* and they were like, *Naw, naw, naw! Just do a shout-out. Say who you is.*"

And so Yungstar's first appearance on a Screw tape ended with him handing back the mic before doing any damage. It wasn't easy to get in that house if you didn't know Screw, but he would sling into that orbit another way, through a couple of guys he knew from Long Drive—DeMo and Key-C—both of whom had been telling him they were going to take him over to Screw's house since they'd first heard him rapping. He was supposed to go with them on the night they made *Dancing Candy*, but it never happened. To boot, DeMo fully intended to freestyle on that tape himself, but he passed out on drank before he ever got a chance. Key-C picked up the slack, covering nine minutes of UGK's "One Day" with Big

Moe and Third Ward's Big Pokey, a football player turned rapper from Yellowstone who was fast becoming one of the biggest voices in the Screwed Up Click. It was Key-C's first tape, and one of Big Moe's, too.

Yungstar "DeMo always orchestrated. That's the way he was with his tapes. He gon' orchestrate the list of songs, the playlist, who rap on what, who rap first. With that *Dancing Candy*, I was 'posed to have made it with him. By that time I was doin' a little writin'. DeMo used to tell me, *Write your thoughts! Write it down. You know how to write?* I was like, *Man, no?* . . . *Man, this, this here—every time, you break it down.* So one time when he gave me a couple of tracks to write under, he showed me how to write it down and do it. Then it was like, *Tomorrow we got the studio time, why don't you come in there. Be ready. Stay writin', stay practicin'. We tryin' to go to the studio.* So we go straight in there, and that's how we learned. When I was a teenager—well, really like a *minor* minor—I wrote a song, 'I'ma kill a man, 187, you know, I'm a pimp,' some shit like that. So I didn't know that writin' was in me, but that's that age, like fourteen and fifteen, messin' with DeMo, and now, *Oh, I can do it. Aight. I got it.*"

Moe created a space that night, a stream of consciousness born from melodies teased out slowly, like he was pumping them straight from his heart. He was channeling, feeding something new into the living thing that was the Screwed Up Click. Moe was *singing*. Ronnie Spencer sang, too, and there were others, but Moe brought an entirely unique new voice into the Screwed Up Click, and it turned out not only that there was room for him to do it, but that it was what the S.U.C. needed, right then. And DeMo was going to bring him right back in.

Key-C "When DeMo fell asleep on *Dancing Candy* . . . he fell *asleep!* You know, you be listenin' to music, Screw doin' his thang, you just sittin' down, and pretty soon you nod off . . . *pow!* That was that syrup in him. Man! Screw had one headphone on and another one off, mixin' and scratchin'. Everybody else in the back laughin'. So we did the tape! But he wake up, he like, *Nah, Screw—go ahead and do another tape. We just gon' do it on my* birthday, *June 27.*"

1 DDDD1 DDScrew

ScSc

111111111111111111111111111111 1 1111111111111111111 11111111111111111111111111111111111111111111111111111111

So come June 27, Thursday, it's DeMo's birthday, and he's off to Screw's house to make a tape. This time, he brought somebody else with him. When they got to the house, Yungstar reintroduced himself to Screw. Other folks started coming through. Reggie "Bird" Oliver showed up. Man Poo was there. Big Pokey and Big Moe were expected later on. Screw was on the turntables all day but didn't start recording the first side until around midnight.

He started out slow with a skit, sliding into "Crossroads" from Bone Thugs, pitched *way* down, with Screw seeming to take a particular joy in how much time he had to stretch out the chopping, considering how fast the R&B group would usually spit their verses. "All About U" by 2Pac follows, and then, midway through the first side, Screw starts looping an instrumental of the laid-back 1994 beat by West Coast rapper K-Dee, "The Freshest MC in the World." Produced by Ice Cube, it was a Screw tape favorite, and it featured a sample of "Free," a 1976 R&B song of the "quiet storm" variety by Deniece Williams that Screw would have heard from his mother's record collection. Once he mixed that in, the shout-outs began.

Big DeMo (from *June 27th*) "1996. DeMo back up in this bitch once again, baby. It's my birthday. I got . . . first, I'ma show love to all these niggas that's in here. Just takin' time out, not hittin' that Carro's tonight. Come up here and chill. I got my boy Goldie up in here, straight off the L, got my boy Yungstar in here representin' that Sand*piper*. I got my boy Big Boy in here, we up in here regulatin'. I got that boy Mark, we got Clay, you know Screw in here, Key-C up in here. Man, it's so many mo' people 'round the corner! Big Moe and Pokey and them all forgot. Man Poo up in here. They comin' through late night just . . . you know, we *thirsty*, and we gon' just . . . you know, I'ma let everybody get on here and holler at some people."

The "Freshest MC" freestyle set the tone for the entire tape, grinding on for twelve and a half minutes. Man Poo took the mic, followed by Bird. Next thing we're hearing Big Moe, who came in singing. Screw chopped in Too $hort's "Gettin' It" and Botany Boys' "Try'n to Survive." With that, he had recorded the first side.

DJ Screw (from *June 27th*) "Say. Fuckin' with them boys out that Drive. Fittin' to get up outta here, know what I'm talkin' 'bout. Gettin' fucked up in here tonight, know'm sayin'. Southside. Stay up. Stay real."

Key-C "It was late. About two. Everybody was there. Everybody chillin'. Everybody start poppin' up. I had been with Pokey, though. Pokey went to school with my brother. They graduated in the same class, one of my brothers. Me and Pokey, we would freestyle at the car wash, goin' back and forth. Wasn't no competition—we'd just back each other up."

Chris Cooley "I had to hype up Yungstar to rap. He was nervous! Went in there and told Screw, *Man you need to put this dude on your tape.* Big Moe and them doin' they parts in the other room. Everybody in the other room freestylin', Yungstar was freestylin' in the livin' room. I was like, *Man, you need to get in there and get on that tape.* He was like, *I don't know, man!* It was a full house that day."

DJ Screw (from *June 27th*) "Lemme holler at some of my boys. First, I'ma flip through the Tre, Clay 'n' them . . . Let's go to Fourth Ward, what's up, Dave? I'm hollerin' at ya, baby. Six years in Long Drive."

Screw cued up an instrumental, the Jermaine Dupri–produced beat for Kris Kross's "Da Streets Ain't Right." The song itself samples the bass line for the Romantics' "Talking in Your Sleep" and the Notorious B.I.G.'s "Warning," the latter of which derives from Isaac Hayes's version of "Walk On By." With that musical foundation, Moe started singing. Then Bird came in rapping, Moe again singing, DeMo, Moe again, Key-C with the longest verse of all in the middle, and then Moe again, who introduced the newest voice in the wood room: "I'm gonna bring young G in on this mic / his name is Yungstar / you know that he's rolling tight / I'm gonna bring him in and I'm coming down."

And with that finally entered Yungstar, who started out low-key, confidence building with every word. He was taking in the room, at the same time establishing himself like he'd been there the whole time, "As I slow the beat down, see the diamond face crown / wrecking whole H-Town, coming through and we down / with them hoes wanna see me, yellows in bikinis / break 'em off for DeMo, it's his birthday and that Key-C."

Moe sang again, Big Pokey following with a long freestyle of his own, Moe again, K-Luv, Moe, Haircut Joe, Moe, DeMo again, Moe, Key-C, Moe, and then Yungstar once more. By night's end—with all of the thunder and lightning caught on tape in that half hour—when Yungstar finished it off, breathless, he had clearly made an impression.

Screw finished up the tape with a chopped and screwed mix of "Roller Skates," by the English reggae group Steel Pulse, 2Pac's "High Till I Die," and then an instrumental of "100 Spokes," by the Cali group Above the Law. Responding to the space he'd left between the tracks after the thirty-five-minute freestyle had sucked all the air out of the room, Screw only said a few words before letting the "Spokes" beat ride out for almost two minutes, closing out the vibe slow, like he liked it. Then, despite the excitement of an epic freestyle they couldn't wait to hear, that's exactly what they were going to have to do.

Key-C "Once you do the Screw tape, you gonna have to wait. You can't get that tape that same day. You can't. It's impossible. He had people comin' in there thinkin' they had special privileges. You know how that is. I done seen it happen a bunch of times. People come in there with drank, a pint, and Screw there, and they're all, *Screw, man, I want my tape, man, I brought you a pint.* And Screw would look at 'em and say, *Aight.* And make 'em play that *wait* game. They on that wait game!"

Yungstar "I was in the back seat—DeMo was drivin', Key-C was in the passenger seat. And I said, I leaned to the front and I said, *Ay, turn that down right quick.* They turned it down. I said, *Man, what's that mean, Screw say 'You in.' What's that mean?* DeMo told Key-C, *Aye, cut that down a little bit mo'.* So Key-C reached over and turned it down, and DeMo say, *Tell him what you just said—what'd Screw tell you?* I said, *He say, 'You in.'* And DeMo looked, he said, *You know what that means, don't you? . . . Nah, what?* He said, *Listen, you better be in there, nigga. You good. Nigga, you better be in there every day you can, tryin' to make your thang known.* I say, *Why you say that? I'm still tryna . . .* He say, *Nigga, if he say, 'You in,' you good! You ain't got to go with me. You 'posed to go over there and get on* the next '3 'N the Mornin'.' You need to go over there and try to get on that! Key-C was like, I told ya. Well, he was sayin' I told you, like Screw real—he gonna like you. They were back and forth talkin' about, I knew it. I knew Screw was gonna . . . you hard, boy!"

About a week later, just in time for July 4, Screw released dubs of June 27th, and the people who had been lining up at his gate every night during the allotted hours went wild for it. The legend of DeMo Sherman's birthday takes off from there. Those guys in the house that night might not have known they'd recorded a hit, but the Houston listening public knew it, and made it so. When people went down to Galveston's East Beach for the holiday, June 27th was the Screw tape of choice, and it has continued to be the most popular of all of them over the years.

Key-C "Everybody that knew him, it wasn't nothin' to go over there, chill, we'd do freestyles. Nobody meant to go there and make a classic, you know? It was like magic. You know what it really is, is that Screw brought everybody together. He got South Park, Sunnyside, Third Ward, Fourth Ward, he brought 'em all together. They from different sections of history, you know? There really wasn't no animosity, hate, you really don't have that, you know? Even Southwest. It helped a lot. You can get on there and express yourself."

Russell Washington "If Screw put something behind you, there was gonna be some fire to it. Every time. He definitely had an ear. Them Screw tapes, some of them Screw tapes—he could work magic right there. I think he was sellin' tapes, but there was definitely—in between that '95, late '96, there was a drastic change in his life, just period. I remember that first car was a four-door kind of car he bought after he got paid from BigTyme, and then I remember him gettin' an Impala after he got paid from 3 'N the Mornin', and I was at his house when he was doin' that, and there was some people comin' for tapes. I remember it being a madhouse after 3 'N the Mornin', but he didn't do anything to promote those tapes. Some of those tapes got to have sold into the millions. Between all the people who bootlegged 'em, how many times . . . I mean, where is June 27th as it stands? That's gotta be two million records!"

RIDIN' DIRTY

July 29, 1996—UGK releases the album *Ridin' Dirty* on Jive Records. It was a national release, but the duo's third album kept Houston front and center, featuring Mr. 3-2 and Ronnie Spencer on the album's hit song "One Day." For the cover, Keith Bardin shot photos of the group in the wood room with Screw and then staged a fake carjacking scene outside courtesy of the Botany Boys, who were honored to be the ones pictured robbing UGK.

Bun B "We took the picture in the wood room because the album is kinda dedicated to life on the Southside of Houston, especially 'Diamonds Against the Wood.' When I gave him the test vinyl, he nailed it on the wall."

Around the time of the album's release, Pimp and Bun went over to Screw's house to make a tape. They started off freestyling over an instrumental of their own "Fuck My Car," with Bun changing the song's hook from "They ain't trippin' on me, they wanna fuck my car" to "You ain't kickin' it with me, you wanna sip my Barre." Somehow seamlessly blending Pimp C's fluttering keyboard movements and rich, funky bass lines into the tinny, compressed synthesizers and gated beats of Total's "No One Else," Screw put another song to work off the same Kris Kross album from which the beat for *June 27th* was drawn. That single, "Live and Die for Hip Hop" was culled from a sample of Regina Belle's 1989 single "Baby Come to Me," which went gold in 1990 at the hands of magic-making R&B producer Narada Michael Walden, with the Kris Kross version again produced by Jermaine Dupri. The musical selections for the night were coming together. UGK wanted one more element in the room.

Macc Grace (a.k.a. Dat Boy Grace) "I was in Mo City ridin' with my pot-nahs and Screw called on the phone. Said, *What you doin'?* . . . *Man, just chillin'* . . . *You need to get some more drank, and y'all need to come straight over here.* I said, *You ain't even know how much drank I got!* He said, *Man, get some more drank—and come.* . . . *What's up?* He like, *Man, Pimp and*

Bun over here right now. They fittin' to do a tape. I asked them who they wanted me to call from the Click to come rap with them. Nigga, they said you. You need to get over here right now. Are they gonna bring you right now or do I need to come get you? I'm like, Man I'm on my way!"

Screw and Pimp C had become closer in the years since UGK started coming to the house on Greenstone. Six months earlier, they'd been jailed together one night for smoking weed in Pimp C's car outside of a store around the corner from Carro's—on a night they were supposed to record together. They had very different public and private personas—Screw was quiet and kept a low profile, while Pimp C had a foul mouth and was confrontational in his lyrics—but each of them in his own way was innovative and fearless with his music and generous when it came to the skills of others.

K Dubb (producer, promoter) "By that time, he had a real soldier behind him in terms of Pimp C, who was *always* speakin' on Screw and like, he really . . . a lot of people don't get it, but Pimp was someone that would so *go hard* for Screw. Everywhere he went, he was jammin' Screw, and lettin' people know, *This is how we do it.* I think there were a combination of things that led to Screw being exposed to a much wider audience, because people were really spreading the word organically. I know 8Ball & MJG were certainly spreadin' the word. South Circle was spreadin' the word. UGK was spreadin' the word—they were spreadin' the word! So these guys were *doin'* shows in Denver, and they're doin' shows in Las Vegas, and whether it's before the show or after the show or *on* the radio station that they're doin' their interviews or their in-stores, there was *constantly* a reference, because people were *curious* about it. And so to have these top-line artists speaking so glowingly about Screw, I really believe, like I say, '95, this was a time when the South got somethin' to say, right?"

LOS (Macc Grace's brother) "That's why I really love Pimp, man. He was a real one, mane. I'll be hollerin' at and keepin' in contact with his son, Lil' Chad, man, he a good dude, too. Pimp was a solid dude, man. Pimp had plans for my brother when he got out. When Pimp got out, he was still locked up. He was fittin' to do somethin' for the G. He was ready to give him a look. He was ready to push him, man."

Bun B "Screw was such a big influence on [the] *Ridin' Dirty* album. The feel of it was tryin' to replicate what a Screw tape *felt* like. What life on the Southside of Houston kinda felt like, and all of the things . . . it encompassed a day in the life of somebody on the Southside of Houston."

7. Screwed Up Click
1997

Screw had established a frequency. Not as far as how often he was releasing tapes—though he was in the thick of his most prolific stretch—but more like a vibration only he was putting out there. The pulse of his music was something people had been listening for all of their lives. A wave that moves like that, anybody can catch a ride. But the slowness was only part of what was speaking to Screw's fans.

Screw played some drums growing up. Not for long, but maybe long enough. Behind the turntables, he put the whole of his body to work in much the same way a drummer uses their limbs behind the drum kit, like coils from the nervous system, down through the legs and arms and all the way out to the fingertips. He knew how to fill the space because he could hear it in his head. All of that scratching and chopping wasn't random, but *specific*. Screw interrupted the course of the song to pull new rhythms from the ether and deal them into the deck of his sound. Maybe he did that on the fly, or maybe he thought about or even practiced how he would cut songs together. Nobody could tell by watching him. All they knew was that he was in the moment, and no movement felt second-guessed. Listening back, those cuts got deeper with repeated listens. Everybody wore out their Screw tapes.

Emerging through the stratosphere of bass was the message. Screw moved things around, and wasn't shy about splitting apart and cutting lines of vocals back together—backward, even. Verse and chorus swapped spots, lyrics took on new shades in the retread, and a song's entire linear meaning was disrupted—with purpose. Screw was emphasizing what was being said in the song, but he was also unafraid to contradict in the way he spliced them together, as he did on Lil' Keke's 1995 personal tape *Don't Make Dollars, Don't Make Sense.*

In that session, throughout the course of a nine-minute mix of "Blow Dem Hoes Up" by South Park Coalition duo the Terrorists, Screw runs rapper Dope E.'s verses into a bottleneck and quilts them back together into brand-new meanings. Keke was on the mic, ruminating on the hardships in people's lives: "We already got a battle against them folks. One foot on the banana, one foot in the jailhouse. That's why Southside gotta stay together. Gotta watch them prejudiced bastards, man."

That was a reference to Dope's refrain, "*Prejudiced* bastards." After giving his DJ time to let the song breathe, Don Ke gave him a nudge: "Screw . . . make 'em feel ya, baby." And with that, a couple of minutes in, Screw lets the track drop out to an empty beat that runs for a spell before a couple of quick cuts count it off like a drumroll and the track explodes in a barrage of synth bass and trumpets over a big, wet beat throttling underneath Dope's delivery—sharp and direct, like the anti-racist message the song carried with it.

But it doesn't feel like Screw is tracking the beat so much as he is Dope's lyrics, at one point slicing, "You're obsessed with the fact that I'm Black / and I'm obsessed with the fact that I'm Black with a bat," into "You're obsessed with the fact that I'm Black / I'm obsessed with the fact that I'm *prejudiced*," the last part cut from the song's refrain. And then, Screw slides things back to normal like nothing happened, charging along with the song's original intent, a masterful interruption forcing questions from the tape deck, on the dance floor, in the slab—making sure everybody out there listening is paying attention.

That was always the idea—to get them *really* listening. Screw took everybody's favorite songs and ripped them wide open, tearing into the fabric of the original sound, decompressing, adding earth, adding sky, adding *voice*. People describe songs on Screw tapes as being more emotional. Maybe that was the point—to open up the music until it bleeds.

Screw slowed it down to reveal more complicated notes, and to find the nerve endings in the music.

By 1997, the public had gotten used to the sound of a compact disc, the popularity of which neatly pushed past cassettes and vinyl earlier in the decade. Record stores still stocked tapes, and drugstores still sold blanks, but it was a dying format. For Screwheads, though, that was part of the vibe, his sound embedded deep in the tape and made alive by the complicated set of plastic jaws that go into motion when one presses play on the cassette deck. Besides, there was pride in it. Screw tapes were supernatural. He came on the scene as the cassette was entering its decline in the early '90s, and Screw tapes not only outlived the format but arguably extended the life of the cassette tape in Houston. People still played tapes in H-Town because that was how DJ Screw released his music.

Screw had put a flag up, and new stars were being added to it all the time—Big Toon, Fooly Wayne, Tyte Eyez, Horace, Mantny, Larro, Big Duck, Big Troy, Big Lenny, Big Ant, Baytown, Hen Duce, King, Bubba Luv, Wacky J, Lil' Chuck, Lil' Boo, D-Pac, Gee-Ree, Tolu, T-Bone, Cripple Jr., Ken Bell, Lil' Black, Robot, Phenon, Skinny Shaun, Lil' Randy's brother Ron O—each of them with a different origin story and a different dynamic with Screw. Rappers from different backgrounds and styles cross-pollinated onto his tapes, and then that porridge of sound traveled in cars all over the city, state, and beyond, making local superstars out of underground heroes and creating a sound from one man's touch. It was unlike any movement before it in Houston.

Jhiame Bradshaw "Rap-A-Lot was Fifth Ward culture! They wasn't screamin', *Houston!* They was screamin', *Fifth Ward!* Screw was the original culture of Houston, you feel me? And I didn't even *like* Screw tapes! Then after I start seein' what the hell was goin' on, I said, *Screwed up? These boys on to somethin'!* And then I start sippin' a little lean, sittin' back, listenin' to it . . . *What I gotta do to get there?* I'm an R&B producer! I said, *What the fuck?* But then I start *listenin',* and I said, *Hold up! This dude got some ingenuity.* It was an art form. I stopped lookin' at it . . . because I don't like fry, and I always thought that was a fry thang, like you gotta be

on some ant water or somethin'. But once I really *listened*, I start respec-
tin' the art form, 'cuz I could hear the *feel*. He was choppin' at the right
time, on the snap. I start seein' what the *art form* was because I could
appreciate what the DJ was doin'. The *DJ* sold me on that."

Big Floyd (from "Cocktails") "Give me my music / man I'll straight Screw
it / give it to the DJ / he's the fuckin' man / comin' down the sand / drums
beatin' like a band / it's that Big Floyd / livin' large in that game / only
out for fame / on my name / Mary Jane / that's what I smoke / never will
I choke."

Fat Pat (from *Show Up and Pour Up*) "Y'all feel us in here? Look here—it's
going *down*. We been sayin' things for a long time, and them boys be
feelin' us out there in the world. They *know* we real. We done *showed*
up, we done screwed up your tiny English city. And it's a trip now. Y'all
pourin' killah drank and syrup, bein' like, *Look!* Know'm sayin'? How we
slang it how *we* do . . . Funkin' it *up* / I got five on the weed / and fifty on
the drank / I'm comin' down / Got my mind on bank / What the fuck they
thinkin' about? / P-A-T / Think I don't capitalize / on the motherfuckin'
industry?"

For the rappers who appeared on Screw tapes, now was the chance to
move beyond the house on Greenstone. Screw had gone back and forth
about whether or not to start a label, and still hadn't moved on it by the
time record deals started happening for the rappers on his tapes. But his
sound carried on with them, as they worked off of one another, always
in new combinations, every night. Some of them writing, all of them
ready to improvise. Screw made them appreciate being in the moment,
teaching them even in their twenties that life was fragile.

Everyone around Screw was reminded of that on New Year's Day in
1997, when Pat Lemon, "Drank Man," was murdered by his wife in their
home when they got into an argument in the kitchen and she stabbed
him. Lemon wasn't the first death in Screw's life, or the first life taken
violently—Michael Price was just a few years earlier—and Screw probably sensed that it wouldn't be the last. But the Screwed Up Click was
family, and they moved forward as one.

Kiwi (Kingsgate) "Screw definition of the Screwed Up Click at that time, it wasn't about . . . it wasn't just rappers. Screw definition was like us comin' together, it was like he was like, *Man, the Screwed Up Click is a group of people—we all come together as one, as a family.* 'Cuz you know, you had hustlers, you did have the rappers, you had a couple dudes that was doin' all other thangs, but it was comin' from different hoods, and as one people. *We Screwed Up Click.* So it wasn't all about the *rap*, but that's what actually pushed it."

DJ Screw (writing in *Platinum* magazine) "Music really can change a lot of things. I like to keep heads up. As a DJ, I remember times when some niggas couldn't kick it in other neighborhoods. With my music, I brought a lot of people together. Right now, it's off the hook. A lot of people in the underground heard my music, so when they get to Houston, all they scream is Screw, Screw, Screw. You know what I'm sayin'?"

Al-D (as told to Jason Culberson) "I told Screw, I said, *Man, you gonna be big, man. Everybody who we look up to gonna look up to us one day, man.* Screw laughed his ass off. Man, he never had the big head. That's one thing I love about Screw—Robert Earl Davis. He never had the big head. You know how long it took this boy—*with* money—to get a slab? To get the piece and the chain and the ring? One ring, one piece, one chain. *Not* flamboyant. I remember right before he passed he said, *Al, what do you think about a grill?* I say, *Mane, get it!* He always needed that approval from his real niggas, his brothers. Because he never wanted to go overboard with anything. Screw had a hoop for the longest, with just no paint on it, no rims, and bangin'! You feel me? He was just never flamboyant, never had a big head, never capped not one day in his life. But he coulda capped! He coulda did all that. And he didn't. He was down to earth. He was humble. He was a peaceful spirit, man."

Enjoli (rapper on Screw tapes) "I was a lil sister. It's like everybody had my back. I'm the female artist, and it was just like nobody could touch that. Nobody could take my spot. It's just like, *She the queen, that's what it is.* It never did bother me, like goin' to shows and bein' on the road and in the hotel room with all the guys. You know, it didn't bother me because like those were my *brothers*. That's how Screw made you feel. I mean, even if you listen to him on his tapes, it's just like a real person lookin' you in the eye and sayin' they love you. Anybody can say they love you, but when a person could look you in your eye and say they love you instead of lookin' off, you know, that person really loves you."

PSK-13 (South Park Coalition) "Me and Screw *never* talked about music. We always talked about life, and he would ask me how was it bein' married, and how did you know that was the one? And, *How is it havin' kids? I'm gettin' my credit straight, I'm tryin' to get a car.* That's the stuff Screw talked to me about. And every time Screw would see me, no matter whose hood, and whoever was there, he would come to me and hand me his cup."

Ida Mae (as told to Matt Sonzala) "He knew what was doing and he knew he was good at it, but he didn't let it go to his head. He was just cool as a cucumber. And he was happy 'cuz he loved his music. Other than that he was the same old kid. Every time you met him he was the same person."

Chris Ward (rapper from Yellowstone) "But he wasn't cool with e'rebody. 'Cuz a lot of people was tryin' to mimic him, you know, just different things that was goin' on. And you know, in his business you gotta be cool with everybody, but he had a relationship with a lot of people that was deeper than the music. I met him through my homies just goin' to his house so many times. You know, we was *hopin'* to be cool with Screw. Who wouldn't wanna be cool with him?"

Big Jut (barber, as told to Jason Culberson) "I used to cut his hair, and I told him, *Man, I don't wanna cut your hair at your house. Lemme brang you to the barbershop.* So I brought him to the barbershop, and I cut his hair. Screw didn't really go out to clubs, and this was back when Jamaica Jamaica was crunk, and I told him, I said, *Man, I just passed by the club, they fittin' to let out.* And he was like, *Alright, we can go by there.* So, we went to the club, it's two o'clock, I ran up on one of my potnahs named Sunday, and Sunday like, *Man, whatchu doin'?* I was like, *Man, just up here chillin'.* He say, *Who you up here with?* I say, *I'm up here with DJ Screw.*

And man, when I said that, I promise you, this whole club that came out was surrounding this man. The police thought it was a big fight and e'rething. They like, *Man, what's goin' on?* I'm talkin' 'bout *the whole club.* So you know me, I'm like, *Man, who is this cat gettin' all this love like this?* But the funny part about it, when we got back in the car, he was countin' money. He was countin' money that people just pinnin' on him! Just givin' it to him! I was like, *Man, who are you, bro? Where people just givin' you this money like this?* Man, ever since then I knew he was somethin'. I knew he was somethin'. I mean it just tripped me out because I never seen nobody just give you money just because who you are. You know, he was a special dude. And there's one thing I like to say about him, he had a lot of fame. E'rebody know that. He ran Texas. And he never let that go to his head. That was the special part about him. He coulda been one of the ones that don't wanna speak, like some of these rappin' dudes do. He was always one hundred."

DJ Screw (writing in *Platinum* magazine) "I remember one day, this lady came over to my house. She told me she had a son, know what I'm sayin'. His name was Jason, and he was dying of cancer. She asked him, *Son, before you die, what do you wanna do?* You know what I'm sayin', *Before you die, what's the biggest thing you wanna do?* He said, *Before I die, I wanna meet DJ Screw and make a Screw tape.* And I told her to bring him through. So, shit, she brought him through. We kicked it. He was a cool little dude and everything."

Al-D (as told to Jason Culberson) "The kid was already to the stage where the hair was gone and he was goin' through the process and the medicine wasn't workin'. The kid was fixin' to die, and his mama kept it real, and said, *You know you're gonna pass. You know you're dying. What do you wanna do before you die?* She brought that lil kid down here, and he met Screw. And it hurt that boy—it didn't *hurt* him . . . what can you say . . . it tripped him [Screw] out so bad, that he didn't show any emotions or feelin's in front of this child or the people that was there, but he came to me, and he broke down, and he hugged me. He say, *Man, Al, you was right, man. You was right.* And I say, *Didn't I tell you, Screw, how important you are to all these people out here?*"

DJ Screw (writing in *Platinum*) "He wanted to be a rapper. He made his tape and met the Click. . . . He had a birthday coming up. I went to his party and hung out with him. That really touched me, for somebody just to love what I was doin' through these tapes. To me, it was just mixed tapes. But to them, it was something different."

Reggie "Bird" Oliver "He didn't even want people to know who we was. I accidentally said his name one day in the mall. He wasn't a selfish person—you'd never have to pay for food when you're around him—but I used to sneak into it sometimes. I'd say, *I gotta use the restroom right quick.* And then I'd go pay for the food, and then he'd go to the lady and say, *How much was . . . I want to pay for everybody.* Then she'd be like, *Well he already paid for it.* He's like, *Man, I told you—I got it! Don't pull your money out when you're around me.* He always wanted to pay for everything. Whenever the Jordans come out he'd go buy me and his girl, Nik-Nak, and a few other people the new Jordans, even if we weren't there. He'd know our size, he'd buy like fifteen pair of shoes. So one day we were in Foot Locker and I said, *Screw, what's such and such?* I accidentally said this dude's name in Foot Locker, and *everybody*—people are like, *Screw? That's DJ Screw? DJ Screw in here?* Everybody ran in there."

ACT "He came down to Smithville one year, man—you know how they have like parents' night at football games? Well, we walked on the field with Doug. He [Screw] had trouble gettin' out there, and then after he was comin' off the field, the damn bleachers damn near cleared. They come over to ask for autographs. And it was so crazy. I'm standin' up here, man, by the fence where he fittin' to come through there, and some lil girl—he signed some lil girl arm and she ran up to the law and say, *I'm more important than you!* She say, *I'm more important than you,* and showed the laws Screw had signed her arm. She say, *He signed my arm.* Man, I looked at that law, man, he didn't *like* that, man! Don't you know them laws escorted us from the football game, went to my mama house, and then escorted us from my mama house out of Smithville? Yeah, man. They didn't like that, mane. We was leavin' anyway, but they followed us. We was all together. But they followed us. They followed us like a motherfucker, man."

THE GATE

Screw had Fat Pat's uncle put up a gated fence around he and Nikki's front porch to keep people from walking up and knocking right on the door, but they still needed some peace around them, so he set some hours. Those hours varied, but in general folks could come buy Screw tapes from the house starting at 8 p.m. Sometimes earlier. Screw himself would usually stand at the gate taking money, sending helpers back into the house to retrieve whatever tapes were being requested. Nikki helped with the dubbing at all hours and kept things organized, and Screw kept buying double-cassette decks to increase his capacity. Some nights, they'd start with full boxes and still run out of tapes.

DJ Screw (writing in *Platinum* magazine) "I had a lot of people at my house, and everybody thought I was a drug dealer. I used to set a time to do business. From eight to ten, I was gonna sell my tapes. So, by 7:30 p.m., my whole driveway and street was filled with cars waitin' on me to open my gates. And to the rest of the neighbors, they really believed I was conducting illegal transactions. They never saw me come outside. I didn't wake up every morning like normal people that got a job, wearing uniforms and shit. It was like, shit, I was at the crib everyday making tapes. When eight o'clock would come, I would have around fifty cars all lined up in the streets to get these tapes."

Knock "I remember times we used to be in Screw house and we'll be waitin' to rap on a cassette and he'll be openin' his doors for people to come buy tapes. And there used to be people from Louisiana, Mississippi, Beaumont, from *everywhere* comin' to buy this dude's tapes. I'm talkin' about buyin' forty, fifty at a time, 'cuz I guess they goin' back down there sellin' 'em all. There used to be people from everywhere, man. There would be times we would set up and Screw had two or three hundred cassettes, man, just in a box, and within thirty to forty minutes' time, man, they gone. And that's because he sold out. It wasn't because there wasn't no more people out there. It's 'cuz he was sold out."

Chris Cooley "Once it start floodin' the streets, people comin' from out of town, just not even knowin' that he's *home*. They comin' from out of state and grabbin' the cassettes. And every time I would come from San Antonio to Houston, I'd see more. He'd have like the Sam's Club edition of blank tapes? You know, just a big case of blank tapes and stacks of cassette recorders, just dubbin' all day. Just all day long. When we leave to go to the store or somethin', Nikki does the house, makin' sure to flip the tapes over or whatever."

Kiwi "It wasn't right away, but it spreaded like the flu, mane. I'm talmbout when it came and people was understandin'—when they found out they had a concrete spot where I can, *Hey, this where we can go get 'em from.* It was like, man, it was havoc, man. I'm talmbout whatever he had sold out. I'm talkin' 'bout it wasn't *nothin'.* You know, it was gone. Back then, you know how tapes pop and you know I done people with screwdrivers open they Screw tapes up tryin' to patch 'em together, and they get to a spot in they tape deck where that spot will pick up and start playin' again—'cuz you gotta fix your tape! Scotch tape, whatever! Until I can get there Friday."

ACT "I used to stay over there, man, and people used to line up outside. That boy open the gate, cars pull up everywhere. What used to kill me was people used to knock, and Screw didn't have no tapes, and they go back to they car, damn near break the window out they car, they so mad they ain't get no Screw tapes, slam the shit out they door! Yeah, man, they gonna be mad as hell they ain't get them Screw tapes, man."

D-Ray (as told to Jason Culberson) "When I finally knew he kinda had made it, shit . . . probably when niggas wouldn't stop stealin' my damn Screw tapes! For Christmas one year, Screw Zulu, he said he wasn't gettin' nobody nothin' for Christmas. Screw said he wasn't gettin' nobody nothin' for Christmas. But you and Lil' D? I'm givin' y'all some Screw tapes for Christmas. So that's what we got! We got like seventy-five Screw tapes from DJ Screw hisself, and we had 'em here in Smithville, know what I'm sayin'? And our objective wasn't to gain money off of his tapes. Our objective was just to jam 'em! And let our potnahs jam 'em. You know, it's a Smithville thang. You know how we do out here. But there's some snakes in the grass. So, my brother end up goin' to the hospital, and I end up goin' to the hospital with him, and when I left to go to the hospital with my brother, that's when somebody broke into my T Jones house, stole my Screws—about seventy of 'em! I was *mad*, you feel me? I was hot. Shit . . . I was hot, man! I was mad."

ACT "When we started havin' them shows—we had a show I can't think of what club, I don't know if it was Carrington's or Jamaica Jamaica, but it was a concert with Hawk, Pat, Pokey, Al, me, Shorty Mac, Screw, Gold . . . it was a lot of folks there. I mean, Moe . . . everybody was there to perform. They had a door for people to pay and then they had a door for the artist to go in. And when me, Screw, Shorty Mac, and Al-D pulled up and got out the truck and started walkin' to the door, man, all them people just swarmed us! We had to hold hands to get in the club. I knew—I was like, *This somethin' serious.* That's when I knew it was big."

Nikki "He never took a deep breath. He never relaxed. For Screw, it wasn't about money. I feel a lot of DJs now, it's about fame, it's about . . . now, who produces the record is bigger than who's rappin' on the record! It wasn't like that for Screw. Screw didn't care if you mentioned his name or not, as long as he was doin' what he was passionate about, he didn't care if he made a dime. It wasn't about the money for him, so he never did take a breather. He wanted to make music. He wanted to do those tapes. He wanted to mix. That's what he wanted to do. We just happened to be able to pay the bills. That was just like a lil treat—we could actually pay the bills doin' what you love. That's what he really, really liked. That was his passion. Music was his passion for real."

FLOSS MODE

One constant through all of the growth of culture around Screw and his music were the slabs. People were rapping about their cars on his tapes—the metallic "candy" paint, the thirty-spoke "swanger" chrome rims, the "peanut butter" or "tight white" leather interiors—because that was the culture all over the streets, and because those cars were the primary broadcast system for Screw tapes. By this time, Lil' Ike had set up shop on the Eastside and was perfecting the art of the candy paint job, and other customizers were working all over town. And the massive Los Magnificos Car Show at the Astrohall—an exhibition and trade-show convention center with a footprint even bigger than that of the neighboring Astrodome—was a central gathering place for that culture each year. Hundreds of lowriders, trucks, and bikes were driven into the facility, with concerts throughout the day (South Park Mexican was known to bring his own system in there) and thousands of fans moving around the booths set up in the complex. As the show was still reeling from the death of its founder Joel Carmona in early 1996, attendees came out in the tens of thousands, and were treated to a rare public opportunity to get close to their beloved Houston artists. Screw had a space for a booth, but he initially didn't think anyone would stop by to see him.

Orian "Lump" Lumpkin (producer, promoter) "He got there late. They almost didn't let us in the damn car show! I was ready to fight Screw ass. So he had this big-ass dolly, them big push dollies that you have at Sam's? And it was full of tapes. I had him make a banner. We was like the first door when you open the car show—as soon as you opened up to the public, as soon as you walk in, we was the first booth on the left-hand side. We supposed to be set up and in there by nine, Screw didn't get there 'em ten. I had to talk shit to get him into the car show. And all we could do was set up. Man, do you know, from eleven o'clock until six o'clock, that boy made almost $30,000 in tape sales, sellin' mixtapes? People were comin' up givin' him one-hundred-dollar bills, *Just give me ten tapes, as long as they different.* People stood there the whole time. I had my pistol in a damn Ziploc, and I had my ice chest in there, because they used to let you bring an ice chest in there, right? So I put the ice in there, I put the pistol in a Ziploc, then I put ice over the top so we could have our guns in there. Because I knew we were going to have a lot of money, but I had no idea it was going to be *that* kind of money. We had to make Nikki stand behind us with a Gucci canopy purse and have to walk out of there with $30,000 cash, man. It was so crazy we had to give away tapes like every thirty minutes. You couldn't just sit there and sell tapes because we was *that* packed, and they just kept crowdin' in on us."

It was the most tapes Screw ever sold in one day. The car show meant something else that year, too. For most all of the trips he'd made to Sam's Club to buy cartons of tapes, to Soundwaves for records, or to Hartz Chicken, Dot's, or Frank's Grill to eat, Screw did not own a car himself. People always drove him everywhere he needed to go. In 1995, he had bought himself a burgundy Oldsmobile Delta 88, but by the fall of the next year, he was ready to upgrade and purchased a black '96 Chevy Impala off the lot. Screw later had the Impala painted his favorite royal blue, even though he was a Southsider and that would usually mean red. But as everyone who rode with him or drove near him would learn in the years that followed, the color of the paint didn't matter. It was about Screw having wheels, and what it meant for everyone else on the road.

E.S.G. "People tell me I can't drive, but I know I can drive, because I seen that nigga *Screw* drive! Screw couldn't drive at all, man. Oh my God. To this day, I'll do lil shit where I'll drive off with the gas thing still in the car. I'll pro'ly done tore about two or three of them motherfuckers off, just drivin' away. But Screw? That nigga gonna back up over some shit, he gonna pull up over your curb. That nigga could *not* drive!"

Pamela Davis (niece) "No, he could not drive. He felt like he was the only car on the road. And then, for a while, that Impala didn't have AC for a few months, and it was the middle of summer, and he would not let the windows down!"

Big Bubb "I remember when he got it—everybody was tellin' me! I had seen his old man, he told me about it. I was still workin' at Dr. Pepper at the time. Just e'rebody sayin', *It's nice! It's nice, man.* My old man, he had seen it, all that shit. I was like, *I'ma see it!* Man, one day I got off work, I was walkin' to my car, big black Impala sittin' out there. He done pulled up to the job! So we left there and went to my mama house, dropped my car off, jumped in the Impala. He had put two fifteens in it already by then, and it was knockin' like a motherfucker! And it sounded different because he had bought the right shit. Just clarity and *all* that shit. And we went ridin' that night. I think we end up goin' to shoot pool."

Pamela Davis "His music was so loud in his Impala, we could hear him coming *into* Smithville. And we lived out in the country! We would stand on the porch waiting for him to pull up. We would be like, *He's getting closer—it's getting louder!* You could hear him out on 71. There was a little mobile place where my grandma and her husband lived. It's a little trailer park out in the country, and we would hear him come in from 71 and we would stand on the porch and wait. And it'd be like an hour, because he drives like five miles an hour."

DON'T MESS WITH TEXAS

July 1, 1997—Lil' Keke is the first to leave the nest as a solo artist when he drops his first album, *Don't Mess Wit Texas*, on Jam Down. The title came from a 1980s Texas Department of Transportation antilittering slogan, "Don't mess with Texas." Screwed Up Click's Botany Boys had just released an album, but Keke was the first to strike out on his own, and for Houston, it marked the beginning of a new era. Keke had come up freestyling on Screw tapes. Now he had a record deal and a product in stores.

Jam Down had released the Triple Threat cassette that Screw produced years earlier. Screw told folks he felt like they slowed his career down, but Pat Lewis had some money to throw around, and Keke took it. In a recording session at Kevin Bomar's South Coast Recorders, he knocked out fifteen songs, the most electric of which being "Southside." The beat sampled the Larry Smith-produced 1984 song "Friends" by Whodini (which by then had already been sampled by 2Pac, Nas, and Dr. Dre), but Lil' Keke had a different vision for it.

Double D (producer, Platinum Soul) "Keke had kept askin' me to redo that 'Friends.' And I had never did it, but I had did another song, and when we were in the studio he asked again, and I just start doin' it right there. I just start puttin' little stuff in there, and then when I got there he was like, *Right there. That's it.* It didn't take that long. I don't know if he had his lyrics or what—I don't think I was there when he laid it—but he already had his idea."

Sean "Solo" Jemison also produced, and Keke invited Screw, Madd Hatta,

Mr. 3-2, Al-D, Mike-D, Big Moe, and Herschelwood Hardheadz into the booth. And of course there was Fat Pat, whom Don Ke had been taking around with him to open up his shows as his popularity grew from the album. Keke, Fat Pat, and Pymp Tyte played a legendary show together at Chocolate City in Orange, Texas, where the crowd boiled over capacity. *Don't Mess Wit Texas* was a local, then regional hit for the twenty-one-year-old rapper, and its momentum took Keke all over, even to the Northside (where Screw tapes were all but forbidden) and into the former location of the second Rhinestone Wrangler.

Lil' Keke "I done a show at the biggest club on the Northside, Chocolate Town. *Hey, man—they say we goin' to Chocolate Town. I say, No we ain't!* We in the middle of the Northside-Southside war for *real* right now, and my album just came out. But lemme tell you somethin' crazy—I sold forty thousand albums the first week that my album came out. Twenty-eight thousand in Houston! Nineteen thousand on the Northside. This when we used to really have numbers and SoundScans and you really know what's goin' on. So, they called! *Man, we gonna give Lil' Keke $10,000 to come to this Chocolate Town.* And in 1997, that's the equivalent of twenty to thirty thousand! I said, *Listen, they tough as hell but we goin' to get that ten.* So look what we do—everybody tryin' to figure out how we gonna go do what we gonna do. We get a limo, right? We gonna all pile in this one limo with guns. We got guns, we all in the limo, everybody. Now that I think about it, I say, *Man, we so crazy. We think we doin' somethin' safe by gettin' a limo, now dudes can just shoot up this one motherfuckin' car and kill e'rebody!* So we done went out here, man, listen—this shit is wall to wall all the way to the street, man. Listen, man, we nervous as shit! So they pull us in the back, *Man, I'm rockin' this shit.* This when you did songs and did *all* the verses. You know how we do one now? Oh shit, you doin' 'Southside,' you doin' *three* verses! So we rockin' it, we gettin' ready to go, man, they turned that joker *on!* Fifth Ward. Then I tell you—we ran out that back door and got in that limo and *tore ass!*"

OUTLAWS

The further the tapes were spreading, the more they got away from Screw.

People dubbed cassettes back then. Not everyone had a CD burner, even if most folks had converted over to CDs, so people were still copying tapes, and Screw tapes became some of the most dubbed because they were worth something even as copies. So his tapes went wherever people could play them, selling cassettes even if it was just folks buying them to get a dub of somebody's Screw.

Tommie Langston "When we would go do shows, tapes would be sold as a concession. Typically—and this is depending on where we went—there wouldn't be too many that we would bring back to be warehoused, okay? Selling out was a typical situation as far as that goes. It would be basically as many as we could bring. So if we brought several thousand tapes, we might be in the situation where's there's more money made off of the actual sales of the tapes that night than there was off of the show, and the show may be a nice round figure! But you made a lot more off the sales of your tapes than anything else."

DJ Gold (from *Houston Rap Tapes*) "We never came back with tapes. Bottom line. All them nights, man, we *never* came back with tapes. Not one."

Nikki "Sam's on 610. We kept them in business, and then if they didn't have them, we'd go to the one on Fuqua. And there was this guy that Screw had got real close with, and the crazy thing is if I see him, I cannot call his name. All we called him was '610.' He worked at Sam's, and he used to get Screw's tapes for him, and bring them to the house. Screw called him '610.' To this day, I cannot tell you his name, but he would bring Screw the tapes, and he would pay him back."

Big DeMo "I mean, so many people met Screw just in Sam's, buyin' up thousands of blank tapes. People wouldn't know who he was, but they'd figure it out real quick. *Man this dude got a whole bunch of—he's buyin' a whole lot of . . . gray tapes! Why would somebody need a thousand blank tapes? That's got to be DJ Screw!*"

Screw's one-hundred-minute Maxell cassette tapes followed all kinds of routes, copied and resold through mom-and-pop record stores, with lesser generations in the streets—some of them dubs, some of them slowed and chopped by hustlers and DJs who knew that the style was hot because they kept getting asked to slow things down, and so they made their own versions. The sound had folks begging for more, and they were searching for it anywhere they could get it, even from other DJs. And the very social nature of tape trading meant that things spread in reverse, too. That's how Screw knew about Master P and Hot Boys early on, and they all knew about him.

Dubbing his tapes was one thing, but he wanted to leave no doubt as to the source of the real Screw tapes, and where you could buy them. Screw tapes had proven so popular that other folks figured out a way to make money off of them. Bootleggers were buying up their own Maxell grays and making copies of original Screws, forging the handwriting on the cassette as best they could and then selling them on the streets, in shops, or at the car shows. Plenty of times they got busted, and the bootlegs were destroyed. All of this was leading Screw in the same direction.

Orian "Lump" Lumpkin "When Screw caught people bootleggin', he would go in there and snatch *all* of their shit. He would personally go do it. Man! In Houston? Shit yeah. He didn't play about his tapes. He did it at this store in Missouri City, right there where Jut used to cut hair at, right next door, on the corner of Chimney Rock and Fuqua. Music Zone 2000. Screw went in there and took all of his shit. Went behind the counter. Screw wasn't playin' about his money. He would buy them from Screw and then he would dub 'em. Screw would take his tapes and his money. He didn't play."

Great Black Shark "He'd grab 'em and ask you how you got 'em! *How did you get these?* That's the first question. There was never a answer. That's why he just walked off with it. Because that's his *work.* That was his blood, man!"

Al-D "Point Blank went the fuck off on one dude. I didn't even know what the fuck was happenin'. Screw was like, *Chill out, chill.* We went to King's Flea Market and there were some dudes sellin' Screw's shit, and the dudes that was with us, they went in his motherfuckin' store, went to the back, and took boxes and boxes and boxes of shit. In broad daylight, and King's Flea Market had fuckin' security, man! Walked right out of that bitch, man. They say, *Man, this old trash-ass shit.*"

DJ Screw (from *South Siders*) "Let Screw holler, know'm sayin'? We goin' late night, gettin' crunk, know'm talkin' 'bout. This ain't no flea market shit, 'cuz... know'm talkin' 'bout? For *real*, 'cuz, know'm sayin'. All these imitators, duplicators, player haters. Can't fade us! Screwed Up *Click*, mane. Y'all gonna wreck off, know'm talkin' 'bout."

But to James Prince over at Rap-A-Lot, and Tony Draper at Suave House, and folks at the major-label level, *Screw* was the bootlegger. He was the one putting songs by their artists on his mixtapes, making money from their catalog, new and old. And they had a point. There was a legal issue left gray. The majors had more of a problem with it than anyone—at first. That's because there was a parallel reality at work. Screw could just stop putting tracks from those labels on his mixtapes, and the result would be that those artists wouldn't be heard by his mixtape audience, which everybody knew by then was substantial. Screw had untold numbers of tapes in circulation, like thousands of different radio stations all playing mixes by the same DJ at the same time to thousands of different ears. For any label that understood Screw's reach, it was hard to argue with the publicity.

Orian "Lump" Lumpkin "I had Cash Money [Records], and nobody at the radio station would play Cash Money, so Baby [a.k.a. Birdman, Cash Money cofounder] just said, *Hey, man, give it to Screw.* I was like, *Man, he sell tapes.* He was like, *Slim, man, give them records to that dude. Let that dude make his money. We need the exposure.* And it worked! And that's why Screw—when Cash Money got big, the first in-store that Cash Money did in Houston was at Screw's shop. They had a live remote. Cash Money pulled up in the tour buses and everythang. Baby loved Screw. Lil' Wayne really did, too."

Lil' Randy (Southside DJ) "It turned from, *Screw bootleggin'*, to people *wantin'* they music on them tapes because he had so much popularity.

It was almost like free market. His marketing scheme was bigger than the radio. In Houston, you wasn't goin' to the record store no more. If it wasn't on a Screw tape, you weren't listenin' to it. That's why Screw was able to open up his *own* record store. In Houston, you had to go through Screw to get your record heard."

There was the bootlegging, and then there were people selling tapes that said "Screw," or "Screwed," or "Chopped & Screwed." That added to the tension between the Northside and the Southside, which by then had been simmering for years. Screw didn't say a whole lot about the Northside on his tapes, but other folks did. He didn't want bad blood between Northside and Southside, but neither could he suffer through other DJs taking on his style—especially if they invoked his name.

DJ Screw (from *What They Wearin?*) "I'ma say it again—this *ain't* no flea market shit. Know what I'm talkin' about? They dubbin' a nigga's shit, slowin' that shit down, callin' it 'Screw.' How the fuck they gonna call it 'Screw' and I ain't make it? Know'm sayin'? [*laughs*] Shit be a trip, though. Southside, what's up? Yeah, and I'm fittin' to tear this Northside shit up. Really I don't give a *damn*, know'm talkin' about? Whoever's in the South. Southside all the time, know'm talkin' about? I don't know *shit* over there, so I ain't gonna speak on that over there in the North, know what I'm sayin'? Nigga talk about a nigga be hatin' the North. North be hatin' *us*! For what? Know'm sayin'? I'm a deal with *e'rebody*, know'm talkin' about? I don't give a damn where you from. Shit . . . I ain't gotta explain myself to nobody."

That whole Northside-Southside beef was something *other* folks got their hands dirty with, starting in the early '90s and going on for years, like a drawn-out soap opera or wrestling match fought in streets and nightclubs all over town. The history was that it started over some rims, but it blew up way beyond that, and was a lyrical cornerstone of 1990s Houston rap music. Screw overwhelmingly stayed out of it. The venom slung from the Southside to the Northside on his tapes always came out of somebody else's mouth. He didn't stop it, nor fuel the fire, but he *did* give the Southside a platform. The Northside wouldn't have something like that until 1997, when DJs Michael "5000" Watts and OG Ron C started up the Swishahouse label to expand in a growing mixtape empire. Watts was from Homestead and Ron C from Fifth Ward, so they began promoting on that side of town—which was just as populous as the Southside—where folks were hungry to hear music slowed down that wasn't talking bad about the Northside.

It was natural for Screw to bristle at the fact that other folks were starting to slow music down, too, but his big problem was with people calling their form of slowing down a record "Screwing" that music. That's when he had to point out that he was the only one who could "Screw" a song, because it took Screw and only Screw in order to do it. If DJ Screw didn't do it, it wasn't a Screw tape. And it *wasn't* chopped and screwed. Didn't matter if it was from the Northside, like Michael Watts, or from the Southside, like DJ Bone, who made his own slowed and chopped mixes for CD buyers, or DJ AK-47, who was making tapes that were slow where he was talking slow, too.

Lil' Sock "Screw used to kinda be trippin' because Bone was emulatin' Screw. It's like somebody tryin' to take your money. Screw used to be cappin'! Screw used to be sprayin' it out, because they was emulatin' what he would do, and they had a few of his customers. And we were fuckin' with Bone, too! Because Bone had start bein' on CD before Screw was on CD. Screw was still on tapes! That shit was a little bit more *quality* than Screw. But you know, Screw was the originator! Screw was havin' money now!"

Nikki "His thing is, like now you look at it like it's a compliment, like it's supposed to be a compliment, *Oh, I Screwed this up.* Well, Screw was a *person.* It was his name, and the story goes—he tells the story all the time. His mom gave him that nickname because he used to use screws on her records! That's where it came from. It wasn't like somebody down the street—Ray Ray started tellin' him, *Oh, I'm with this guy, you're DJ Screw.* No. That started with his mom. That's why I say people don't know him and his mom had this bond that was unreal. So it's like . . . the bootleggin' wasn't an issue, but the calling your music 'Screw music'? That was bigger. He didn't really care what you did with the music because he had people that helped *him* start. Darryl Scott was instrumental in what Screw did. He *loved* Darryl. Like that was his boy, that was his big brother, that was his mentor. He loved Darryl. At the same time, it's like ... he didn't call himself 'Darryl Scott,' like *I'ma Darryl Scott the music*. No, that was Darryl's stuff! That was Darryl's trademark. So Screw developed his own, it became *his*. So for someone to say, *I Screwed this*, or, *I'ma DJ Screw that*, that was an issue for him."

GHETTO DREAMS

December 4, 1997—Late fall wind blows in big cold gusts down Greenstone on a Thursday night. It was Fat Pat's twenty-seventh birthday, and folks were still recovering from the Bayou Classic, a Texas-Louisiana football holiday that, for the gumbo of families that make up East Texas and all of the Boot, is no lesser an occasion than the Thanksgiving and Christmas it falls between. They started playing the game in New Orleans in 1974, and in this particular installment, Southern had beaten Grambling 30–7. Screw was still feeling the New Orleans vibe in the house that night, and pulled some records to tease out the feeling. It was shortly before the release of Pat's debut album *Ghetto Dreams*, which was to be put out by D-Reck's Wreckshop Records early in the new year. *Ghetto Dreams*—and Pat—had traveled a long road.

Double D "Pat had already told me from when he came over and got on a track that I had did for Keke, you know, when I was with Jam Down. He was like, *Man, you can rap. When I work on my album, I'ma have you do my beats* and *rap on it*. And, you know, I ain't really think much of it, but it played out just like that! We had a chemistry. We was puttin' in a lot of work, because I guess at that time, too, the rest of the producers, like Noke D and all them, they was still in Beaumont, so they would be back and forth to Beaumont. But I was in the studio all the time, and I was ready. I was like, *I got beats, let's do it*. It got to the point where I would call Pat every morning, *I got a lil beat*. Because a lot of times, I'd stay up and work all night. We wasn't sleepin', man. I'm serious. We wasn't sleepin'. We saw the dream! So of course we tryin' to do it, tryin' to make it happen. So he would be like, *Yeah, man. I'm about to get up and I'ma grab somethin' to smoke and I'll be through there.* And he'd come through, and when he'd come in, I'd already have one pulled up and he'd start bobbin' his head."

K-Rino (as told to Matt Sonzala) "I went to Sterling with Pat and Screw. Screw was a couple years earlier. I took home economics with Pat. This is how I knew, 'cuz I was rapping and Pat was a class clown. He'd be rapping, singing, doing everything, but I mean I didn't know he *rapped*. I thought he was just acting a fool in the class. Then I started hearing, *Fat Pat, Fat Pat*, in the streets. And I had no idea, I thought, *I guess there's a new dude called Fat Pat.* And I went to the Stadium Bowl. They used to have these shows . . . I don't know how I ended up in Stadium Bowl, I'm coming in and everybody coming out. There was twenty thousand people in the Stadium Bowl, and I look up and it's Pat, Patrick Hawkins. I said, *Man, you Fat Pat?* My God! That messed my head up. But right then is when I knew how big it was. 'Cuz I mean the streets was just on him so hard. That whole crowd knew every word."

On the tape they made that Thursday night, *It's All Good*, Screw channeled NOLA through Master P and Hot Boys. He also dropped in Mr. Mike of South Circle, who had just released his first solo record with Suave House, and of course he mixed in Fat Pat. "Tops Drop" was produced by J Slash and sampled the Yarbrough & Peoples 1980 disco-boogie single "Don't Stop the Music." Screw had a copy on vinyl, and Pat was more than happy to introduce the song.

Fat Pat "What's up? Southside. H-Tine. We doin' this here, representin', mane, this for that Mr. Fat Pat album comin' out in February. In stores soon. On the shelf."

Lil' Keke was in the house, but he and Pat didn't freestyle on the first side, or on most of the second side. The space between the songs was static until the very end of the tape, when Screw cued up a Nile

Rodgers–produced instrumental of David Bowie's "Let's Dance," and Pat and Keke went *in*.

Fat Pat (from "Been Around the World") "Swing down, sweet chariots, let us ride / we do the 'Body Roc' and we do the 'Southside.'"

Lil' Keke (from "Been Around the World") "Swing / down / please let us ride / when I come through / please, I can't be denied / 'cuz I'm on fours and I only screen chrome / when I'm on the King / you know I got my screens on."

Fat Pat (from "Been Around the World") "I'ma grab the mic and give the haters hell / it's the Mr. Fat Pat / got a story to tell / I'ma blow big weed down the highway, too / ain't nothin' that you can't jam on the Screw / 'cuz I'm grippin' on wood and I'm feelin' fine / got a big ol' sack so I'm comin' down / everybody wanna see Mister Mister in the place / I'ma show up in my cup got a taste / Gucci on my waist and Gucci on my feet / every time I jump out / I'm lookin' so neat / just look at that big nigga piece and chain / every motherfuckin' bopper wanna know my name / but I ain't gon' slow down / I'ma put it in your face / I'm all up in your stores / body rockin' with my waist / you can get the flip side of the P-A-T 'cuz ain't nothin' but player in my damn family / and that's the congregation / ain't no player hatin' / Man Poo what we gonna do? come through / Big Snoop in the Lincoln right behind me and we comin' down baby reppin' P-A-to-the-T."

For good and bad, most everything passing between Texas and Louisiana goes through Houston. Sometimes, even on their way to somewhere else, people only make it as far as the Bayou City. And then they stay there, even if just for a while. Houston is transient. It's a big junction. *Everybody* has business there, and if they don't, it's always a place to scratch something up.

Such was the case with Kenneth "Weasel" Watson, a promoter and hustler from Austin whom Pat and D-Reck had met in New Orleans the previous weekend. Weasel's business was a lot of things—plenty of it illegal—but at this point in time his interest was in Fat Pat and the S.U.C., both of whom he was trying to persuade to come and perform in Austin. He also had an apartment in Houston, and that was how, on the night of Pat's birthday, Weasel ended up in Screw's house.

Derrick "D-Reck" Dixon (Wreckshop Records) "We met that clown-ass motherfucker Weasel, we met him at the Bayou Classic in November, the weekend after Thanksgiving. The '97 Bayou Classic. That's when we met that motherfucker. We was walkin' down the street and he came up and he wanted to do a record with Pat. And so you can imagine—between late November and December, that was after I caught my case. So me and Pat, we were still rocky, but he was lookin' for his next bag, you know what I mean? Next money man."

Fat Pat (from "Been Around the World") "I'm gonna act just like a nigga do / I'ma put it all in your face / one time that you know / ain't no fuckin' with these niggas on this instrumental / let you know straight wreck gotta numb your necktie / Fat to the Pat and smokin' motherfuckin' fry / I'm so high on fuckin' cloud nine / fittin' to come down in my low bubba recline / trunk blowin' up and I'm showin' out G / screens fallin' from the ceilin' / can you see me? / Mister Mister / got the pistol in my lap / always stay strapped / twenty-four seven / send your ass to heaven on the motherfuckin' two / eleven on the beat / Mike-D come through / got your paid / I'm all the rage / next day Keke on the stage / got paid / big large pockets / don't even knock it / we in the Summit / got the whole motherfucker rockin'."

C-Note "I was exitin' the Beltway one night in my drop-top, and I'm makin' a left comin' toward the neighborhood. And Fat Pat—you know, I'm from Cloverland, he's from Kennedy Heights. They're like right across the street from each other. So I'm comin' down the street—before they built it up, you know, it's dark. Next thing you know, I come across, they pushin' the car in the middle of the darkness, and guess who it is? Fat Pat, pushin' a Lincoln, a candy Lincoln on swangers. He's comin' from the graveyard, because there's a graveyard at the end of Cullen where almost all of us get buried at. You know, it's been there for years. He's comin' from the gravesite of Pat Lemon in the Lincoln that he got from Pat Lemon, and he's pushin' it. He done ran out of gas comin' from the gravesite, he was down there so long. And the gas station was down there at the corner at the end of Cullen. So I say, *Damn, man, what's up?* So I did what I did—I was able to push him into the gas station. You know how you go bumper to bumper? Because the street was long! He had a long way to go, I'm talkin' 'bout a *long* way to go, and he's pushin' and pushin' in the middle of the night. I rolled up to him talkin' 'bout, *I see somebody pushin' 'at car in the middle of the night, and it's yo ass.* He say, *Man, I was at the gravesite visitin' Pat Lemon and shit, I ran outta gas on the way back—damn!* I was supposed to run into him, man. It was meant to be. It ended up bein' one of the last times I remember."

Man Poo "We all went down to Prairie View, and we end up down there fightin', squabblin' out there. We was out there fightin' like a motherfucker. We was about thirty, forty cars deep that day. That's like the last episode I remember with Pat. He was there. Him and Keke . . . we ended up gettin' into it with some guys, and we had to squab. Fat Pat performed and Keke performed, and they also had Maze and Frankie Beverly there. They performed after Maze. That was in an auditorium. I think it was they homecoming."

Noke D (Wreckshop) "Biggie was hot at the time. Pat wasn't doin' what Biggie was doin', but he found his own niche, you know what I'm sayin'? And Pat started comin' into his own. I remember like when he was wrappin' up his project, the last few songs was like 'Am I Player?' and 'The Last Man Standin'.' 'Ghetto Dreams.' Those were the last three songs to finish up the recording, and I remember tellin' Reck, and him sayin', *Yeah, he comin' into his own, brother.* He had found his shit, man. He was gonna be huge."

Derrick "D-Reck" Dixon "The posters had came in for *Ghetto Dreams*, and he came by and got a bunch of posters. I remember flyin' in kinda late on a Sunday, and I went straight to Carro's. And I knew Pat had got a stack of posters, so I'm gettin' ready to go in the door and this fool pull up. He had that Lincoln Town Car. This was before cars were gettin' wrapped, so he had damn near wrapped the car himself like . . . he had posters lined up, his posters taped on the car, on that Lincoln, all the way across the side on both sides, on the back of the trunk. He had the whole car damn near wrapped with that poster. And then he pulled up to the front of the club, he got the doors open and shit, you know, he a big ol' dude, he get out, you know, he jockin' and rockin' and talkin' shit to his potnah out there, 'cuz he wanted to get all that attention on him, you know? And everybody's lookin', 'cuz his car bangin'! And then he get back in the car, he sittin' in the car for a lil while, he bangin', he blowin' smoke comin' out. Then he had a red carpet—he threw the red carpet out, rolled it out, and got out that motherfucker and walked off into that club on the carpet, man. Then his potnah went and rolled the carpet up, put it back in the car. That's how Mr. Fat Pat came through the door. That dude was a character, man. We was fittin' to have some fuckin' fun."

8. South Park
1998

The idea to open a storefront from which he could sell his tapes had long been on Screw's mind. The fact that he needed to make something happen was evident from the lines of cars trailing down his street and the people knocking on his door around the clock. Screw had set certain hours to limit the traffic, and often sold out of tapes, but it didn't matter. The neighborhood disruptions were a cumulative annoyance that had been building around him for years. The police had been there before, and they would be coming back.

Klondike Kat (South Park Coalition) "I go over there one night and I notice some black cars down the street, man, look like undercovers, so I say, *Hey man, Screw look like they're undercovers parked down the street from your house, man.* He was like, *Yeah?* He looked out there, *Yeah, they've been there for days, man, watchin'.* And probably thought he was sellin' dope—and when they came in there, they see he had tapes!"

Reggie "Bird" Oliver "He said, *If you ever get pulled over, just tell them I'm making tapes for free.* Because he knew he can get called up for money laundering or whatever the case is. Taxes. So he said, *Man, just make sure you just tell the police that you're just getting these tapes.* I got pulled over before, they towed my car, took my money. They thought he was selling weed. The police said, *Man, where is the marijuana?* I said, *You know what? We don't have no marijuana. This is our DJ, he makes tapes.*"

That's all anyone wanted to do—buy tapes. Screw had one thing he sold, in an endless series of underground volumes, and he could see that it was growing well out of the range of what was possible to vend from the other side of the gate in front of his house. And that was just it—*way* too many people knew exactly where he lived.

Lil' Randy "He had to move from there because it really was a hazard. I mean people were starting to jump his gate, people he didn't know, knowin' where he stay. There was too many people—and he didn't do *everybody,* so somebody might get frustrated if he wouldn't do a tape. He just had to move. And plus, you know, he was havin' people comin' to his house thinkin' that he was sellin' drugs. So he had to get a legitimate business, where he opened at a certain time."

Besides the traffic beleaguering the neighborhood, there was heat on him to bring his operation in from the cold and get it on the books. The police were running through his place because they thought he was selling something illegal out of the house. And to a degree, he *was*—it just wasn't drugs. It was music on which he wasn't paying taxes. For someone who dealt almost entirely in cash, and thus had large amounts of it in the house in which he slept, with strangers passing through at all hours of the night, he needed to move operations away from there, and shift the weight of the tapes off his homelife and into a commercial space.

Lil' Rick "He just wanted to keep it away from his house. It got to where his real potnahs was lettin' him know, *It's basically like you runnin' an illegal dope house, a rock house.* Screw started to see some money that some *dope dealers* wasn't seein', and you know, from a dope dealer's perspective and the way we live, you don't sleep where you shit at, you know what I mean? You in this house and motherfuckers tryin' to do somethin', they gonna come *get* your money, mane. So basically it was just for the safety of him and his family, you know. Tryin' to keep it from them. Because at the end of the day, you got total strangers comin' there buyin' music. So that's pretty much what persuaded him to go on out and get that store."

Screw was shifting big gears. His situation now was he needed to lead people away from the place he'd drawn them to for the last four years. He had created a nucleus at Greenstone, and he was making money because of it, and now all he needed to do was transplant that nucleus—intact— into the best spot he could manage near where things were happening on the Southside. And as Darryl Scott had realized thirteen years before, there was no better place to make that happen than in South Park.

THE SOUTHSIDE REUNION

January 4, 1998—On a Sunday afternoon, a caravan of slabs leaves Houston headed toward Austin. Fat Pat was in the line, as were E.S.G., Big Hawk, Big Pokey, Big Moe, and Screw. Pat had taken Weasel up on his offer to come and do a show, and the promoter booked them into a 1,500-capacity venue in northeastern Travis County called Dessau Dance Hall, a relic built by nineteenth-century German settlers of central Texas. It was a one-story venue with a huge wooden dance floor and a red exterior that had members of the S.U.C. outside making jokes about per- forming in a barn when they pulled up.

The concert was organized by Straight Lace Entertainment and billed as the "Southside Reunion." Shorty Mac, Al-D, and ACT also performed. Austin's DJ Harvey D was the house track selector that night, with Screw and his tables set up on the stage. DJ Gold was with Screw, too, selling tapes—sales of which would total around $15,000 by night's end. It was on the eve of the release of *Ghetto Dreams*, and the energy around Pat was turned up. Hundreds of fans packed into the venue. A microphone went missing during the set, and the entire crowd hunted for it until it made its way back to the stage. In one freestyle that night, over Whod- ini's beat for "Friends" (which Double D had leveraged for Lil' Keke's hit "Southside"), Pat made a direct reference to the Austin promoter who brought them all there.

Fat Pat "I done flipped the game / put blades on the diesel / got real live with my nigga fuckin' Weasel / we gon' act bad / see me all the time / So Real Entertainment / watch a player grind / at the nigga show / got me free to go / my nigga Weasel brought me in / so now you know."

The reason a transcript of Pat's freestyle is possible is because someone made a recording of the show from the soundboard that night. The Screwed Up Click left the venue's muddy parking lot without getting paid all of their money, and while they were partying back at their hotel off Highway 183, Weasel was already making plans to sell bootlegged copies of the show to a public hungry to hear more Fat Pat.

Derrick "D-Reck" Dixon "We did the show down there with Weasel, and instead of Weasel following protocol and fuckin' with me, with the money and the business, he was dealin' directly with Pat. Which is always a dead giveaway a lot of times, you know?"

Meanwhile, the S.U.C. returned to Houston. A release party for *Ghetto Dreams* had been planned for the third weekend of February at JJI Entertainment in Bay City, Texas, but it would never happen. On Tuesday, February 3, Weasel was in Houston, and he phoned Pat and asked him to meet over at the Onyx Apartments off of Wilcrest on the southwest side, near the community of Alief. The visit was arranged on the premise that Pat was going to be paid the rest of the money he was owed for the January show. What Weasel didn't mention on the phone to Pat was that he had been robbed, and that he thought Pat had something to do with it (he didn't). The call was a setup. When Pat arrived and opened the door to the apartment, Weasel pulled a gun and shot him, then ran through the parking lot and out of the complex. Fat Pat was dead.

Kiwi "At the time, Hawk was workin' for American General, and my homeboy Will-Lean from the Botany Boys, his mama worked at American General also. We had a couple of rooms at Shorty's Inn, right there by Reliant, and a few of us at the room—I remember Will-Lean, me, Runn G, 380 . . . we had a couple rooms and somebody called and made a statement like it was . . . there was something happened to Pat. Pat got shot, or somethin'. We didn't know nothin'. Somebody just called and said somethin'. We was like, *What?! Man, we ain't heard of nothin' like that, man, they trippin'.* I called Hawk phone on his line, his extension to his desk. He didn't *answer* the phone, but I knew he was supposed to've been at work, so I'm tellin' Will-Lean, man, *Call your mama and see if she seen Hawk today.* So when he, Will-Lean, called, his mama was like, *Yeah, John was here but he had a family emergency—like he left real—like there was somethin' goin' on. He had to leave.*"

MoMo (Nikki's friend) "We were at the shop when we found out Pat had died. We were there, and Nikki and I were sittin' in the back, and Screw came through the door. He was with Tommie Langston, and they were in the van, and they drove up, and he was like . . . I guess they were *sayin'* that Pat had died, but Screw didn't believe it, so Screw went down there to Pat's house, and he came back and he told us—it was true. He said he wasn't listenin' to nobody until he went down to Pat's mama's house."

Kiwi "Hawk and them was already over there by the time we pulled up. And we stood out there for a while 'em we saw 'em pull the body out, you know, then Hawk, he left, he was like, *I'm fittin' to go to my mama's.* And on the way home, he knew his mama was tellin' everybody she wanted all his friends, that she wanted all his friends to come over to the house. Yeah, then he was like, *My mama want all his friends to come to the circle.* You know, at they mama house, where they stayed at. So we all pull up at the circle, and I remember Corey Blount had one of his cars out there. He was playin' Fat Pat album. You know, Fat Pat died before—he ain't ever see his album drop."

DJ Screw (as told to Daika Bray) "What happened to Fat Pat was just getting caught up with a shysty promoter. We were doin' a show down in Austin, Texas. Come to find out the dude who we done the show with named Weasel videotaped and audiotaped the show without tellin' us. I found out about it, asked him about, he tried to deny it. A while later he wanted us to come back and do another show. We were like, fuck that, we ain't gonna go back there. First, he disrespected by tapin' the show and sellin' it, sellin' it on the street and everything."

Derrick "D-Reck" Dixon "Had I not been fightin' a legal case, I woulda ran his ass to the other side of the earth, but I was kinda . . . I was not in position at that time. I was just trying to get the record done. But yeah, the end of November to the beginning of February, that's when he met Weasel, and that's what caused his death. That quick."

Fat Pat (freestyle from "Been Around the World") "1998, Fat Pat still sho-vin' / I'ma tell you how I had to pay the cost / that's why they call me Don Corleone / or the big boss / of the damn thing / got so much clientele / might as well get my nails done / 'cuz I can't fail / biggest goddamn Dave / showin' my lane / make my fingers shine with the damn pinky ring / hold up big baby 'cuz I'm mobbin' Mercedes / big twenties / big money / Fat Pat lookin' funny at these damn haters that wanna throw up on my mug / bullshit motherfuckers man hold up I done fucked up but I came right back 'cuz I hollered at that boy Sock-a-lock and the cat / where the party at I got the big Kroger sack / from feel feelin' so real pop a pill / what's the motherfuckin' deal / that's my fuckin' slang / what's my motherfuckin' name F-A-to-the-T / my phone rang / it's a ho / I go to go slow / down Fondren hummin' / trunks keep it comin' / a long-ass way don't play / Southside holdin' in the trunk today / I'ma swang to the left I'ma swang to the right / do the 'Body Roc' and we'll do the 'Southside' / don't show I as a villain of the curb / I done struck a nigga nerve / you really gonna deserve / Pat ass-whooping / trunk still shookin' / '84 swangin', wood grain danglin' all up your block and don't stop got my mask on / slidin' on chrome when I'm headed to the bopper home / me and the Ke so what it's gonna be? What we gonna do?"

E.S.G. "I'll never forget, when Fat Pat died, that boy sold four thousand cassette tapes that first week. Cassette tapes. Boys weren't doin' them kinda numbers like that, man. It's just crazy, man. Goose bumps."

Despite there being a police investigation, and common knowledge of the killer's identity, no one has ever been arrested for the murder of Patrick Hawkins. Weasel was never officially charged with Pat's murder, but in 2007 police did catch up with him in central Texas on unrelated charges, for which he was convicted and sent to prison. He is currently incarcerated in Atlanta, Georgia, where he won't be eligible for release until 2040, when he will be sixty-seven years old.

SCREWED UP RECORDS & TAPES

Fat Pat's death put an ache in Screw's heart at a time when he should have been his proudest. Near the end of 1997, Screw had signed a lease for a commercial warehouse space in the corner unit of a tiny sand-colored stucco strip center at 7717 Cullen Boulevard, right at the dividing line between South Park and Sunnyside—central enough to where you could argue which of those neighborhoods could claim the shop. It was right in the middle of Screw's world—south of Loop 610 and the neighborhood of Yellowstone, adjacent to Herschelwood and Cloverland, and right up the road from South Acres and the Dead End. The shop was blocks away from King's Flea Market, where nearly everybody on the Southside went to shop for *something*, and just off the freeway near the car wash where folks shined up the slabs in which they were banging the Screw tapes they could now buy on the boulevard. To boot, for Screw it was only a fifteen-minute drive from the house on Greenstone.

DJ Screw (as told to Daika Bray) "I got my own lil record shop, Screwed Up Records & Tapes. Screwed up Texas, that's what's we call this. Down South, Third Coast. It's in your face, for real. Showin' up, pourin' up, growin' up."

When Screwed Up Records & Tapes opened in February of 1998, the price of a Screw tape jumped from a flat ten dollars to $10.81 with tax. There were still no CDs, just cassettes, but the most important thing for Screw was that in opening a shop, he had fully converted his art form to a business—on his terms. Now he had a storefront, a cash register, and an organizational system that would have him getting ahead instead of being buried in boxes of tapes, the way it was at the house. He also started getting the tapes manufactured instead of dubbing them himself. Nikki handled a lot of the day-to-day operations of the shop, and her friend Monique—MoMo—soon joined her behind the counter.

MoMo "I would come into the shop with Nikki when they first opened, and on the first day they opened—or they weren't even *open* yet—he was there, getting everything together. I walked in, he was sittin' in there, and he had on a coat. He had the hood on his head and he was sittin' behind the desk, and so I remember he was like . . . every day I would come up there and just sit and talk with Nikki, and he asked me was I still working, and I was like, *No, the business closed down.* He say, *You wanna work here?* I was like, *What!? Me??* And so he said, *Yeah, you!* He said, *You always up here! You always sittin' up here with Nikki!"*

Ida Mae (as told to Matt Sonzala) "I was so happy because you know when he had that house on Greenstone, the cops bugged the heck out of him because they thought it was a dope house. And when they came in and busted down the door one time when I was there and they were looking for dope, I said, *Mister, all we sell here is tapes, but you're welcome to come in and look through this house. Just help yourself, all gonna find is boxes and boxes of tapes.* And they looked so stupid. You know cars would be coming down the street and that's why he opened the shop. He was so proud, and I was so proud. I said, *When I come visit you I don't want the cops kicking in this door and scaring me to death. I'll pull a gun on them and get shot in the process."*

IN GOD WE TRUST

In August of 1997, Stick 1 had been released from prison and went to live in a halfway house to finish out the terms of his sentence. On one of his approved weekend excursions, he came by Screw's house and recorded a tape called *Mind on My Money.* As was Screw's preference, he went heavy on the West Coast selections, mixing in go-to artists like MC Eiht, Ice Cube, and Too $hort, some Houston love with Crime Boss and PSK-13 with UGK. There were also a couple of songs by Spice 1—who in his own way could represent for both Houston *and* the West Coast. But for Stick, who intended to land on his feet after prison and turn over a new leaf, the visit wasn't just about the tape.

Stick 1 "When I came home, man, the vibe wasn't the same. Like I say, I'm kinda real heavy and deep, you know, mentally. And the vibe wasn't the same. And in between those times, you know, me and Screw . . . the roles kinda changed. He would have to come steal off to *me*, and come get *me* now, you see what I'm sayin'? I'm fresh home, you know, *he* doin' better than I was. So the roles done changed now. So, when he would get time away from them, it would flip to where he would call me and we would just have talks. I would come down from my apartment and we would just sit in the car and talk. And you could tell what was bein' said and what he was hearin', 'cuz he looked at me, man, and he said—one day we was just sittin' down—he came to holler at me, we was just sittin' there, man, he said, *Man, you ain't changed. People wanna say you different, man. You still the same.* The talk with me was a little bit more militant when I came home. It was a little bit more militant, a little bit more focused, you know, church oriented. I was still *me*, but I wouldn't let people get close to me because the *vibe* was different. I didn't really wanna live that *life* again. But now, this dude—we connected on a different level, so as we talk and open up, he like, *Nah, you still Stick, man. They trippin'.* He knew it. But *that* tell me what was bein' said when I wasn't around. So yeah, man, it was somethin', and I could really see it, man, and I just seen 'em on a different level, to where he had took our thing of pleasure to another level. It wasn't so much more of a *we chillin'* thang. It was a lifestyle. And that was kinda bothersome to me, because I was seein' the things we did for recreation—it was his *lifestyle*, and I was like, *Man, we did this to pass time, to chill.* This wasn't our every move. And you could see that part of it."

After Fat Pat's death, Stick was ready to move into another phase of his life. He and Screw remained close, and he still had a good relationship with Big Hawk, because he'd been close to him since they'd grown up together in the Dead End. But his time in prison had produced a profound change, if not in him as a person then in his direction in life. Some folks were put off by Stick's new outlook, but Screw wasn't one of them. The two of them had many conversations about how different they had been as youths, and how they had moved on from that in so many ways, beyond what was expected of them. That new path would eventually lead Stick 1 to the church, where he would become a pastor and minister to young people in an attempt to divert them from a path that would take away their freedom, as had happened to him.

But before Stick moved on, he would visit Screw's house to make one last tape: *In God We Trust*. This was in February 1998, and Big Moe was in the house, as were T-Bone, Will-Lean, and a young rapper named Clay-Doe, who would go on to inherit Fat Pat's spot in the group Southside Playaz. Screw was loading up the first side of the tape with Ice Cube and Westside Connection, and was headed toward finishing the whole mix with a long freestyle session over the beat for WC and the Maad Circle's 1995 track "West Up," which leaned heavily on a sample of the title track from jazz legend George Duke's 1977 gold record *Reach For It*.

DJ Screw (from *In God We Trust*) "Stick 1. Glad to see you home, boy, know'm sayin'? Boys been missin' you, boy. But we been *kickin'* it these last days!"

Stick took the mic and went back and forth with Screw. He would end up freestyling when Screw dropped the needle on "West Up," but first he was going to get a show of just how much things had changed at Screw's house. He did know that Screw had gone from buying records to *receiving* records. The labels had caught on to the fact that Screw was promoting their releases rather than disrupting sales, and had taken to sending him boxes of new vinyl. What Stick didn't know was that sometimes the record companies didn't just send stuff, but brought it—as they did that evening, dropping off a record that made it onto *In God We Trust* that very night.

Stick 1 "You get to the fifty-one minute of that tape, you hear me and him talkin' at the end of the song, there's just one of them deals where I'm sayin', *Man, you my potnah, man, I love you, man.* We just talkin' through, waitin' on the first side to be done with. So we just kinda talkin' that side out, and we fittin' to flip over and go to side B. So you get to the fifty-one minute of that tape, man, you'll hear Screw say, *Who at my door?* And from that point, he gets up, he goes to the door, somebody had already answered . . . man, this was amazin' to me, man. It was Priority Records. It was somebody runnin' errands for Priority. I had never heard this song on the radio or nothin'—the thing they dropped off for Screw to sample Ice Cube, that was my big—Ice Cube was my favorite rapper at the time.

Ice Cube and Pac. They want him to sample 'Bend a Corner Wit Me.' They had just dropped it off, the people from Priority. We listened to it, and man—I said, *Man, I need that on my tape.* We threw it in there—man, if you listen to that song, the way we talkin' through that song, it's almost like we rehearsed it, like we done heard that song about forty times. It was me, Big Moe, Will-Lean, and this guy named Clay, man. And you know Big Moe—he could *sing*, so that was a good night for me, man, bein' back, like *wow*. And that was the last Screw tape I ever done right there. That was the very last one."

SO MANY WAYS

September 15, 1998—The album *Screwed for Life* is released on Dead End Records. The cover featured a photo of Fat Pat, Big Hawk, Kay-K, and DJ Screw, but the provenance of the group, Dead End Alliance, went back years, and Screw really only played a small part. And while Kay-K, who had grown up in Kingsgate with Lil' Troy, was known as the man behind D.E.A., the album was the product of a complex journey.

Kay-K "Koldjak was the first one to say he wanted to form a group. He called it Dead End Alliance. But he wasn't backin' it or payin' or any situation like that, so I ended up start—financially start payin' for it, and when I looked up I was the only one takin' care of the business, payin' for thangs, doin' everything we needed for it to come out. And at that particular time, Ke had a probation violation or somethin' like that, so he slid on down to Jam Down, and Pat left and did Wreckshop, but before he left, we had finished all the D.E.A. stuff first. So that caused confusion. That's why you get just me, Pat, Hawk, and Screw on the cover."

D.E.A. had evolved since its inception, but just about everyone who ended up on the record was already a part of the Screwed Up Click: Screw, Big Hawk, Lil' Keke, Big Moe, Big Pokey, Mr. 3-2, Mike-D, E.S.G., C-Note, and the late Fat Pat. Southside rapper Rowdy Bone was on there, too. The sessions were recorded at producer Jus Fresh's studio on the southwest side, where E.S.G., Godfather, Big Love, Criminal Elament, Half Dead, and Street Military had all recorded classic Houston rap records. D-Red of

Botany Boys, Harvey Luv, Bruce "Grim" Rhodes, Sean Solo, J Slash, and Big Swift produced.

Kay-K "We had worked on D.E.A. before anything—before *Don't Mess Wit Texas*, before *Ghetto Dreams*, all that. We had already had the music made, but by bein' young and not really knowin' the game, just tryin' to figure it out, it just take a little longer than somebody that knew how to make albums and push albums so they came out quicker. It developed from the *Popped Up Smoked Up* tape that I did. It was my tape. Me, Screw, Hawk, and Keke—we was on that tape."

Kay-K ended up in prison before the album's release, so Screw's friend Runn G, Koldjak, stepped in as the money man behind the project. Though the album is sometimes credited to "DJ Screw & the Screwed Up Click Presents Dead End Alliance," Screw mostly worked in the studio and only appears on one of the album's fourteen tracks, "Screw'ed 4 Life." But on that song, Screw rapped! Not only did he make a rare appearance in the vocal booth, but it was among his best performances. His verse followed Big Hawk's.

DJ Screw (from "Screw'ed 4 Life") "Nigga, it's the don of the crew / slowed-down originator DJ Screw / well it's plain to see that you can't stop me / from jammin' that tree in this R-A-P / remember the shit that you said about my style was no good / well I done Screwed up every city, state, town, and hood / I'm up to no good / gettin' the stress off my chest / catch me leanin' with my strap and my black headset / all about my chips / nigga five to dip / gon' mix up a sip / and watch them records get ripped / for years and years / I done paid my dues / hold out! me and my dick will forever be screwed."

Koldjak "When Screw come in there, it's tripping Jus Fresh out, 'cuz Screw actually know how to work this automated board! We *all* trippin' off that! It's like, *How the fuck you know how to do that?* But he doin' the *3 'N the Mornin'* with Russell'n them, he in and out the studios with Russell'n them. This motherfucker really know how to turn these knobs! It was *mind-blowin'* at the time. Man, Screw came to mix. Screw mixed and recorded

'Screw'ed 4 Life,' and 'Dead End Representative,' *cold* mixed that whole motherfucker down. We were like, *Goddamn, this motherfucker really know how to turn these knobs, bro!* I'm talmbout was goin', hookin' up shit to the compressor to reverb and turnin' knobs, *What* that *do, Screw?* Shit, he just *fuckin'* wit' it. Wild! Exactly what he wanted to hear. All you had to do was show him what knob that do, and he knew it, *bam!* He turned it."

On December 22, 1998, another group forged from the Screwed Up Click, Southside Playaz, released *You Gottus Fuxxed Up* on LafTex Records. The original group was Fat Pat, Mr. 3-2, and Mike-D. After Pat's death in February of 1998, Clay-Doe, who had appeared on Stick 1's last Screw tape, was drafted into taking his place in the group. Swift, Slack, and E-Man produced. Much like the Dead End Alliance record that preceded it by a few months, *You Gottus Fuxxed Up* was marketed as "DJ Screw & Screwed Up Click Presents Southside Playaz," though this time Screw did not appear on the album at all.

Mr. 3-2 (as told to Polow's Mob TV) "Me, Mike-D Corleone, and Fat Pat. Southside Playaz, which we got off a Screw tape, the name. And I came with the whole idea about it, brought Mike-D and Fat Pat together because I knew 'em both from just hangin' out with 'em, and so there was a Screw tape out that Screw had made called *South Side Players*, and I just took the name and ran with it."

Mike-D "People say, *Man, why didn't Screw have a label with all y'all on it?* That was never his plan, you feel what I'm sayin'? That was never his plan. See, me, Kay-K, and Runn G . . . well, actually it was me and Kay-K, and Runn G was a part of D.E.A., but Kay-K had D.E.A., I was financing Southside Playaz, which was originally Fat Pat, 3-2, and Mike-D. D.E.A. was originally Kay-K, Pokey, Keke, and Hawk, okay? We would have friendly competition, but we was all Screwed Up Click."

SCREW DUB
By the time the shop was opening up, the culture around Screw tapes had been evolving for years, and change was the only thing promised.

Fat Pat was gone. Corey Blount went to prison not long after the shop opened. Plenty of the Screwed Up Click had signed record deals or moved on to other phases of their careers. Keke had already released a second album, *The Commission*, with Jam Down. E.S.G. was also on his way to linking up with Wreckshop, as would Big Moe, and Big Pokey would be signing with Paul Chevis's local label on his way to working with Universal. So a second wave of artists now had the space to get in and make themselves heard, and it was a generation that had grown up listening to the Screwed Up Click.

Chris Ward "Me and Pokey from the same neighborhood. I went to Screw house like '97, but I was in high school when I was goin', and I graduated in '98, but I had already made like two Screw tapes, in high school. And then along with that I just started doin' music with Poke, and then I met Hawk. I met Mike-D in '98. I was like seventeen years old at the time when I end up meetin' everybody, so I was just a little brother to everybody."

Wood (rapper from Third Ward) "Screw was lookin' for some new guys to rebuild the name, because Keke was the hottest member, Pat was goin' to sign with somebody, and he's like, *Fuck it, I need some new hot guys.* So me and Grace was like the new young regime. And they brought me to Screw house and Screw looked at me like, *Nigga, I know a million niggas that rap. Don't come in here with that rap shit. We're just kickin' it. We're just doin' music.* I'm like, *Alright! I feel you.* And then I look up and Grace is playin' a tape and Screw got my music on, and I'm like, *Damn, you Screw my music already?* And he's like, *Nah, that's Grace tape. Grace put that song on there. I like this song, but Grace put that song on there.* So I said, *Okay, you got my song—you already Screwed one of my songs—when I'm gonna get to rap?* Screw looked at me like, *Nigga . . . wait. Nigga calm down. Not right now.* And you know, I'm lookin' at everything 'cuz I was fifteen years old but I done read management, marketing books, and all that crap. I'm just like, *Man, you actually Screwin' me!* He looked me in my eye and said, *Now, here's the thing: we are gonna do music.* And I'm lookin' at him like, *How you know we're gonna do music? I'm mad right now—how do you know we're gonna do music?* And he's like, *We might* not do it today, we might not do it two weeks from today, we might not do it two months from today, we might not do it two years from today, but we're gonna do somethin'. And when he said that I was like, *Man, that's the most . . . bunch of bullshit I ever heard in my life.*"

Macc Grace "I ain't never rapped a day in my life before I met Screw. No. I used to *talk* about rappers. I thought it was the dumbest shit in the world. Niggas go into a studio and rap and make all these songs and then wait ninety days and get 10 percent of the shit—I just thought it was stupid. *I'ma be y'all manager.* I was sellin' dope and shit, so all them boys, they ain't playin', them niggas . . . I was really actin' like they manager! Until I met Screw, and then I don't know what the fuck happened. That was Screw, though, just his spirit. Just his will like that. He brought it out of 'em."

Grace's younger brother LOS started coming around, too. There was Lil' Flip, whom Screw would go on to honor as the "Freestyle King," Den Den, Enjoli, Lil' O, Dez, Big Steve, Sherro, Trae Tha Truth, Dougie D, and a young artist from Missouri City, Texas, who, to Screw's ears, was doing something altogether new. Joseph McVey was from the area of Mo City known as Ridgemont, where he always said he came from nothing, and thus called himself Z-Ro. His rapping and singing back then were faster than anybody else in the S.U.C., but that didn't put Screw off. He was hearing something deep and full of pain, even at that speed. In the summer of 1998, Herman Fisher's Fisherboy label released Z-Ro's debut album, *Look What You Did to Me,* at a point when he was coming under the wing of Screw and learning things from him that would later turn him into one of the biggest artists in Houston.

Reggie "Bird" Oliver "The first time Z-Ro ever rapped for Screw, I was over there. Z-Ro said, *I wanna be Screwed Up Click.* So Screw like, *Okay, let me hear something.* Man, Z-Ro started goin' off. You know how he rap fast. Screw say, *Hold up, come here right quick.* Screw was like, *Come in. You can step in.* He pulled him in from that day forward. He let him step in and then Z-Ro just started comin' over there every day. He looked up to Screw. He started comin' over there every day and Screw started teachin' him how to write his sixteenths. He's like, *Here, write it down like this.* Screw knew how to play the keyboard a little bit. A lot of people don't know that. He taught Z-Ro how he sing his hooks. Z-Ro didn't really know he had that pattern like that. Screw was like, *Hey, sing this.* Screw would be playing on the keyboard and he like, *Ah da dah,* and he'll be singin' it. Z-Ro already had a talent, but Screw would be like, *Hey, sing this here, sing this to this hook, or sing this to this.* And they'll be in there singing it and, man, it was *days.* Z-Ro used to be fallin' asleep on a pallet at Screw house. Not sayin' he was dirty or nothing. He just gonna be over there so much, he'd just fall asleep. You know, Screw gonna get food and everything. He can have food and he'll just get him a pallet and fall asleep. I come over there, I might leave in the morning. Z-Ro over there, and I might go do what I need to do and come back, Z-Ro *still* over there."

Z-Ro (from *Houston Rap Tapes*) "Screw was fuckin' with me because I was *different.* I was the only one in that bitch that wasn't talkin' about how, you know . . . how everybody else was doin' they style. The different motherfuckers you had in there were like E.S.G.—when *he* freestyled, it was like . . . it was real rap. Like . . . all this shit was real rap, but he was actually gettin' in that bitch and he was talkin' about shit that was goin' on . . . he could look around the room and rap about your shirt, your shoes was too tight, you know what I'm sayin', your haircut didn't quite just . . . *blend* right. He was gonna *rap.* And like me, I was gonna *rap.* Big Moe was different because he was gonna come in that motherfucker and *sing.* You got all this *real* shit around, so it was kinda like *Man, I need you in my Click. You kinda like, complete the gumbo. We got boys who freestyle rap, we got boys who really rap, and then we got people who* really rap. *We got people who sing, and then we just got homeboys.* I mean, it was like . . . it was just a whole lot of different genres, and that shit was cool for me because I got to be around all that shit. And I got to create my own lane outta that shit."

Larry B "I met Z-Ro when he didn't have no record deal. When he was just flat bottom without a nickel in his pocket. They sleepin' on the floor at the studio, everybody was tryin' to come up. Screw helped a lot of them cats out. He really did."

DJ Screw (from "One Life to Live") "Shit be a trip in the city streets, know'm sayin'. Nigga just tryin' to put it down, try to survive, know what I'm talkin' 'bout? Al-D. Grace. Wood. *Shiiit* . . . all we gotta do is maintain, stay on top of our game, mane. Fresh from the detail shop. It's comin' through, know'm sayin'? So you're a wheel watcher, huh? Like the way these twenties spin? It's alright to look, *shit* . . . but if you got a mind of a crook, I'm watchin' you watchin' *me.*"

DEAD END REPRESENTATIVE

By default, Screw's business and creative lives had been intertwined. He did everything at street level, cash, and always had financial freedom that way. But now he enjoyed the relief that came with fiscal legitimacy— a storefront where people would come to buy his tapes, where they were charged tax, and he could come in from the cold with the IRS. He had applied for a trademark on his name near the end of 1995—though the process was never completed—but it was the shop that established him as a member of the Houston business community. Local ABC station KTRK even sent a reporter and a camera out to do a profile.

For the interview, Screw sat on a chair in the wood room, answering questions comfortably and matter-of-factly as if he'd done it a million times. At one point, he even stepped behind a microphone and rapped for the camera, performing Lil' Keke's "Still Pimpin Pens" from *Don't Mess Wit Texas*. On the broadcast, they showed Screw rapping the lines, "The devil's beneath me / to God ain't no stoppin' me / It's syrup, not Hennessy / blowin' up independently / I done Screwed up the industry!"

The segment was about a minute and a half long, airing on Houston's channel 13 in February of 1998. Latrina Thompson from BigTyme also appeared in the piece. It brought new attention to what Screw was doing at an important time to promote the shop and splinter his traffic. Screwheads were now going to the store, but artists were still coming to his house to record tapes, and what he was doing was garnering interest from all over—including Rap-A-Lot.

Mike-D "We all went to Lil' J [James Prince]. We sat in Lil' J office, and Lil' J was like—Troy took us up there—and Lil' J was like, *Man, how can*

I get *y'all?* And Screw was like—this was Screw's response: *You gotta talk to Mike-D and Kay-K, because Mike-D is Southside Playaz and Kay-K is D.E.A.* He [Prince] wanted to kill all the Southside-Northside beef, and of course, him bein' the godfather in the city, you know, he wanna have a hand on how the city *move,* you know what I mean? My response to J, and why me and J bond is so good today, is because this is what I told him—and I just be truthful with him—I tell everybody if you wanna be real, just be *real* with J, you know? You know, I told him, *I'm not gonna lie, J—I'm tryin' to be* you. *I'm tryin' to build a you.* And Kay-K uncle already—which is Lil' C—he locked up, call him Joshua—he ran Rap-A-Lot West, and he was like, *Man, I got a uncle works for ya.* And that's what I wanted to do out there with him, with all due respect, we just tryin' to build a Rap-A-Lot on the Southside like you got. And Screw respected that, and he was like, *Man, I'm behind whatever my boys wanna do. If they wanna sign with Rap-A-Lot, we'll sign with Rap-A-Lot.* And there was no disrespect to Rap-A-Lot, but we was just tryin' to build our own brand on the Southside. We had *much* respect for J. I still do to this day, you feel what I'm sayin'? That's why Screw never—he had the potential to do all the record-executive stuff, but he—it was never his *desire* to do it, because he never wanted to be in *charge* of nobody. He just wanted us to be our own businessmen and run it like we knew we could do it."

Devin the Dude "I knew it was big when Rap-A-Lot came after him! And was really tryin' to get him to do a deal with them for a while, man! He was really tryin' to get a deal together for him to come on board, and that's when I knew he had his own thing. That's when you *got* it."

E.S.G. "All this was going to be under one tree—Screwed Up Entertainment. Lil' J sent Benzes, tour buses to my house, courted the hell outta Keke, *Hey, come over here.* Did the same with Pokey. Screw—we just had a different vision, and we was some young bosses who wanted to do our own thing, and that's how Screwed Up Click was born. That's how we done sold millions of records independent."

Koldjak "When D.E.A. dropped, man, there was a guy, there was a guy named Marvin. He was an A&R for Epic Records. I'm talkin' 'bout the man tracked my baby's *mother* down to find my ass. Tasha said, *Man, there some guy steadin' callin', talmbout he from Epic Records lookin' for you.* So I end up callin' him back, right. We was Heatseekers! I'm talmbout no streets, no radio play, no commercials, no nothin', just straight-up tapes in the store, we sold twenty thousand records in two weeks. The guy flew down, we go meet him. He's stayin' right across the street from the Galleria, an' we end up meetin' him at Pappadeaux on Westheimer. I'm tellin' Screw, I'm like, *Hey Screw, there's a dude down here, he wanna talk. He say he from Epic Records.* He like, *No shit? Where he at?* I say, *Man, he wanna meet with us, today at Pappadeaux.* So he was like, *Shit, aight. I'ma come. I'll be there.* Because I was like, *I need ya there, mane!* Because I ain't fittin' to do nothin' without him! You feel me? So guy pulled up, we end up sittin' on the patio, so *bam.* At this time, Screw got that blue Impala. He pulls up, so when he pulls up, the guy is sittin' there, and he don't know who Screw is, so Screw pulls up, I guess the people in the parkin' lot notice it's Screw! And people runnin' up to Screw, sayin', *Aye, Screw!* This guy witnessin' this, this dude go to the trunk, pop the trunk, and sellin' tapes! *Boom!* Screw closed the trunk, Screw start walkin' back to where we was at. Before he could get to us, some more people done stopped him, he gotta turn back around, go back to the trunk, sell some more. Dude picked up on that. He lookin', he like, *Who that is? I ain't never seen nothin' like that. Who that is?* By this time, our waitress, it's this lil Chinese girl, she run up, she say, *Oh, Screw! Screw!* She literally done stopped our order, and went over there, and gave Screw a hug and she tryin' to get her some tapes! That man was like, *Dog, I don't know if you orchestrated this shit or whatever, man, but I'm sold!*"

DJ Screw (as told to Desmond Lewis) "I got nieces and nephews, my brother, my sister, and then I got family members around me, friends— and if I can go out and do something and make some money, and be able to help them, that's what I wanna do. And just really . . . Run-DMC, the whole pioneers of the rap game, Whodini when they first came out, Ice-T and all that, Ice Cube. Seein' them do this make me wanna do it more, really. Try to create jobs for people around me so we ain't gotta go out and do no dumb shit. We can have our own lil Black businesses and stuff and feed our own families and everything. We ain't gotta turn to drugs and guns and all that. But every day I wake up, I see my lil nieces and nephews . . . shit I went through when I was little, I don't want them to go through that. For them, that's what make me really make this music, for my family and the people around me. 'Cuz I wanna get out there and get it where, in case something happen to them, I can help them out and just by me bein' there and havin' it right now, helpin' them out, I can change their life where they can do stuff and be able to help other people out. And really that's how it basically is—help one another."

Major labels were courting him, and the shop was hitting its stride as its visibility grew from its location on Cullen Boulevard. Screw was now getting the cassettes manufactured to keep up with demand, and as that demand grew, so did Screw's profile. Music video director Dr. Teeth came to the shop to shoot an interview with him for a segment on BET. His favorite rapper C-Bo even came by the house one time, but Screw was in one of his hibernating sleeps, and his cousin didn't wake him up. Rap-A-Lot's Big Mello had been coming around. Lots of folks wanted a chance to meet Screw.

Will-Lean "Shaq and Screw met. That probably was like around '98, '99. My sister was at a little sports bar club off of Shepherd and 59. It used to close like at twelve thirty. Me and Screw just happened to be in Quail Valley, at the house on Hilton Head. So my sister call, and she talkin' 'bout, *Man, we up here talkin' to Shaq, the basketball player. I was tellin' him about my brother, how he rap with Screw. He say he wanna meet DJ Screw, because he heard Screw put his songs on some of his dubs.* So I'm like, *Man, you lyin'. You just want me to bring you some drank.* She like, *Man, I'm tellin' you—I promise I be up here with Shaq.* So I get off the phone with her, *Man, quit playin'.* I'm like, *Man, why Chanel tell me she got Shaquille O'Neal over there?* Screw said, *It might be true.* So shit, we went up there—she wasn't lyin'! So we got in the car with him. He was in a Benz . . . I don't know how they made them mugs. His seat was so super huge, he musta had it like custom made for him. Man, we sat in that car and listened to some of Shaq's songs, chopped it up . . . we was up there so long like the place closed at twelve, all the cars had left. It was just our two cars out there. So I stood outside the car smokin' and him and Screw chopped it up, man. We chopped it up with Shaq for about three hours. Man I *know* he remembers that! I know because he probably be tellin' people, *Man, I met Screw,* and people be like, *Boy, you ain't met Screw!* We really ain't talk nothin' about sports. We just talked about music."

9. New Territory
1999

Screw's move to the southwest side took him and Nikki *out* of the city of Houston. By the fall of 1998, he had rented a house on Hilton Head in Missouri City—which would become his new studio—and bought a house in Sugar Land's New Territory. Both areas had a totally different vibe than the Southside. While Missouri City had experienced a growing Black population for decades, Sugar Land had once been the site of sugar and cotton plantations that used slave labor (until they switched over to prison labor) and by the late '90s was primarily white. Each spot was a half hour's drive away from the shop and from one another, both of them far-off suburban neighborhoods past Beltway 8 and away from all the noise. DJ Screw was no longer any kind of mystery around Houston. Because of the shop, more people had access, more people became fans, and everybody knew what he looked like. He just wanted somewhere to work.

MoMo "One time, we were lookin' for him. He wouldn't answer his phone. He wouldn't answer his phone for Nikki, for *nobody*. And we got *worried*! We were like, *Where's Screw? Where's Screw?* By *this* time, he was in Missouri City. The studio was in Missouri City, and they were livin' in Sugar Land at that time, so we were lookin' for him, like late night, and you can ask Nikki this story. We were afraid because we hadn't heard from him in like three days. I mean, we were lookin' for him. We wasn't gonna put out no police report, because, you know . . . we just wouldn't *do* that, just to alert anyone. So we finally went over there. And he put the car in the garage—he was in there! He finally opened the door. He was in there, he had on a sweater, his boxers, he had a refrigerator full of Lunchables—which, he loved Lunchables—and he had made ten tapes by himself. He closed up, didn't answer anything. Didn't bother with *anyone*. And that was his mode! That's how he got like in that Screw mode, you know? He had the little bounce rock when he mixin'. That was his little dance, you know?"

Big Pokey (as told to Jason Culberson) "One of the craziest things I seen, mane, was this nigga was in there makin' the tape, you know he on the ones and twos, shit . . . and a motherfucker be in here, be *in* the motherfucker. So he'll be up. He tireder than a motherfucker, too. So he tired, everybody, you know, doin' what they do, feelin' . . . it was a cool atmosphere, and I seen the nigga, he doin' it—and he noddin' off! I seen him nod off! But you know how a motherfucker nod off and then catch theyself and act like they wasn't doin' nothin'? Man, that nigga'll be on the tables, man, noddin' off, mane, and we just sit there watch that nigga like . . . and a nigga wake up and he'll catch that, and won't miss the beat that he fittin' to do. Wake up—tap, tap! Right on! That's literally, nigga, like a motherfucker say, *Man, I can do this shit in my sleep.* That nigga—when I seen that, it's funny 'cuz, nigga, you noddin' off and I'm talkin' about you noddin' off, your knees bucklin', and you wake up and *catch* that motherfucker, mane!"

Nikki "Screw would be so entrenched in his music that he would forget, *Wait, did I sleep? Did I take a shower today? Did I brush my teeth?* Like, it would be situations like that, where I would go to sleep and wake up and he'd be standin' in the same spot. Like they tease and they talk about it now, but I swear to God Screw was makin' a tape one night—we was livin' on Greenstone, and that boy had that turntable and that mixer, and he was 'sleep! Never skipped a beat. He was 'sleep, like you hear snoring, and they like, *Man, Screw! You 'sleep!* He, *Yeah! Aight*, and never missed a beat. That was him."

IT'S GONNA GET BETTER

January 9, 1999—Late on a Saturday night, Screw drives into a park and ride on the southwest side to turn around and is pulled over by police waiting there in the lot. They found a weapon in the vehicle, and Screw was the one driving so he was charged. He pled no contest, paid a fine of $300, and had a short stay in jail. Screw would ultimately use the incident as incentive to steer clear of trouble and focus on his music, but another flash of violence soon shocked his circle.

Only a couple of days after Screw's arrest, Hiram Clarke rapper Big Steve, also known as Granpappy Mafioso (or Mafio), a member of Johnathan Coleman's Southside collective Woss Ness, was killed in a shooting in a Southside parking lot. The shots were meant for a guy named Big Rue, not for Mafio, but both of them were killed in the gunfire. It was a surreal turn of events for Screw because Big Steve had just been at his house.

Chris Cooley "We was at Hilton Head and Mafio was over there. He was goin' to the store. He was like, *Kinfolk? You wanna ride with me to the store? I'll let you hear some of my album.* That's when he let me hear a lot of stuff that's on C-Note's album, the songs he did. And when we get back from the store, he was like, *Screw, man, I like Kinfolk!* And he like, *Man, you know what, man? I like the vibe over here. We gonna go get some clothes and I'ma come here and stay about a week with y'all.* And he never made it back. That morning, that was when Screw was gettin' calls, *Hey, man— they say Mafio got kilt!* He like, *Aw, man, he just left here!* We thought he was comin' back. We didn't believe 'em."

Man Poo "They had just dropped Pokey off. The night Big Rue and Mafio got killed, they just dropped Pokey off. If Pokey wouldn't have got out that car, he would have been hit, too."

DJ Screw (as told to Daika Bray) "Big Steve—up and comin' ghetto superstar, just got caught up. Wrong place the wrong time. Some people were doin' bad shit on the streets. Steve just happened to be in the same place when the shit was gonna go down. He got caught up in it. It's like Steve got it just by bein' with the dude. The dude was just messin' people over in the streets. Business—wasn't takin' care of business the way it's supposed to been done. Hustlin'. You know how you hustle—you owe people money, steal from them, do all typa' stuff like that. Niggas ain't gonna put up with that. Just can't keep takin' 'em. Sooner or later it's gonna go down. Niggas comin' back, get revenge on this cat. You with him—everybody gotta go. How you gonna just shoot this dude and not shoot *this* dude? That's a witness, and you sure don't wanna be in trouble, so you've gotta kill two birds . . . that's how that happened. It's fucked up. I miss my potnah. He had a bright future in the rap game. I'm gonna miss him. But he's always gonna be here. We're gonna keep him alive. I love you, man, I miss you. You're always gonna be around, sho' nuff. *Rap it, scratch it.* That's Big Steve talkin' to us."

ALL WORK, NO PLAY

January 26, 1999—Screw's album *All Work, No Play* is released on Jam Down. Much like the BigTyme albums that preceded it (*All Screwed Up* and *3 'N the Mornin'*), it was basically a Screw tape recorded in the studio, but without any freestyles. The sessions were produced by Simon "Crazy C" Cullins, who was from Missouri City—Ridgemont specifically—and had come up in the early '90s making beats for nearly everyone on the Rap-A-Lot label (Geto Boys, Raheem, Choice, Big Mello) and plenty more Houstonians (H-Town, Ganksta N-I-P, Jazzie Redd) before expanding into work with artists that took him beyond Texas (Method Man and Wu-Tang Clan). In the past, he had given Screw some sounds for making beats, but they hadn't actually worked together yet.

Crazy C "My first time seein' him work was when he came into the studio to record. He did have a game plan. He had a list of songs—because this was a Jam Down project, so he was usin' all of the Jam Down artists—and he had a flowchart of what songs he wanted to blend with what songs. We hooked all of the equipment up and it was like clockwork, man. It was just amazing to actually see him work."

There was one big difference for Screw. By the late '90s, two-inch reel-to-reel tape was being phased out in favor of digital-to-tape (DAT) cartridges, and that was how Crazy C recorded Screw, to a TASCAM DA-88. DATs are tape, but digital, and make an exact clone of the sound, like compact discs. For Screw, that turned on a different set of lights, because he no doubt had an awareness that essential to his sound was the fact that he recorded straight to tape. Some folks might think of tape as lessening the sound a generation, but for Screw, dubbing was a tool, the destination for his sound. Even if he recorded through the multitrack and then recorded to tape again to slow it down, that was still a couple of generations to 1/8-inch tape—sound on sound stacked in a tiny flat shell. Screw used that to his advantage, each time taking a little more shine off the original, burying it deeper in the smoky ceiling that fattened the sound, embracing the fact that he was losing something with each dub. Even though Screw tapes would later end up being released digitally, the origin of their sound was always cassette tape.

These sessions were also more fine-tuned and controlled than the pandemonium of a session at his house. Every song on *All Work, No Play* had already been released by Jam Down. Nobody came into the studio to record, or even to hang out. Patrick Lewis and his general manager Vincent Perry were in the house to get things underway on the first day, but after that, for a few muggy nights in the summer of 1998, it was just Crazy C and DJ Screw—with Screw leaning and both of them learning. Screw knew his way around the songs—Herschelwood Hardheadz, Mr. 3-2, Double D, Fat Pat, Lil' Keke—and left himself room to stretch out the beats. He was a seasoned artist by that point. It was organic.

Crazy C "A couple of times, he actually wanted to do some sections over. He was like, *Man, I wanna redo that.* It sounded good to me! But he was like, *Nah, man. It just don't feel right.* I had them separated on different tracks, so I was like, *Alright, if we're gonna punch in for this section, I need you to blend that same song, and then once I catch the right blend, I'ma punch it in.* And dude was like right in there! Like *right on it!* Normally, it'll take you some time to sync it, because all this was done manually. Naw, man, it's like he had an internal clock going, and he got it *right* on beat, every time. When you listen to the CD, you don't hear those in it, but yeah, there was a couple of times he wanted to redo some things, so we had to punch in and catch it on the fly. I punched it in and kept goin'. I could see his point afterwards. I couldn't hear it before, but *he* could."

UNCLE EARL

Even as he moved around, Screw's family and his connection to Smith-ville remained a constant in his life. Ida Mae came to stay with them in Sugar Land for a little while. His cousin Chuck was around, and Big Bubb had started working at the shop, applying what he knew from working for a beverage distributor to the workflow around Screw tapes. Shorty Mac was also working, and in the summer of 1999, another cousin from Smithville, Lil' Doug (Lil' D), came to live with Screw and Nikki while Screw was paying for him to attend business school in Houston. The house in Sugar Land was where they would sleep, but sometimes Screw's late nights meant Lil' D stayed over at the house in Missouri City, even if it wasn't meant for that.

Lil' Doug "There wasn't really too much furniture in there. We stayed a lot of nights there, showered up and everythang. I mean, you could almost live there, but we would basically be sleepin' on the carpet. I'm tryin' to remember, did he even have a couch. You know, he didn't really wanna get too much there. He didn't want people to get too comfortable over there. We was back and forth from the studio to his house in Sugar Land, and then once he got kicked out of that house, he went and got that other—the new studio, and we went over there. But we was layin' on floors a lot. Yeah! We was."

Ida Mae (as told to Michael Hall) "He was under so much stress from helping so many people. He didn't *know* the word 'no.' He would say, *PawPaw Jack, you need any money? Please take care of my mother.*"

Nikki (as told to Jason Culberson) "There were no conditions on anything. If you need it and he gave, he didn't want it back. If he loved you, he loved you genuinely, wholeheartedly. He didn't need nothin' back. If you never said to him, *I love you, Screw,* it wouldn't bother him at all. He gonna still love you. And that's what I miss about him. I miss the fact that he was just a good dude. He was just a genuine person. You know, he was very forgiving. Because, I'm not gonna lie. I've said some things, and some things have come out of my mouth in anger, and he would be so *mad*. But the Cancer in him, made him emotional, and he would get so, so pissed at me. And then he'd be like, *Man, I love your bigheaded ass*, and just walk off. That was him. That was him, and instantly, at that very moment, I was forgiven."

Ida Mae (as told to Michael Hall) "He had guys from prison—Huntsville and in New York City—call him from prison and he would send them money. I'd say something to him but he'd say, *Mom, they just want to talk*. If he had two dollars, he would give you one."

DJ Zo Tha Affiliate (cousin) "He would come to my house when we had my mom's birthday party and stuff. He would make sure he would be there. So I would blackmail him, like, *My mom made you a sweet potato pie. If you would like the sweet potato, I need to see something in my hands when you pull up*. And I would definitely get like two or three Screw tapes, and he would autograph stuff for my friends in the neighborhood. He'd know most of my friend's names and stuff. *What's up, Pancho?* All the people in the neighborhood would be like, *Oh, you're not DJ Screw's cousin*, a lot of the older kids. And everybody would be like, *Yes he is, bro! Watch*. And sure enough, he'd come around in the Impala. I stayed in Crestmont where Big Steve and all them stayed. I stayed right in the front, so we would always see Mafio and Screw and them comin' in the neighborhood, because they had to turn on my street. So we'd be sittin' there, and Screw turned in, and everybody's like, *That looks like Screw Impala comin' down the street!* He'd pull up, him and D Drew hopped out the car, *What's up, cuz?* I'd be like, *What's up, y'all?* And they'd be like, *Damn!* And then he'll be like, *What's up, Pancho? What's up, Juan?* And then everybody was like, *Bro, Screw was at your house!* He always kept it real with everybody. Even though he'd already wrote my friends autographs, he would write one again. He gave me the tapes, he'd be like, *Where's my pie?* . . . *It's on the counter inside*. I'm like, *I don't know why you did this—you know my mom's gonna give it to you anyway*. It was always cool, man."

LOS "Screw and my wife birthday are three days apart. So every year, Screw and us would go to a club. Screw would say, *Let's go.* You know, we ain't drink alcohol like that! But we would go to a club for like three, four years in a row for they birthday, and we'd go get a shot, and Screw would buy the whole club a shot. *E'rebody come to the bar right now—DJ Screw in the buildin', it's her birthday, he buyin' e'rebody a shot, but you gotta be here in the next five minutes.* And man, when we walked out, he was like, *You like that, huh? That was live.* I was like, *Hell yeah it was live!* He say, *Man, I love ya.* He loved to see other people happy."

Larry B "He looked out for my cousin Big Bubb. Because Bubb used to work for Dr. Pepper. And Bubb was goin' in for a promotion and he . . . you know, you hang out with Screw, so he liked to smoke, too, a little weed or whatever. And he went in for a big promotion, he done did good and they were gonna allow him to move up in the company, and they did a lil ol' drug screen on him in the process, and they found the weed on him. He had been smokin' the marijuana, so it came out dirty. And that's how he end up workin' for the shop."

Jason Culberson (a.k.a. K.i.d) "I was sixteen, and I had rode down there with Lil' D. Lil' Doug, that's his kinfolk that stay with him, from Smithville. But we had rode down there with him, in my car, and we went over to the studio in Mo City. And the Impala was flat, so we had needed a ride, and I was like . . . Doug was like, *Man, K.i.d wanna sip, Screw!* He was like, *Well what y'all got on it?* I pulled out like ten, fifteen dollars. You know, we youngstas! He's like, *Man, y'all can't even buy the cups and ice with that!* And we ended up goin' to the store, and man, I promise you—I think he was meetin' Dave on the other side of the store or whatever—man, *two hours.* I mean, he went in there to get some soda, and he was like, *Man, I'm just fittin' to go get some soda.* We was sittin' in the parking lot *two hours,* and we did not know what was goin' on. It was always like that, though! And his late nights."

Ida Mae (as told to Matt Sonzala) "He was working that job, in that store by himself. Stayed up all night making tapes, then he had to get up and open up the shop at ten o'clock. Then stay there 'til nine and go home.

Maybe eat some fast food, which he didn't need. And then go back and make some more tapes, and then he might stay at the studio till five o'clock in the morning, go home and take a shower. He wasn't getting any rest. I have seen my son, he was so tired that when he walked into the house he'd fall asleep on the couch. He wouldn't even go upstairs. And he'd sleep there for maybe two hours. I have lifted that boy off the floor 'cuz he had rolled off the sofa. I had to lift him up, and my son was a big dude. I have lifted him up off the floor and put him on that couch. His girlfriend would say, *How can you lift him?* And I'd say, *That's my baby.* And he'll sleep for two hours and get up and take a shower, and it was like he slept eight hours. He would say, *How did I get off the floor?* And I'd say, *Your mama lifted you.* I said, *Baby, you my baby. I lifted you when you was a baby.* And he had this little crooked grin on his face."

99 LIVE

In the summer of 1999, Screw was interviewed by Daika Bray, a native of Third Ward who had been writing and working in film production since 1994, when she got her start on a music video with director Dr. Teeth (also *his* first video) for the Greenspoint rapper Fesu. She would go on to work on videos for Geto Boys and Blac Monks, and in the late '90s was writing for a magazine called *Dialect.* Bray was then married to Henry LeBlanc, who grew up in Beaumont knowing D-Reck from Wreckshop and was working on a movie with Reck called *The Dirty 3rd*—a film in which Screw would appear, in a scene filmed at his shop. Bray pitched the idea for a story about the Screwed Up Click to the hip-hop magazine *XXL*, and the article was given a green light for their December issue. It would be the most in-depth interview Screw had done to that point.

DJ Screw (as told to Daika Bray) "Everybody in Screwed Up Click, we all got dreams of what we wanna be and what we wanna do, what we wanna accomplish in life. Business, home, record shops, lawyers, businessmen, whatever. Everybody got their ghetto dreams. My plan is do the best I can do. Everybody wanna help theyself. If they got their heart into it, they really gonna do something. I know I got my heart into it.

I live and die for this shit, every day. I'll do the best I can, try to keep my name up high. For my family, the ones that's with us, upcoming generations. The young BGs, they see us rappin', they really like that. I'm tryna pave the way so they can shine, too. 'Cuz the sun will shine on everybody. Everybody will get their time to shine. It don't happen overnight though. Gotta be dedicated. Gotta be real about it, can't just do it 'cuz everybody else doin' it. You really wanna do it, you just gotta put your heart into it. Be true to you, be true to the ones around you, your loved ones. 'Cuz I ain't gonna fuck with nobody who don't love me. Get real with me, I'm getting real with you. For real."

Daika Bray "There are two things that stick out from that interview. One, he was *really* nice. He was very polite, he was accommodating, he was warm, he was friendly. He had questions for *me*—which was surprising to me because I had heard that he was not friendly and didn't wanna talk to press and all that kind of thing. But I think that he kind of looked at me as more of like . . . I mean, not really like press. More like family. And the other thing is, he was talking about Fat Pat—he was playin' a Screw mix and making me a gray tape of the interview while we talked, right? And as he was talking about Fat Pat, the record skipped, and he was like, *Look! There he is. See, that's him right there, lettin' me know he's here with me.*"

DJ Screw (as told to Daika Bray) "Don't believe all these rumors. 'Cuz I play my music slow, people think you gotta get high, get fucked up, do drugs, just to listen to my music. It ain't like that at all. Or that I just do drugs all day, that's why my music's slow. It ain't all about that. I stopped smokin' weed a while back. Back in the game I was young, so I was smokin' weed, but you get burnt out on that. You don't gotta get high to listen to my music. It ain't no worship-the-devil music. So people think you worshippin' the devil when the music drags. It ain't about that. I'm just bringin' it to you in a different style where you can hear everything and feel everything. Give you something to ride to. I'd like to thank all the people that support me. Without the people supportin' me, I wouldn't be where I'm at today."

STRAWBERRIES

Louisiana was hot for the Screwed Up Click, who had done many a show out there over the years, and one of the places they got the warmest response and the most support was at the club Strawberries in Lafayette. The population of the city itself wasn't much more than one hundred thousand, but the Lafayette metropolitan area sprawled over five parishes and accounted for about a half million people, and plenty of them made their way out of the wilds to the club on a Saturday night.

Strawberries was a venture of Louisiana promoter Bobby Caillier, who was from Lafayette originally but had opened up nightclubs in cities all over the state and knew how to tap into the local culture. Part of the magic in Lafayette was because of Troy DeRouen, a native of nearby New Iberia, Louisiana, who went by DJ Troy-D and had been hyping up crowds in the area since *forever*. That didn't mean he just handed over the mic, though.

E.S.G. "I used to hit all the major clubs in that area, as an unknown artist, and grab the mic! And I still recall at the same club where Tupac got his chain snatched at, I was like, *Hey man, lemme get the mic.* And the DJ looked at me like, *Nigga are you* crazy? *I'm not gonna give you the fuckin' mic!* And everybody around was like, *Naw, you need to give this nigga here* the mic, mane! *Give that nigga the mic!* And the DJ was like, *Naw, I don't really* give the mic. So the *same* DJ, Troy-D, wind up deejayin' at one of the college parties. He ain't wanna gimme the mic at Strawberries, but when he seen me on the mic at one of the college parties, oh *shit!* That nigga gave me the mic at Strawberries *every* time after that! That's where I met UGK at, Strawberries. I seen Shaquille O'Neal get beat up at Strawberries!"

Louisiana's alcohol laws meant that the establishment was BYOB, which kept it open well past the customary closing time for venues—a good thing for the Screwed Up Click, who always showed up late. Lafayette was three and a half hours from Houston—depending on how fast the slab line was moving. One bill featured Screw with Big Hawk, Point Blank, and Botany Boys, but the show didn't go down like anybody expected, and it wasn't because they got there late.

D-Red (Botany Boys) "I was lookin' at the side of the stage where Screw was, and I remember there was a puddle of water down there and I seen him. Nobody—a lot of cats was standin' around, but I guess they ain't see him. So I looked, I say, *Man, Screw on the ground!* So I jumped offstage—he was shakin' in a puddle of water. He was havin' a seizure! So we took and grabbed him and got him outside on the back, man. That's why we had to stop the show. People ain't really pay attention to what I was doin' until I jumped offstage. He was like on the side of the stage, standin' right there. We called the ambulance. Big Moe was there, too. When we took him outside, he kinda bounced back. He didn't remember. We had to tell him what happened, that he had a seizure."

C-Note "We ain't know what the fuck was goin' on. It scared the shit out of us! We got him out of there, got him to an ambulance and shit. Next thing you know, Screw had rolled up in that ambulance that night. That was one of the first encounters, first time we knew Screw had some sickness goin' on."

THE DAY HELL BROKE LOOSE

December 7, 1999—Swishahouse releases the compilation *The Day Hell Broke Loose*, the first official album from the Northside label founded by OG Ron C, G-Dash, and Michael "5000" Watts. Swishablast, as the movement was called, started off doing regular-speed tapes they called "Swisha Mixes," to coincide with the popularity of Swisher Sweets cigars, which were commonly cut open, emptied of tobacco, refilled with marijuana, and then rolled back up and smoked. The Swishahouse DJs had been on the radio for years before they started slowing and chopping music, but over time DJ Screw's influence started to come out in their music. The biggest difference was that the label had an internet presence, and they were releasing their mixes on compact discs—making them accessible to folks who didn't have tape decks in their cars, or who lived elsewhere and could find Swishahouse on the web but couldn't make it to the Screw shop.

Lil' Keke "We had left the tapes alone, and it was a huge market for freestyle CDs. We had moved into really makin' music now, makin' albums! So we wasn't doin' as much, and that's how they really came up. They picked up where we left off."

The mixtapes kept growing for Swishahouse in the years following, but much like the members of the S.U.C., they were also now pivoting toward making albums, and *The Day Hell Broke Loose* was a way of introducing their roster to the world: Slim Thug, Chamillionaire, Paul Wall, J-Dawg, Archie Lee (not to be confused with Herschelwood's Archie Lee), Lil' Mario, and plenty more. In a Southside-Northside crossover moment, even South Park Mexican made an appearance on the album, and in perhaps a hint of the eventual dissolving of the crosstown beef, C-Note of Botany Boys raps on "Can't Stop from Ballin'," and it was Southsider Billy Cook singing the hooks on three of the album's sixteen tracks.

OG Ron C (Swishahouse) "At first, it just set out to be a chance for the Northside people to represent for theyself, for the rappers to rap about some Northside stuff. People on the Northside had got tired of pickin' up a Screw tape and just hearin' nothin' but Southside shit. Then got tired of hearin' them talkin' *down* on the North, *Fuck the North niggas! I'ma rob them niggas!* It just came to a point where people was like, *Okay, that shit's cool, but damn! We need somebody to represent for us.* And then when people started realizin' that Watts was doin' that, and not even bashin' the Southside *back*—because once I became the MC, it was me! Remember—I had the jump. I was workin' for the radio station, I worked at Jamaica Jamaica, I was on the Southside a lot. I met a lot of Southside girls, so I was tellin' Watts, *Listen, man, they fittin' to put out a tape, man. They dissin' us, I'm tellin' you!* And I'm the MC, so I used to try to respond back! But Watts was like, *Man, don't do that, man! Hell naw.*"

Knock "The Northside-Southside beef started way before Screw. It started like behind rims, man. '84s and '83s, the swangers they would be ridin'. That's really where the beef come from, man. A lot of dudes from Rosewood and Hardy and all that, they used to come out here and steal our cars, you know, jack niggas out here and all that, man. So a couple of people got—a *lot* of people got killed in that lil beef. So when Screw came, that gave us a mouth, you know what I'm sayin'? We was able to talk about it through Screw tapes. And later on down the line, Michael '5000' Watts gave the Northside a mouth, so it's like we was able to go back and forth just through the mixtapes, Screw tapes. But nah, that beef was started before Screw. Screw just gave us a mouth to be able to, you know, put it out there."

Michael "5000" Watts (as told to Chowtime TV) "I met Screw three times, right? And out of the three times that I met him, there has never been no hostility or no negativity. I ain't gon' lie. There's never been none of that. But I heard him talk some shit about me on some of them mixtapes!"

Probably the most infamous meeting between Screw and Watts took place right outside of a Third Ward establishment where Screw, who was known to eat fried chicken nearly every day, was getting his fix. While Watts recalled an amicable encounter where he jumped in Screw's car (Screw wasn't driving that night), Al-D has a more blunt recollection of the evening.

Al-D "It was me, Screw, and Poppy, 3-4 Action. We pulled up at the Frenchy's over there by TSU, and man, all I know, we's walkin' and I'm thinkin' we just gonna go get some chicken. But Screw runs up on this dude, *Say, man—I'm not gon' tell you again, mane. If you gon' put my name—don't put my motherfuckin' name on your tapes. You ain't Screw. Don't put 'screwed and chopped' on your motherfuckin' CD. Put your own motherfuckin' on your CD, man! Do you understand what I'm sayin', man?* And I'm like, *What the fuck is goin' on?* I ain't know who this dude was. All I know is Pop-pop was like, *Man, Al get the car. I'ma run over this nigga.* Pop-pop wanted to run over him in the parking lot of Frenchy's."

Michael "5000" Watts (as told to Chowtime TV) "I am an admirer of DJ Screw, and I always have been, and I am still to this day. You know, but it was a division between the city way before the music. It was . . . the Northside and Southside were like Bloods and Crips. That's how it was at that point."

AI-D "I had just got out of jail, so you know, you have to be out in the streets for a little while, because you still got that lil butterfly thing, that lil urge. You wanna chill the fuck out because you just got out of jail, you know? So when I was put in that predicament right there, I go, *Goddamn.* You know what stopped anything bad from happenin' was when Screw said, *You understand what I'm sayin'?* You say, *Alright, Screw.* He puts the fire out instead of wantin' to be a smart-ass. He was *wise*, you know what I'm sayin'? He didn't pop off at the mouth and say nothin' ignorant, because that's what coulda led on to some violence or some bullshit."

OG Ron C "At the '25 Lighters' video shoot, DJ Screw said to me, *Man, I ain't got no beef with the Northside. I ain't never had no beef with the Northside.* He said, *Me and the Northside, we good.* That's what that man said, outta *his* mouth."

The Day Hell Broke Loose was a distinctly Houston enterprise, influenced by Screw and Rap-A-Lot alike, and perhaps even, in a business sense, a synthesis of the two. Swishahouse started in the streets, as had Screw via the way his tapes were distributed, but they also promoted in ways Screw never had. Of course the DJs drew comparisons to one another, because they were the centers of movements from opposite sides of town, with a growing crew of artists behind them. But Screw was the pioneer of slowed-down music, and he was about to get his shine.

THE RING

December 21, 1999—In the months leading up to his Fourth Annual Mixtape Awards, Justo Faison enlisted help in going through the countless submissions he had been sent for consideration. The awards show was a personal pursuit for Justo. His day job was doing promotions at Epic Records, but since 1995 he had been funding and promoting an awards program to recognize the art of the mixtape, and the event was getting bigger each year.

Tytanic (NYC producer) "We had to go through so many tapes, and Justo couldn't do it all, so he used to hand tapes to me. And basically he handed me damn near a whole crate of DJ Screw tapes. I'm like, *Who is this guy?* And he said it was a DJ from Houston. Really, I was pro–New York when it came to mixtapes. I was into my crews, and upcomin' DJs, which was Kay Slay—he was upcoming, but he was *fire* in New York. Anyway I was given the task of actually listening to some of Screw's mixtapes, and I was like, *Yo, somethin's wrong with this tape.*"

DJ Kay Slay "Justo was like the Grammy Awards for the DJs. He was somebody that recognized who we were, what we meant to the whole culture, us bein' the backbone of the culture from day one. And as modern technology evolved, it kinda pushed us to the back. He wasn't about to just sit there and let that happen, so he took whatever money he had, whatever sponsors he could get, and he *honored* us. He made that his responsibility, to honor us. He was *everything* to a DJ in the late '90s."

Justo (as told to SidLocks for MultiHop) "I did it because all other DJs was gettin' credit for breakin' artists everywhere, and the mixtape guys were, you know, working hard in they cribs and puttin' them together, and puttin' them on the streets for the people. They were breakin' artists, remixing their songs, and they wasn't gettin' credit."

Bun B "At the time, that was the biggest event going for DJ acknowledgement in the world in terms of DJs being honored by other DJs and that kind of thing. DJs being able to show their appreciation for other guys they listen to. I didn't get to go, but I do know it was a big deal, and he was received with open arms, because he was an originator. You know, anytime you go to New York and you talk to different guys about different things, they'd be like, *Yeah, I heard that before*, *Yeah, I saw that before*, or *Yeah, we did that before—my homies used to do that back in the day*, that kind of thing. But what Screw was doin' was actually new. It was totally new. Nobody had ever done anything like that, or seen anything like that before. And so New York people were really taken aback. Because, you know, it was the opposite of—you know, ghetto-style DJs back in the day used to speed music *up*. The Florida DJs, they used to kinda speed music up. You know, that was their thing. But no one had ever slowed music *down*."

Tytanic "I kept playing each one, and all of them were slow. It was some music you were kinda familiar with anyway, but it was slow. I said, *Yo, man. Dude, there's somethin' goin' on.* He's like, *No. You don't understand. This is the style.* I said, *I don't like that style. I don't like it. This is crazy right here.* I still had to listen to it, though. It was still my job to do it. And after listenin' to it, I kinda like . . . like, this thing is gettin' in tune with my mind. I'm like, *Wait a minute. I'm starting to feel this!* Some things sound really good played slow! I was like, *Justo I'm startin' to like this stuff, man.*"

For Screw, the Justos were a chance to put his name up on that stage with the legends of the genre he'd been representing ever since he first touched a turntable. He felt that the work he and the S.U.C. had been doing in Houston belonged up there, and he was finally getting a chance to show what he'd been building—and who he'd been building it *with*— all those years.

Tytanic "Everybody used to get plaques as a Mixtape Award. You know how labels give you a plaque? Justo, as an award for the DJs, he gave them a plaque. So this was the first year that he wanted to give them Mixtape Award *rings*. And I was like, *Why are you givin' these DJs Mixtape Awards rings?* And he did some research, because he wanted the ring to be a Super Bowl ring. So he found the company that actually makes the Super Bowl ring. I actually seen him in possession of the paperwork of the design of the ring, and one of the designs was DJ Screw. I said, *Yo, man. DJ Screw is that popular, that you gonna give a Mixtape Award ring to?* He said, *Yo, you don't understand. This is a movement.* Anyway, when the ring came back, and it was a DJ Screw ring, and I was like, *Yo! This shit is . . .* It had diamonds in it, it looks crazy. I was in a very jealous kinda way! DJ Screw was one of the first rings that he got back, because he named the award after DJ Screw. It was the Chopped and Screwed Award. And that was one of the biggest honors, to have an award named after you."

Den Den (Straight Profit Records) "I remember when he got home. We was at his house, and he was like—I'll never forget this—I had a cup of syrup. He grabbed my cup—he was like, *Lemme hit that*. He grabbed my cup and damn near *kilt* the motherfucker! I'm like, *Man, gimme my shit!* He's like, *Damn, look at this ring, man. It look like a Super Bowl ring, don't it? They gave this to me in New York.* He was proud of that shit, because him goin' to New York was like finally them sayin', *We recognize what you got goin' on down here.* He was proud of that shit. Really proud."

Trae Tha Truth (rapper, activist, ABN, Guerilla Maab) "There was a certain way he used to smile, man, where you knew he had that good feelin', man. I remember when he showed me the ring. For cats like us, who would have thought that he could get up there with the Red Alerts and all that, and actually be recognized? And the fact is, he *did* do that, and that was a blessin', man. It was a blessin' as a introduction for people who weren't from here. They could actually see the talent, and what he was capable of doin'."

Shorty Mac "That made him feel like on a whole 'nother level, like all the work he been puttin' in, it was like. . . *Somebody from New York* noticed *me*. He felt *good* about that, I *do* know that, 'cuz as *soon* as he got back, he came to Smithville. It was around the holidays. When he got here, he pulled up, he parked in my mama driveway in the Impala. Me and him sittin' in the driveway for probably like four or five hours, and he was just tellin' me how good he felt that that happened, you know what I'm sayin'? I guess the way he was lookin' at it is all the work he do around the *city*—but they didn't *have* awards like that in Houston. But that dude felt so good, and that's why . . . like I know it's all on God. I know when God tell you it's your time, it's your time, but man, this dude was on his way to do stuff he had never done before. I think him gettin' that ring is a big part of like . . . it kicked another gear in for him."

DJ Screw (as told to Kyu-Boi) "1999 Justo's Mixtape Awards. New York, New York. Red Alert was hostin' the show. They flew me to New York right before Christmas. They was lovin' H-Town, lovin' Houston. I took everything down there and left it with 'em. Screwed Up Click, know what I'm sayin'?"

PLATINUM

In early 2000, a culture and lifestyle magazine called *Platinum* was just getting started by Desmond Lewis, a young professor at Houston Community College, and Carolyn Chambers, an entrepreneur in Dallas. Lewis, the editor, knew Screw through mutual acquaintances like DJ Gold and Al-D and had a vision for Screw's words to appear in the magazine.

Desmond Lewis "When I came by to talk to him in regards to writing for the magazine, I could tell you he was a hell of a real DJ. I mean like he was really a *DJ DJ*. I didn't know! I came to his house in Missouri City, and on that particular day Lil' O showed up, Big Moe was in the corner. C-Note from Botany was there, and I think Hawk was there. And some other people which, I couldn't tell you who they were. And none of these people knew me, because I just knew Screw. So Screw and I walked through his studio, and in the studio—because we were talking, and I didn't understand how deep he was into musicality—he was like, *Man, hold on Des*, and while we're talkin', he's deejaying! And I'm like, *Bruh, nobody is going to see this.* But the whole time we're talkin', he's deejaying, Screwing stuff up, and that's when I realized that, *Man, you are* really *talented.* Like really, really talented!"

For *Platinum*'s first several issues, Screw contributed a column called "What's Dirty Down South?" In it he interviewed Al-D and Point Blank, and writer Cheryl K. Brown penned a piece about him as well. Lewis took photos of Screw in the Fairchild Building of Texas Southern University, and Point Blank and Lil' Doug came along for the shoot. The pieces were both autobiographical and inspirational in nature, with Screw using the platform to reach a new audience.

DJ Screw (writing in *Platinum*) "A lot of my partners that I went to school with ain't here right now. Some of 'em dead. Some of 'em in jail. It's been a lot of cats that's been in my house that's not here right now. You see a person one day, but never think that you ain't gonna see 'em no more. So, I try to enjoy my life, family and friends. Ain't no plexing with me, it's all good. I do what I do for the kids. It gives them something to strive for. If I can make it, I know these kids can."

Robert Earl Davis Jr. (DJ Screw) outside of his grandmother Jessie's house in Smithville. Courtesy of Michelle Wheeler.

Robert Earl (DJ Screw), Ida Mae Deary Davis, and Michelle "Red" Wheeler. Courtesy of Michelle Wheeler.

Michelle "Red" Wheeler and Robert Earl (DJ Screw). Courtesy of Michelle Wheeler.

Michelle Wheeler holding her daughter Shimeka, Ida Mae Deary Davis, DJ Screw, and Jessie Deary, right before Screw left Smithville for Houston, 1986. Photo: Uncle Buddy Boy. Courtesy of University of Houston Libraries Special Collections, collection of Nikki Williams.

MG/Nation: Trouble House, DJ Screw, and Great Black Shark. Charles Washington got Screw working as a DJ with two of his former classmates at Sterling High School, in the group originally called Legion of Doom, 1990–1991. Courtesy of University of Houston Libraries Special Collections.

Al-D and Big DeMo in the wood room, months before the recording of Screw's most infamous tape, *June 27th*. Photo: DJ Screw. Courtesy of DeMo Sherman and University of Houston Libraries Special Collections.

DJ Screw at Maestro's studio in southwest Houston during the recording of his album *3 'N the Mornin'*, 1996. Photo: DeMo Sherman. Courtesy of DeMo Sherman and University of Houston Libraries Special Collections.

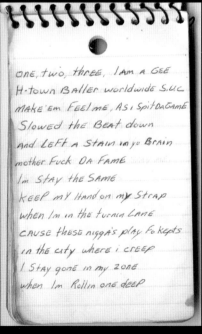

Screw's notebook and a Screw tape from 1999. Courtesy of University of Houston Libraries Special Collections.

Nikki, Poppy (in back), DJ Screw, Stick 1, and Mrs. Chatham at Stick's wedding, 1999. Photo courtesy of Stick 1.

Bamino outside of his shop in South Park, a Houston cultural landmark where DJ Screw went to get his car washed and where everybody still goes to this day, especially for the air freshener, 2014. Bam is the older brother of Mike-D (Southside Playaz). Photo: Lance Scott Walker.

Kay-K, Big Hawk, Fat Pat, and DJ Screw for Dead End Alliance album shoot, 1997. Photo: Deron Neblett.

Front row: E.S.G., Derrick "D-Reck" Dixon, Mr. 3-2, DJ Screw, Noke D, B Hawk, and Darin, by Dallas photographer James Bland for Daika Bray's article in *XXL*, 1999. Photo: jamesblandphotography.com.

Pamela Davis (niece), DJ Screw, PawPaw Jack (Ida Mae's boyfriend), and Poppa Davis (nephew) in Smithville, late 1990s. Courtesy of Michelle Wheeler.

Robert Earl Davis Sr. (Poppa Screw) at home in Southside Houston, 2008.
Photo: Peter Beste.

Meshah Hawkins, Lil' Keke, Lance Scott Walker, Shorty Mac, and E.S.G. at University of Houston, 2012. Big Pokey was there later. Photos behind them: DJ Screw, Fat Pat, Big Hawk, Big Moe, and Pimp C. Photo: Julie Grob.

Screw's family at his grave site on what would have been his forty-seventh birthday, 2018. Back row, left to right: Susan Davis, Poppa Davis, Michelle Wheeler with DaMari, Pamela Davis, and Shimeka Johnson. On the slab, left to right: Kianna, DeMario, Joshua, Jaylon, and Charles Jr. Photo: Lance Scott Walker.

CITY OF SYRUP

July 25, 2000—Wreckshop Records releases Big Moe's debut album, *City of Syrup*, with appearances by Big Hawk, E.S.G., Big Pokey, Z-Ro, Al-D, Will-Lean, and Ronnie Spencer and his young daughter Ronetta (the latter appearing as the voice of the "Barre Baby" on the album's iconic first song). Screw even showed up to the record's release party. He didn't do any cuts on the album, but his voice can be heard on "Leanin'" and the title track. Production was handled by Screw's cousin from Luling, Texas, Salih Williams, along with Blue, Double D, and Wreckshop's own Noke D, who was the one responsible for Moe's album happening in the first place.

Noke D "I had some real personal times with Screw as far as dealin' with Moe, 'cuz Moe didn't wanna leave Screw at all. He was waitin' on Screw to do a record label. But Screw would always tell me, *Man, I just wanna deejay. I don't wanna do no record label.* So that's when him and Reck kinda got together and convinced Moe. I really wanted to do a record with Moe. Nobody else really saw Moe bein' a solo artist! So I went to Reck and was like, *Lemme do this*, basically, you know what I'm sayin'? So he was like, *You think so?* I say, *Yeah, man, I got some ideas. I can work for Moe.* We talked to Screw about it, Screw told me, *Man, if anybody can do a record with Moe, it's pro'ly gonna be you. You know, 'cuz you got patience and you got some ideas and direction for him, and he'll listen to you.*"

The album made a splash on the charts, with a video to accompany the song "Maan!" that featured E.S.G. and Big Pokey and plenty of references to drank. Three 6 Mafia's hit song "Sippin' on Some Syrup," released a few months before, may have emboldened some folks to talk a bit more about syrup, but it was Moe's language they were speaking.

D-Gotti (a.k.a. Sonny BoBo) "Moe was the Barre Baby, you know? Everybody and they mama loved Moe. I ain't met a person didn't love Moe or had nothin' good to say about him. That was like him and Screw. Them was the two people that you know ain't no flaw—there wasn't no flaws in they character, man."

FOUR CORNERS OF THE WORLD

September 3, 2000—On the Sunday afternoon of Labor Day weekend, Screw returns to Smithville for a concert called Rap Fest at Vernon Richards Riverbend Park. On the bill were artists from Wreckshop, Presidential, Jam Central, LafTex, and the rosters of several other labels. This being Smithville, Screwed Up Entertainment was also listed, but Screw never did appear onstage that night, instead sleeping in a car for most of the show.

Back in Houston, his life was full of new pressures. He and Nikki had broken up in the aftermath of having lost the house in Sugar Land to foreclosure. That relegated Screw to the Mo City house, which was more studio than home, and his creative morale suffered in the process of dealing with his neighbors there. New people were coming around, but that was also because a lot of the people who used to be at his house weren't coming anymore, and Screw couldn't help but feel abandoned. The shop was rolling along, but Screw's output of tapes dwindled drastically in the year 2000.

Lil' Doug "He was stayin' with Dee, one of his female friends, and he was tryin' to get another house. He was really hurt from that house that he lost with Nikki. He was almost cryin' talkin' to us about it. He was like, *Man, this next house I'ma buy, it's gonna be bigger and better, and I'ma just pay for it cash. I'ma just pay for it cash.* But he never got around to it."

By summer's end, Shorty Mac, Big Bubb, Screw's cousin Lil' Doug, and his eldest niece, Shimeka, were all working at the shop in some capacity. Shimeka and her younger sister, Pam, Screw's other niece, had stayed in Houston over the summer, and when it was time to leave, the eldest didn't want to return to Smithville. Screw was living with his new girlfriend, Dee, in her apartment in Chinatown, and she agreed to let Shimeka move in with them. That was the arrangement in place while Screw focused on relocating his studio.

DJ Screw (from a 2000 interview) "My next door neighbor, she kinda prejudiced, so I'm in the process of movin' my studio and shit. And I make Screw tapes every day. Still do 'em, but it's been kinda slowin' down 'cuz a lot been happenin' with workin' on my label and my two shops. It's just me. It takes a lot to run a company, so actually . . . just my next-door neighbor's bitch hatin', that's why I ain't really been doin' no tapes, because every time I try to make a tape, she knock at the door and shit. I know it ain't the music. It's just prejudice. She ain't gonna stop it."

Reggie "Bird" Oliver "Soon as she see four or five cars, this lady would call the police. There were several times, and Screw was like, *Watch this.* Soon as these cars pull up, watch the laws come. We wouldn't even be playing no music. They'd knock on the door, he'd say, *What is it, Officer? . . . I'm getting complaints you having too loud music.* He'd say, *Did you hear any music when you came up?* They say, *You probably turned it down, turned it out, when you seen our car pull up.* He'd say, *I didn't even have any music on. This lady really hating on me. Any time she see two or three cars, she call y'all. I don't even have no music playing. As a matter of fact, we don't even have a session going on, nothing musical, we not even doing that. We just over here talking about the next project that we're going to be doing, and we not even playing no music tonight.* They still would come over there messing with him. They gave him tickets. He would have to go to court. That's why he moved. That's why he moved, because of this lady."

Lil' Rick "His clientele just wasn't nothin' but youngstas! You can be in any neighborhood and you see three, four youngstas come up, you gonna automatically think they doin' somethin' they ain't got no business doin'. So just imagine twenty, thirty cars at one time, and then most of the traffic don't come 'em after 10 p.m. at night. You in a community and a neighborhood where it's nothin' but working people, and you the only dude that draw this kind of traffic, you got niggas pullin' up bangin' and gettin' out, runnin' over to the potnahs, *What's up, bubba? What's up?* You know, your voices carry, and smokin' in the street, everybody got cups. *Damn, why everybody got a cup?* You know what I mean? Shit like that. You got motherfuckers gotta get up at four, five in the mornin' shit. Shit just really in its *prime* around that time."

Enjoli "I guess a lot of dudes feel like, because when they were doin' bad and lost their game or whatever, Screw came around and looked out for everybody. He looked out for a lot of them, and put 'em back on feet, you know what I mean? He had their back, but a lot of people didn't have *his,* you know what I mean? I saw the ups and downs, and I saw the real niggas and fake niggas. It was a lot of bullshit goin' on around him."

Lil' Doug "After he got over there, you know, them neighbors started callin' the police on him, the laws, because it was so much traffic and so much noise, and you know he had to eliminate a lot of that. You know, there was times people wanted to make tapes—even me myself, I can't! I can't. And *that's* when he went and got that studio off of Commerce over by Bissonnet and 59."

PITCH CONTROL

October 29, 2000—Screw sits down for what would be the longest interview of his life, with Ariel "REL" Santschi, a film student who would go on to create a series of video-magazine DVDs called *Pitch Control.* REL met Screw at a Botany Boys concert in Austin the previous year and then later linked up with him back in Houston on the Sunday night before Halloween. Santschi's long-ranging interview, filmed in a Northside hotel lobby late that night, formed the basis for *Soldiers United for Cash,* which started off as a student film and grew into a project that reached all the way into Screw's past, reenacting his childhood in Smithville, casting Shorty Mac's son and Screw's nephew Poppa as young members of the Z Force Crew. Over the course of several weeks, Santschi was allowed access that showed him a side of Screw not everybody got to see.

Ariel Santschi "There would be just some random person that would start freestylin' for him, and Screw was so humble that he would just give them his number. Like, *Alright, well call me.* I don't know if he did that with everybody, but I witnessed that. It was somebody he didn't know, and he gave them his number. You know how some people have like an ego or they don't really wanna mess with people? He was open. He was receptive to all that."

DJ Screw (as told to Ariel Santschi) "Niggas know who started this shit, know what I'm saying? I had a lot of partners, know what I'm sayin', tell me through my music and through my tapes, know what I'm saying, I done changed their lives by the type of music, the type of songs I done put on my tapes. Know what I'm saying, that inspired a person, you know what I'm saying. To most people, they think it's gangsta rap, it's, you know what I'm saying, talking about killing and selling drugs and shit. But shit. That's reality, that's real shit. Shit, just like you watch the news and you see motherfuckers getting shot and robbed and all that. You go rent a movie and you see motherfuckers killing motherfuckers and all that. Shit, this music, this is our way of expression, you know what I'm saying? To wake people up across the world."

South Park Coalition rapper Kyu-Boi also shot video of Screw around that time, at the house in Mo City. On that night, in the interior room of the house where Screw had his studio, were Point Blank, Enjoli, Big Jut, D Drew, and plenty of smoke in the air. Screw worked at the turntables while everyone stood around, nobody freestyling—just listening. When Screw finally stepped away from the tables and addressed the camera, Kyu-Boi asked him how he was holding up against the stresses—mostly concerning his neighbors—that were catching up with him.

DJ Screw (as told to Kyu-Boi) "It's been alright 'cuz I've been *livin'*, but really it's been hell because I'm under surveillance. Punk motherfuckin' laws and shit, think I'm sellin' drugs and all that shit. Like I'm the leader of the Crips and all this shit here. But all I'm tryin' to do is make music. It ain't nothin' but *music*! I'm an entertainer and a stainer. Keep it *real*. Keep it real, you feel me?"

Kay-K "He never got a chance to sleep. Somebody at his house twenty-four seven. When do he sleep? They there all night, man. Then it's different groups of people. He might sleep in the daytime, but I'm tellin' you, Screw would stay up for *days*. The drugs and stayin' up two, three days is just not healthy."

Stick 1 "People who wasn't able at first to get into the house was in the house. And I start noticin' that it growed so much, it came to the point where to me, on a heavy level, I think that's what got his life, man, is he became just involved in bein' a part of the party to *bein'* the party. You know, as his life changed, now who's around him to say, *Say, man, let's chill out. Say man, let's not smoke too much, and let's not mess with that dipper. We doin' too much drank.* Because if *you* the party, if I tell you to stop, that cut *me* off. So Screw became a person who was just a part of it to *bein'* it."

Cory Nelson (neighbor, Sugar Land) "People were always comin' and goin' and buggin' him, and so he'd come to my house and hang out. It was more like he'd go off the map for a second. You know, I'd get home, *I'm home!* And my mom would be like, *Shhh! DJ's on the couch asleep. Be quiet!* You know, my parents are sittin' there watching *Wheel of Fortune*, and there's Screw on the couch with a half-eaten sandwich on his chest, passed out."

Ida Mae (as told to Matt Sonzala) "I know one thing. I know the problem that he had was his heart, and he didn't want me to find that out. He had heart problems, and he kept that a secret from a lot of people. The only reason I found out was because I went to the doctor with him several times. He didn't want me to know, but as a mother I got nosy. And that wasn't the first heart attack he had. He already had five. I think two of them was like a tremor or something like that, but then the last two was bad, and he didn't want me to know. But the next time I went to the doctor with him, I asked the nurse when they took him to get that EKG. So I said *Are you okay?* 'Cuz he had gained a lot of weight. He said, *Yeah, Mama, I'm fine.* And I said, *Naw, there must be something wrong, you better talk to me.* But I had talked to the nurse already, and she had told me what the deal was. That it wasn't the first one or the second one."

Al-D "Me and Nikki brang Screw in to the hospital at least six or seven times, man. He would just get stressed out on phone calls and shit. You look in the back seat, and he got his motherfuckin' hands and shit all crossed up, like when you see when you gettin' ready to have a heart attack and it's just like you're grippin' a baseball or somethin'. Your hands start lockin' up and shit like that. So we was runnin' him to the hospital.

Shit like that. Just stayin' up late and workin' all the time. I mean, eatin' greasy-ass goddamn food, not eatin' right, no proper sleep, stress. That was enough to kill you by yourself. No exercise. There wasn't *no* goddamn exercise, period. He didn't know what exercise *was*. Screw didn't ever do no exercise."

Reggie "Bird" Oliver "He had a heart attack, and when we went to go see him in the hospital, the nurse wanted to know . . . because they didn't want to give him something and then it, you know, triggered something else. They was like, *What drugs do he do, is he on heroin?* They just wanted to know. Anytime you fall out or pass out, they need to know 'cuz they don't want to give you the wrong things and it'll make it worse. So I tell them he drink a little bit. She says, *Do he smoke marijuana?* He didn't smoke, he just drank a little bit, and then he would take No-Doz, so that was even worse. She say, *What in the world?* She say, *He drinking and drinking, and that puts you to sleep, and then you take No-Doz to keep you up, and it's like your body and your heart don't know what to do—go to sleep or stay up.* So she told me to look in the room, and I looked in the room and he was just snoring. And she said, *That's his problem right there.* And I say, *What's the problem?* She say, *He's tired.* She said, *This guy is really tired.*"

C-Note "I was in Hiram Clarke, and I seen Screw drive by in his Impala and pull into a corner store. I had kept goin', and when I came back *out* the neighborhood, he was at the store—and I was at somebody house for a few minutes! I was like, *Man! Screw still at this store.* Now, keep in mind there's a couple guys hangin' out there, and Screw was in this Impala, on blades, candy blue . . . so I'm like, *Lemme go see if my potnah still at this store.* Because I know at least fifteen, twenty minutes may have passed. I just knew he should have been long gone. So I pulled in there just to talk to him, and man, don't you know, I went in the store, and Screw was standing there on the drink aisle where you buy the beverages at, standing there leanin', tired or whatever, basically asleep standin' up. With a chain on his neck. I'm lookin' around, he got his nice jewelry on, nice car outside, *Man, Screw, what's up, my nigga? What you doin'?* I got him up out of there. I ain't have to carry him or nothin', I mean he just woke right up and continued with his day. But that's how I found him, though! I'm lookin' around like, *Ain't nobody hit him upside the head and took his jewelry?* 'Cuz he was really asleep standin' up, and the necklace so big and long, you coulda just slipped it over his head. And I seen guys standin' around there, but I guess they knew who he was, and out of respect for him, nobody touched him, 'cuz he was alright."

Ida Mae (as told to Michael Hall) "He knew he was dying. He came up here before Thanksgiving, said, *Mom, won't be back for Thanksgiving.* He wouldn't say why. Didn't want to worry me. He had had five heart attacks. I got to cooking, made all of his favorite foods. He kept hugging me, saying, *I love you.* He was well rested that night. He stayed up late, not sleeping, nodding off."

DJ Zo Tha Affiliate "They had Thanksgiving dinner early, and that was crazy because he called the whole family, like he called our house but I was at football practice. He called to talk to me and my mom, and then he called my cousin Brandy, and my cousin was like, *Hey, Robert Earl tried to call y'all but y'all was gone.* And then my mom tried to call him back but he didn't answer. And then just after that we had the dinner with Mama Screw, and it was like he kinda had a feelin' something was about to happen and he started callin' and tellin' everybody he loved them and all of that."

DJ Screw (as told to Daika Bray) "They say the world gonna come to an end. I think the world gonna come to an end for the people that's been doin' bad stuff. Their world gonna come to an end. That's how I look at it. The world ain't gonna stop. All the people that done messed over our generation, they world gonna come to an end, for all the bad stuff they done to us. And the success and all that, the talent I got, I ain't never gonna let that go to my head. It's like the Man gave me the talent, I'm just tryin' to stick with it. We're all here on this earth for a purpose. I'm tryin' to reach people through my music. Keep the faith. Believe in yourself. Keep it real with the ones that's real with you, take care of your family . . . you be alright."

COMMERCE PARK

November 15, 2000—Houston pride is teeming on a Wednesday, what with local group Destiny's Child having the no. 1 song in the country with "Independent Women Part I" and Hakeem Olajuwon's Rockets beating the Chicago Bulls the night before. Screw was working in the warehouse he was converting into a studio near Sharpstown. The facade of 8181 Commerce Park looked like any of the hundreds of baked-concrete, cream-brick buildings that popped up around Houston in the mid-1970s—nondescript and not easy to find—and that was the point.

Inside, things were still being built out, but Screw was crafting a vision for a recording studio and manufacturing and mail-order operation, along with another shop, and eventually a label. His turntables were again set up against the wall, but now he had a concrete floor underneath him and speakers set up on stands for him to broadcast what he was spinning up into the space's fourteen-foot ceilings. There were still milk crates on the ground, but also wooden farm stands set up with his records accessible and easy to flip through—like shopping in his own record store. He had always depended on just *knowing*, with a savant-like accuracy, where every last record could be found, but now he could mix, pull records without having to bend over, and dream up a whole new filing system.

He had made three tapes since getting the warehouse, *Screwed Up Texas* being the most recent. But that afternoon, Screw was just playing records. That was something he didn't always get—time to just listen. He came across his copy of Nirvana's 1991 album *Nevermind*, a record Screw loved, even if he never put it on a tape. He dropped the needle down on "Smells Like Teen Spirit" and blasted it through the system in the warehouse, with no next-door neighbors there to tell him to turn it down. He didn't even really have *business* neighbors, because he didn't work business hours, and he wasn't about to start.

Everyone seems to have a recollection of seeing Screw that day, or the night before. J Doe, Manny Sauce. Earlier in the week, Klondike Kat drove past the shop on Cullen around five in the morning and saw Screw sitting outside in the Impala. D-Gotti stopped by the house in Mo City and found Screw kneeling on the lawn. There were phone calls that weren't returned, with plenty of people just barely missing him. Looking back, anybody could see his world was spinning.

ACT "I went down to Houston 'cuz we was gonna make me a birthday tape. When I got down there, Al picked me up from the bus station and we went back to his apartment, put my stuff up. We was sittin' up there chillin' and Al was like, *Man, let's go to the shop, go over there and holler at Screw'n them.* So we rode over there—Screw was gone. He had left. But his car was there. So me and Al got some tapes and shit and we went back to Al house and then Al was like, *Fuck it, well let's go get some drank.* So we go to get some drank and Screw car is at this woman house. And we pulled up, and you know how you got on one side, we parked on the other side of her street, not facing the traffic but with the ongoing traffic. And the woman, she just kinda was actin' funny and we just kinda went on in there, and Screw was sittin' off in there, man, Screw was choppin' it up and Chris Cooley—him and Chris Cooley were together."

Chris Cooley "We had a whole bunch of records in the record pool, and we were goin' through his records, and then he said South Park Mexican had called, and that's when we came to celebrate. He gave me the keys to the car and wanted me to go and get a lil syrup, and he just stayed with his records at the studio. I went, came back, and I come up to the door, and you know, I'm knockin' on the door, knockin' on the door, and forgettin' that I had the keys, so I opened the door and he was dozing off. His face was just about to hit the record. He woke up and then he was just lookin' at the Nirvana album cover for a long time. It was weird. I mean, he was just at peace, just chillin', and we had just like . . . the three days before that night, I remember we stayed up like three days in a row. That's when Big Moe shot the video for 'Barre Baby' and the song 'Maan!'"

For Screw and many others, South Park Mexican (Carlos Coy) was *the* pipeline into the Hispanic and Latino communities of Houston. His Dope House label had focused on developing talent from all over Houston, but particularly the Southside. Although relatively few Latino rappers appeared on Screw tapes, a lot of those cars lined up outside of Screw's house had been turned on to his music by SPM. On the night of November 15, he called Screw to talk business.

South Park Mexican "I gave him my idea of how we could Screw the world, which was ultimately his dream, was to Screw the world, and I had ideas how we could talk to major record labels and get in major catalogs and just Screw the fuckin' world! And of course, he's out of his mind, but he can hear a little bit! And he was like, *Yeah, that sounds alright. That sounds good. Let's meet up tomorrow.* And I said, *Okay, I'll call you tomorrow.*"

Big Jut (as told to Jason Culberson) "I went to this club we used to go to, a pool hall called Cornbread's, and there wasn't really nobody up there so I say, *I'ma go by the studio and see Screw.* So, when I knocked on the door, him and Chris Cooley, his cousin, was there. And you know, we was sittin' around, just talkin', and Chris . . . I ain't gonna lie—we was drankin'— and me and Chris, we went to go get some breakfast and came *back*, and when we got back, Screw was like . . . he was kinda . . . you know, he was out of it a little bit. But, you know, he woke up, and like Chris said, you know, he went and got the ice cream and he was eatin' that. But so after I ate my breakfast, you know, when you full of that drank, you gonna pass out, so I lay down—I mean I just sat on the couch, and we was just like . . . Screw was walkin' out the room, but he touch me on my leg, and it was like a . . . it was more like a *goodbye*, because when I woke up, I seen him from *behind*, and he was goin' in the bathroom, and I said, *He just gonna go use the restroom, pro'ly fall asleep,* you know."

Chris Cooley "It was three, four o'clock in the mornin' at that time. He had some mattresses that were up against the wall and I grabbed me one. 'Cuz I saw him in the restroom, and I didn't think nothin' of it because that was his favorite . . . you know, that was like his privacy, his office. And, but these were like school restrooms, with the door, you know the door you close and put the little latch. But it was just . . . it didn't have doors, or if it did, he didn't use it. It was just wide open. He was just sittin' on the toilet like a chair. Just sittin' there eatin' an ice cream cone. And I said, *Screw, why don't you go lay down?* And he would just look at me and smile, and put his head back down. And he did that *everywhere*, in the restroom—in the restroom in his house. That's the thing—he would be goin' in there like he had counted money over there, I dunno. And Screw was so damn heavy, lil stubby, it was like man . . . I'm like, *Man, go lay down*, and he don't say nothin'. So I just—just made sure he was alright and pulled a mattress over there. Fell asleep."

ACT "After we left, we went back to the apartment and was supposed to hook up with him later, and Al-D jumped up and said somethin' was wrong. I said, *What's wrong?* He said, *Man, somebody just like . . .* He felt something rub across the top of his head, and he said, *Screw the only one do that . . . when I'm fuckin' with that keyboard or somethin', Screw'll walk by and do that. Man, we gotta go check on Screw.* So we get to where he at, the warehouse at, and we pull up in the back and there's no car there. We thinkin' that they gone somewhere, they still ain't made it."

At around five thirty in the morning, a light rain began to fall over Houston. It was about an hour before sunrise on the morning of November 16. Al-D and ACT sat out in the parking lot for a while, but having not seen Screw's car and figuring he was elsewhere, they left Commerce Park and drove back to Al's. What happened was that Chris Cooley had parked Screw's Impala around the *back* of the building, hours before, and he, Screw, and Big Jut were all inside asleep.

Chris Cooley "I woke up just like I was doin' push-ups. And just comin' to check on him, I already knew something was wrong because I never seen him like that. He was layin' down on the side, where his hand was on the side of the . . . kinda behind the toilet on the floor, and then his left hand was kinda *in* the toilet, and his leg was—his foot was kinda stuck behind the little peg of the wall to the restroom, and when I moved his foot to get it from around that peg, I already knew somethin' was wrong because his leg was stiff. And I couldn't see his face because he was kinda behind that toilet, around the side, until I pulled him out and he turned over. That's when I freaked out. His eyes were closed. It was just like he was 'sleep."

Big Jut (as told to Jason Culberson) "I fell asleep, and then before you know it, Chris shakin' me, talkin' 'bout, *Wake up, Jut! Screw dead!* I said, *Naw, man, you trippin'!* And I used to always pour water on him, to wake him up. So I grabbed—he just moved to this new studio, and the refrigerator was right in front of it—so I grabbed a pitcher of water, and I ran in the bathroom, and I poured it on him. But that water cleared his face, and I seen that he was in there—I mean, he turnt dark. I say, *He gone.* And Chris, you know, he was scared, he was tryin' to . . . CPR, brang him back. And that same ice cream he was eatin', it rushed out his *nose.* I was like, *Chris, he gone. He gone.*"

2000 TEARS

Nikki (as told to Jason Culberson) "I was at my grandmother's house. I was layin' down, and I was 'sleep. And my grandmother's phone rang, the house phone, and my grandmother said, *Nikki, telephone.* And I said, *Ma, I'm 'sleep.* And she said, *No, it sound important.* She didn't know, though—all she said was the person on the phone didn't sound right. She said, *No, it sounds important.* So I got on the phone, I said, *Hello.* And my friend—it was Shatoria, and all she said, *Nikki, I'm so sorry.* And I said, *What are you talking about?* And she said, *I'm so sorry. He tried to get me to call you, and I wouldn't call you because I knew you just couldn't deal right then. Nikki, I'm so sorry.* And I said, *Toria, what are you talking about?* There are three chicks. There's Shatori, Jaron, and Toni. Y'all know the E.S.G. song 'Float On'? They were the three girls from that. So we all went to concerts together, these was my ride-and-dies for real. We still cool. I'm her child's godmother. And Shatoria just kept sayin', *Nikki, nobody called you? Nobody talked to you?* I said, *What are you talking about?* And she said, *Screw died.* And I said, *What!* And I sat up, and all I remember was I screamed, and my grandmother came runnin' into the room, and she said, *What is wrong? What is wrong?* And I could not . . . I remember crying. I don't remember gettin' off the phone. I remember crying, like *excessively,* and within an hour, my friends were at my grandmother's house. Now, keep in mind—all my people—all my friends and stuff, lived on the Southside. Yellowstone, all in that area. I lived on the East.

I had moved to my grandmother's house on the Eastside. It's a nice lil journey. Within an hour, they were at the house, and they were like, *You just need to get out the house.* But I still was not—it was not *registered* to me what was said, so I'm like, *What?* They said, *Get dressed, we need to move around. You need to get dressed.* So I said, *Did anybody call his mama? Where's his sister?* I remember saying that. Because by this time, I think shock had set in, because I couldn't cry anymore."

Shimeka (niece) "The night before, I was at the studio with him, and he was actually supposed to bring me to Dee house, but like I said, he move so slow! And that's just him, so it's just messin' with me sometimes, the *waiting* game with him. And she ended up finally coming to pick me up, and I went on to her house, went to bed, got ready for school, and by the time I . . . a little bit before I got out of school, people kept telling me my uncle passed away. Ain't—I ain't really take heed to it right away. None of that, you know? So then by the time the bell rang, and more and more people kept saying it, I was like, *How do y'all know this?* . . . *They're saying it on the radio.* I'm like, *I ain't heard nothin' on no radio*, you know? But I get to where I go after school, and the first thing I do is I call his cell phone. I think I called the shop, because usually he was at the shop. I called the shop, nobody answered the shop phone, so I called his cell phone, and I think Dee answered the phone. I was like, *Well this is weird.* You know, why is she answering his phone? And then from there it was a confirmed thing. She didn't even specify. I just asked her, *Is it true?* And she never said anything. By that time, my mom and them had already made it up here. They were already on their way to me."

Poppa Davis (nephew) "Out the blue they come get me out of class. When I got home I could tell my mom had been crying. I'm ten at the time, mind you. So I could tell that my mother's been crying, because her eyes are real dark. I'm like, *Mama, what's wrong?* And she's like, *I got some bad news to tell y'all.* We called him 'Uncle Earl.' She was like, *Uncle Earl died.* My older sister was already in Houston, Shimeka. She had stayed there. So it was me and Pam at the house. We got taken out of school. Pam immediately broke down, and it's like my whole body just went numb. I couldn't cry, I probably couldn't even tell you my fuckin' name at the time. And all I could do was just think about my grandma, who was stayin' across the street. So I walk out the house, goin' to my grandma's. It's a little dirt road that separated us from our front porch. And all I hear is, *Naw, they got the wrong one. Not my baby. Not my baby.*"

Frank Popa Watts "I was locked up. I had just talked to him, and then we go on lockdown, because we had a riot, so we was on lockdown, and it was on the radio that Screw had passed or whatever. But I had just talked to him! Everybody was like, *Pop! Pop!* And I couldn't believe it . . . like my whole dreams, my plans, like comin' out and doin' my album or whatever. Because I used to always tell Screw, like, *Man, Screw, I don't wanna come home and be havin' to go through this or whatever* . . . so Screw was like, *I got it, man, I'll talk to everybody we need to be plugged in with so we don't have to worry about nothin'. I got you. Just come home.* So, man, when he passed, man, I didn't wanna . . . I didn't really eat, come out, or nothin' for like three months, and then one day I just broke in the shower. It finally hit me, and I finally broke down. I didn't even wanna accept it, you know? It was hard for me."

Enjoli "It was a shock but it *wasn't* a shock. To me, I was young and I really didn't know that drugs could take you under like that. I didn't know drugs could *kill* you. I know when we were in elementary—you gotta remember I was around them in my middle school, high school era—so I'm still young! And when you're still young, you're still learning, so I didn't know that the things that we were doing, that it could kill us. I didn't know that. So when he died, it's just like, *Wow* . . . Oh, I left codeine *alone*, strictly. I was like, *Hell no!* You know what I mean? I stopped completely. It freaked me out."

DJ Chill "My potnah was a workaholic. He worked himself to his demise. It wasn't . . . you know, yeah, he did other stuff that wasn't conducive to his life, physically, you know what I'm sayin'. But my potnah, he *worked*, man. He *worked*. Everybody, when they hear about Screw, they hear about the parties, they hear about the heights of his career, and things like that, and the people he *helped*. But *they do not know the struggle!*"

Big DeMo "This was our voice, this was our medium. This is how we got out our stresses, whatever we needed to say about music in general or anything that was goin' on. I mean, we talked about it on Screw tapes, during the intermissions. *Yeah I wanna say a shout-out to Clinton, 'cuz my mama opened a new business.* You know, stuff like that. He was our avenue, man, and it was gone just like that, man. God don't show favoritism. He'll take anybody out of here, you know? And it was—people were like, *Well, what'd he die of?* This and that . . . none of that stuff was important, man. The important thing was we lost Screw. We lost our Kid Capri. We lost our voice. It was just so devastatin', man."

Al-D "I lost my mind for about three fuckin' years. After Screw I lost my fuckin' *mind*, man. Man, I was in the streets, man. I left, went to Austin. I lost my fuckin' mind. I never wanted to make music again. I probably got around three albums since. But I didn't wanna fuck with music no more, man. When he died, it's like my fire, you know, my ambition to keep doin' the music, it kinda died, too. Every time I tried to do a song, it wasn't happy. It wasn't a happy song. I started gettin' crazy with the fuckin' music."

Ida Mae (as told to Matt Sonzala) "I knew my son. But I knew also in my heart that my son was sort of sick, but he didn't tell me how sick he was. Nurse told me how sick he was. I went to the doctor with him. Sometimes you can get too high up there and want to kill yourself and get it over with 'cuz you can't handle the publicity or you can't handle this, but that wasn't my son. That wasn't DJ Screw. He had too many plans in progress for me and him. All the places that we was supposed to go together . . . now why is he going to kill himself and leave his mama hanging? We had plans for the beach, for Las Vegas, to go to Louisiana, to go to New York City, everything. So why would he go off and leave me hanging?"

Nikki "The first service was in this big building where everybody could go, and then the second was in this teeny tiny funeral home. Then they took him home to Smithville for the funeral, and when I drove into

Smithville that morning, his mama called me and said, *Are you going to the church?* I said, *Yeah, I'm on my way.* She said, *No, come to my house.* I get out there and it's me and my mom in the car together. Ida was like, *You goin' to the church with me,* and that lady got in the car with me and my mama! She defied everything they wanted her to do. And when we walked in that church, we walked in that church hand in hand. That pissed some people off! But at the same time, it was a defining moment for *me,* because right then I knew I was going to be okay."

10. The Legend

Everyone has a vibration in their head, an echo of when they first heard that sound, a recurring flashback to all the ways their ears tried explaining it to them. On the streets of Houston, it would have been the kick drum they heard first (or maybe the snare—they sound the same on Screw tapes), announcing the shock wave from blocks away, shaking windows, tripping up car alarms, radios, and televisions, knocking pictures off of walls. The loudest thing you'll hear in Houston is a passing Screw tape. The treble shivers up into the atmosphere while the bass just bounces off the earth, the collective ear of the vicinity listening even from indoors for the slab going by with its windows down in the heat, filling a city's streets with its own homegrown vibe.

It's a public service, really, delivering Houston's musical history to its front lawns, through its walls, and over its roofs, maybe to entangle with the sound waves coming out of another car playing a different Screw tape. Bass is an idea that develops as it rides, saturates, and then evaporates. In its natural environment, the long waves of Screw's music ricochet off thickets of trees sprinkled through industrial wilderness, the surrounding concrete factoring in as part of the Houston weather system, and its sound. Ass-flat lowlands might offer us *some* benefit.

Screw's music is all at once under the city's bayous and atop its freeways, coiling and cleaving the wind between patches of skyscrapers making sense of the patches of houses between them. There is a rhythm, forged from the open windows of the cars in Houston, Texas, altogether new compositions sweeping through town and country, day and night. It's not the same sound in idling traffic on long city roads as it is blowing by on one of Houston's short-run arterial parkways to the tony neighborhoods out west, or in the parking lots outside of Vietnamese restaurants, Mexican cantinas, inside and all around the barbershops, tattoo parlors, record stores, clubs, taco trucks and barbecue spots, or any place that has anything to do with cars. The same tape will sound different driving slow, smoking weed on Almeda Genoa at one in the morning, than it does blaring by at eighty-five miles per hour, drinking coffee on the way to the airport, or in the church parking lot on a Sunday afternoon. The tape makes the moment.

Denizens of every street and alleyway in the city have that in common, the echo of Screw tapes having become the blood coursing through their neighborhoods, in open spaces, and off of every freeway exit—both for the people who were already onto Screw music and those who were bewitched when they heard it coming. The tapes resonate differently on the Northside and the Southside, but the music goes everywhere, wrapping big arms of sound around an entire city.

That is the chorus along six thousand miles of street, a collective movement rolling around Houston banging Screw tapes at any given minute, driving just slow enough to live inside their own echo, expanding in the humidity, one with the swamp around which Houston is built. Screw made his tapes sound like driving around Houston *feels*.

I felt it—on a Saturday evening in the spring of 2000, walking from my house to get a drink at a club called the Proletariat. Those of us standing at the corner of Richmond and Montrose waiting to cross heard a thumping and turned to our right to see a short slab line coming up the boulevard—a blue car followed by two red cars, their volume all but engulfing the intersection when they pulled up to the light.

"That's DJ Screw."

"Yessir," I said, by then bobbing my head.

But the guy standing behind me wasn't talking about the music. The blue sedan at the front of that slab line inched up farther into the crosswalk to turn left at the light, and a hand pointed over my shoulder.

"I mean that's *him*."

And behind the wheel of that blue Impala, there he was, arm extended out of the window, ashing a cigarette alongside his door into the street. Traffic got loose on the other side, so he put the smoke in his mouth and hit the gas, skidding out a little on the fresh paint of the crosswalk as he made the left. Our eyes turned with him, none of us ever having seen the *person* DJ Screw. We were the audience as his front tire found the pothole, all of us wincing at the noise the Impala made when it bottomed out. The two candy reds followed behind him, sunset streaking down Richmond into their windshields, the sound of three different Screw tapes circulating throughout the intersection. Screw took the cigarette from his mouth and blew out a column of smoke. As he passed, he turned his eyes in our direction and gave us a glance. He didn't nod. We felt seen.

I never saw a photo of DJ Screw until the news of his death. Remembering back to the volume of his music that day, buckling the air pressure of zip code 77006, I could feel it again on the sides of my skull. It hadn't been that long. You heard about the lines of cars at his house, but it didn't occur to you that he got out in his *own* car and made noise. And for the most part, he didn't. DJ Screw's life was one spent working from home, but the music that came out of that house fit into every corner of the metropolis.

In that, maybe there is no music that is more Houston, no music that more *represents* Houston, than the music of DJ Screw. The city has a rich history of both live and recorded music in rock, tejano, blues, jazz, zydeco, R&B, funk, punk, country, gospel, boogie, soul, and anything else you can think of—but no Houston genre focuses as much of its lyrical energy talking about the different *parts* of the city than hip-hop. And the first place that rappers from all neighborhoods could come together was on Screw tapes. His work is an audio map of the Southside of Houston, Texas.

In Screw's era, that sound was coming primarily from tape decks. Other DJs had been getting in his lane for years, and in the wake of his death, the market opened up, but the path forward wasn't lit well for his beloved format. Plenty of other DJs and producers out there were admittedly and openly influenced by DJ Screw, but by the time most of them were starting to show his influence in their work, both cassettes and vinyl had drastically fallen off the radar, and they were looking to make CDs, not tapes.

And so on November 16, 2000, the slow death of the cassette tape entered a new stage, because DJ Screw was no longer making them. As the compact disc later made way for digital media, a new generation of DJs discovered and have adapted Screw's techniques to the musical landscape of the present day. So that's where Screw's death represents a sticking point in the legacy of his music—after his passing, what is "chopped and screwed," "Screw music," or a "Screw tape"?

Nothing. If DJ Screw didn't do it, it's not a Screw tape, it's not chopped and screwed, and it's not Screw music. There is another school of thought, that if you call it "screwed," then it's a tribute to DJ Screw. That has legs, because that's basically the way it has been ever since he passed, but the people closest to him—and DJ Screw himself—went to great lengths during his lifetime to spell out that it's only *screwed* if it was touched by DJ Screw.

In death, the distinction becomes vivid. Screw was given a funeral in his hometown of Smithville, preceded by private and public services in Houston, and scores of people came through to show their respects—both for the man and for the music. Because really, the mythology and folklore of the work of DJ Screw in the end would mean that his genre—chopped and screwed—died with him, and that in the process, his impact on music was reborn anew. From there, the art form grows wings. Maybe it's "slowed and chopped" or "slowed and throwed," "eighted and chopped," like Mike Moe's Beltway 8 Records, or even "chopped not slopped," like OG Ron C and the Chopstars do it. Entire genres have sprung from channeling Screw (witch house), with whole movie soundtracks slowed and chopped, as Swishahouse did with Barry Jenkins's Oscar-winning 2016 feature film *Moonlight*. The generations following Screw have continued to pursue slowing and chopping as a legitimate art form, year after year, even if they're unaware of where it originated (as with "slowed and reverb"). DJ Screw wasn't just playing with records. He was playing with time. Everybody can relate to that.

In his final studio session, for *All Work, No Play*, Screw recorded on media that could tape for 108 minutes straight. Imagine for a moment that Screw had recorded for that long, and how long the finished tape would end up being once he *really* slowed it down, and then imagine what he would be doing with today's technology—or how he would work around it. His hands would still be on the turntables, no doubt, and people would still be learning about their relationship with music and with themselves through crossing paths with him. How would Screw see our world today?

Decades after his death now, you can still feel him all over Houston. Smithville, too. His legacy is so thick the networks of artists that developed under him can't help but still be connected to one another, and to him. When I first started working on the project that produced this book, Screw had been dead for four years. His lingering presence among the people who surrounded him during his lifetime, even then, was palpable. When people reminisce about Screw, they take on a certain peace. After a while you can't help but think they can still feel him around, even if he hasn't directly paid them a visit from the afterlife. Around the people touched directly by his music, and by him as a person, DJ Screw is very much alive.

CODEINE

Whatever part recreational cough syrup played in Screw's life, his was the first high-profile death associated with its consumption, and thus from the moment his coffin closed began an uphill battle to separate his legacy from it. For an early 2001 article in the *Houston Chronicle*, the headline was "Autopsy Shows Codeine Overdose Killed DJ Screw." The same local news media that had produced the *City Under Siege* TV series in the late 1980s to keep up with the crack epidemic now had a new drug to follow around. Of course they talked about it on the local news, but DJ Screw was also in the *New York Times*. "Rap Is Slower around Houston," read the headline, and in the article they talked about syrup. MTV News wrote the same thing. You didn't see an article on Screw's death that didn't mention it, as his name became synonymous with SYRUP EPIDEMIC. "Drank," "lean," and "syrup" were all of a sudden very bad words.

But it was cigarettes dipped in embalming fluid mixed with PCP—otherwise known as "sherm," "wet," "water," "angel dust"—that were really Screw's drug of choice. PCP (phenylcyclohexyl piperidine) is a hallucinogenic drug that stimulates receptors in the brain controlling muscle movement, which can manifest in a person's muscles locking up on them. Some folks drink milk to unlock, even if there's no science behind it. Screw was known to have locked up, and to have had seizures in the past—also a byproduct of smoking angel dust. Some can smoke it like it's nothing. Others end up running down the street naked and are never quite the same. Screw (like Mr. 3-2) was in the former category.

Overconsumption of codeine-promethazine was a contributing factor in DJ Screw's death, but not the primary cause. Medical examiners detected phencyclidine (PCP), benzodiazepines (Valium), and toxic levels of codeine-promethazine in his blood, and a lifestyle strung together around inconsistent sleep combined with a poor diet, no exercise, and abundant access to substances finally caught up with him. He also had a condition called cardiomegaly, which meant that his heart was abnormally enlarged and had difficulty pumping blood to the rest of his body. At the time his heart finally stopped, Robert Earl Davis Jr. was five-foot-seven and weighed 214 pounds. His heart weight was 450 grams—well above normal for someone his age and size.

Morna Gonsoulin (medical examiner, as told to Michael Hall) "He was a big guy. He had a big heart. The muscle part of [the] wall was thick. You see that in big people. I didn't see evidence of heart attack or physical damage. It was just a big heart. It could have given him some trouble. It wouldn't have helped matters, but it's not clear if it was bad enough to have contributed to his death."

Big DeMo "People stopped sippin' drank as much, because we not sure if this is why he died, but it had to be a part of it, so let's be a little bit more responsible. We do have kids. We do got family. We do got people that depend on us, that count on us to be there today, tomorrow, a year from now, ten years from now, and we gotta be here for them. So let's not drink as much. Let's not drink the whole pint, man. Let's just sip—you know, a deuce is enough. You know, drank is like weed. You get so high on weed, you can't get no higher. But once you leanin' on drank, you can't get no—you can't get no more leaner!"

In the years that followed, rappers were talking more about syrup, and so was the media. Money was swirling, laws were changed. Possession of codeine-promethazine in Texas began to carry stiffer penalties, and the prison-industrial complex always welcomes the expansion of drug codes because the resulting sentences fill their facilities. Syrup had risen in popularity over the years, and Big Pharma were invested in the promotion of codeine-promethazine just like the prison industry, the drug dealers, and the buyers. In 2014, only months after a headline in *MarketWatch* about its pharmaceuticals dominance, Actavis would make the decision to take its codeine-promethazine product off the market by ceasing production and distribution, citing the drug's unintended use and abuse over the years. By then, codeine-promethazine had earned the industry billions.

E.S.G. "People are always gonna connect DJ Screw and the S.U.C. to sippin' syrup, but at that time, there were plenty people—plenty kids, whether they were white, Hispanic, who had never sipped before—and they *still* was jammin' Screw music. I can't say the music had nothin' to do with the drugs—it's just that, like I say, the D-boys in the neighborhoods who was buyin' and gettin' Screw tapes made—those neighborhoods was a little faster than the slower neighborhoods, so at that time, in the faster neighborhoods, everybody was sippin'. And sippin' is just a culture of Down South. It's certain drugs we looked at growin' up in our environment that are just total like . . . that's a no-no. Everybody looks funny at a crackhead. No matter how you try to fake it, we all have 'em in our family and done seen 'em. That's just how it was. You do cocaine? *Aw, that's bad.* Heroin? *Aw, you awful.* But, if you sip and smoke, you were accepted, and that just was a cool thang."

Mike-D "Crack was more like an attack on our people. It took TVs out of homes, removed parents outta homes. Drank never did it like *that*. It was more like a champagne, a player potion. It never took people *last* money. It was for people who had money already. It was not as expensive as it is now. I'm sure if they had it still available as expensive as it is now, it probably would be a problem due to some client demand, because people want it but they can't get it. So if they had those numbers that they had—you know like maybe like it bein' scarce like, maybe that coulda happened, but naw, it wasn't . . . because you could find a bottle for $200. It wasn't—you wouldn't see people drinkin' four or five bottles a week, so there was nothing taken, because at that time crack was so big it had everybody in the ghetto paid. It didn't start goin' super crazy, like with little suburb kids drinkin' it and shit, until later. That's what landed—by the time it hit the suburbs, they was already sayin', *No more.* See, they stopped it in Houston first, and then that's when it moved to Dallas, then it moved to California, so it never got a chance to be *so* available that it was that bad. It was highly addictive, but crack was more like you gotta get it and keep on goin'. You drink a lot of syrup, you gonna go to sleep. Crack, you stay up, and keep spinnin'. If you smoke an ounce of cocaine, you probably gonna stay up still. But if you drink a pint of codeine, you gonna go to sleep."

SOUTHSIDE STILL HOLDING

April 1, 2001—The media landscape around Screw evolves dramatically when an article by Michael Hall entitled "The Slow Life and Fast Death of DJ Screw" appears in *Texas Monthly.* It was a breakthrough piece and remains an important early journalistic work involving Screw's family and loved ones, producing a rich archive of notes from Hall's interviews with Ida Mae Deary Davis and Robert Earl Davis Sr., conducted in the months following Screw's death. Hall's papers are held at the Wittliff Collections, a treasure trove of Texas music history at Texas State University's Alkek Library in San Marcos. Going through a box of old interviews, notes, and letters, I found that Ida Mae Deary Davis was brought to life in her conversations with Hall. Countless stories would be told about her in the years after she passed, but her voice meant a lot to the manuscript of this book, as when she speaks here about Screw's dad.

Ida Mae (as told to Michael Hall) "If I hear him say *I love my son* one more time, I'll kill him."

Their words allowed me to understand Screw's parents through some of the only interviews they ever did, outlining their love for him individually, as parents, mother and father, even if their idea of a family unit had changed over the years.

Robert Earl Davis Sr. (as told to Michael Hall) "I was worried in case he didn't make it. He used to say, *Pops, I'm gonna be a big star.* He told me, *I wanna build a home in the city,* on land we rented from a long time ago. We'd stayed with my mama in the city, and he used to run in the woods with his dogs."

Screw called his dad "Pops." But after Screw passed, everyone began to know Robert Sr. as "Poppa Screw." It hit him especially hard, the death of his son, because their relationship—as witnessed by many who spent time with them both—had its rough patches over the years, culminating in the elder Davis apologizing to Screw during a pool game at Greenstone for doubting him all those years.

Robert Earl Sr. (as told to Michael Hall) "He said, *Pops, you thought I wouldn't make it, but I did.* He held it against me. But our communication got better after that. He told me, *Pops, buy a tour bus like John Madden, and drive around the city.*"

Ida Mae (as told to Michael Hall) "Kids would call me 'Mama Screw.' I don't know why they're giving all this credit to his father. I got him started. Mr. Davis wouldn't even pay $200 a month in child support. I had to buy my son clothes. If he were here today, he'd say, *My mom started me in this biz. My mom started me doin' this.*"

Though a lot of folks might have been unaware, the article's loudest report was buried in a passage about Screw's sister, Michelle. In the course of telling the story of the family unit, it was revealed in the article that Ida Mae "had a young daughter from a previous marriage." That was how Michelle found out Robert wasn't her biological father.

Michelle "Red" Wheeler "I knew something when I was like sixteen. But it just didn't *confirm*, you know. Everybody kept sayin', *That's your daddy*, and I went on with the program. But it didn't hit me like a ton of bricks until he publicized it in that *Texas Monthly* magazine, and he let the whole world know that I was not his child. Shorty Mac was callin' me, everybody kept callin' me, *Are you okay?* I'm like, *Man, what's wrong? . . . You ain't seen the magazine?* And I'm like, *What magazine? . . . The magazine article that your mom and dad did.* I'm like, *No!* And people just kept callin' me. So I called Shorty Mac back, I said, *What is everybody talkin' about? People are callin' me like I'm just about to fall apart. What's wrong?* I didn't know what was *wrong.* And so Shorty Mac said, *You at home?* And at that time Shorty Mac and I lived like four blocks from each other. He said, *I'll be around there.* I was like, *Okay!* So he came around with the magazine and he opened it, and he opened it up to the page where it said—and he says, *Read this paragraph here.* And so that's when I read the paragraph, and that's when Robert told everybody—I guess they must have asked him a question about his daughter, and he said, *She's not my daughter. She was a diaper baby. I raised her, but she's not my daughter.* And I looked at Shorty Mac and I told him, I said, *That's a relief.* It was like it took a weight off my shoulders."

Though the Screwed Up Click largely scattered after Screw's death, almost all of them kept making music. Eventually, even Screwed Up Records & Tapes started not only releasing older recordings they had unearthed, but also commissioning mixes by Screw's cousin DJ Big Baby out of Smithville—slowed and chopped. New music and new mixes for a new generation of Screwheads, with a particular love for works by S.U.C. artists. Big Baby came up watching and learning from Screw, and his tapes were drenched in Trae Tha Truth, Big Hawk, Fat Pat, Big Moe— all the people who had been around him.

DJ Big Baby "For me, man, it was kinda like me comin' in and just like . . . kinda *prove* myself, because I'm the new guy comin' in! Dudes like probably lookin' at me like, *Who is this cat?* So I had to prove myself, and just do my thing and earn different cats' respect, 'cuz like you know you might have some people lookin' at me like, *Oh, he tryin' to take Screw place.* Nah, that wasn't the thing. It was about keepin' what he started alive. I'll tell anybody, you know, I could *never* be Screw. I could never fill those shoes."

December 11, 2001—At the Apollo Theater on 125th Street in Harlem, Justo Faison holds his Sixth Annual Mixtape Awards, with twice as many people in attendance as the event Screw attended two years earlier, this time with a whole lot of internal drama stirred up inside of the eighty-eight-year-old theater. DJ Kool Herc, DJ Premier, Mobb Deep, Craig Mack, and Fat Joe were all there, and Harlem's own DJ Kay Slay took home multiple awards. In the most somber moment of the night, the Pink House Award went to DJ Screw, with Orian "Lump" Lumpkin flying up to New York to accept the award on behalf of his friend.

Orian "Lump" Lumpkin "When I went to New York to go get those awards, it was at the Apollo, and it was wild! They had me come onstage to accept the award, and all of my homeboys were giving me a hard time, but they were praising Screw at the same time!"

Tytanic "Today I'm listenin' to all these influences from what he has done. It's just incredible. It is everywhere. More people need to understand how important to music he was. He was super important, and it's a shame that he passed, that he's not here. He needed to still be here. Certain people need to be here. J Dilla is another person like that. People like that change music, and the influence goes right up here to New York. You talkin' about the A$AP Mob. They use it. I live in Harlem. That's a Harlem act! They usin' all the chopped and screwed stuff."

The event was another level of recognition for the late Houston DJ, but there was a ways to go, even posthumously. Hip-hop was still a few years out from making Houston its mainstream vehicle, when a new generation would retroactively find out about what Screw had been doing in his house all those years. Meanwhile, there was still work to be done, as evidenced by the spelling on the plaque they handed Lump that evening, which read, "DJ Scru."

June 15, 2002—Eight o'clock on a Saturday night, and rapper Big Mello (Curtis Donnell Davis) is driving along South Loop West with a passenger, Jerry Louis Jett Jr., when their vehicle goes off the road, slamming into a pillar and killing them both. Jett was twenty-seven. Davis was thirty-three. It was a loss felt across multiple communities. Mello had become close to Screw over the years and was part of both the Screwed Up Click and the Rap-A-Lot movements, a rare crossover artist who had the respect and awe of his peers and had played his last show in Amarillo only weeks before. His fourth album, *The Gift*, came out a month after he died. He left behind a wife, Tammi, and two children. His son Andrew, who was then only thirteen, would also become a rapper in the years that followed, calling himself The Aspiring Me.

January 31, 2003—Southwest Wholesale closes, effectively pulling an enormous rug out from underneath a whole cross section of artists from all over the city whose labels had depended on the local economy built around its business model. Southwest offered production and distribution, advances on sales to local artists, investing in their careers when they got to a certain level, and helping others just get their product into circulation. They made a lot of things possible for Houston artists, and the framework allowed for a lot of labels to get off the ground. Screw referred a lot of folks to Southwest Wholesale so they could pursue their own thing. When Southwest shut down, the album cover and poster design company Pen & Pixel followed not long after. The effect on Houston's rap economy was devastating and immediate.

Robert Guillerman "It happened pretty quick. There were a lot of things that happened that caused our demise. One was 9/11. The music business *stopped* for about six months right then, and Blockbuster Video, who was our biggest customer, they went bankrupt in that period and owed us about a million dollars. And you know, things were changing. We had some serious internal issues as well."

Den Den "Everybody followed that same structure and the same outline to get them checks from outta Southwest Wholesale. I'm talkin' about everybody that had anything to do with S.U.C. that Screw put his stamp of approval on, they was cuttin' 'em checks! Don't get me wrong—they wasn't cuttin' the checks and wasn't *eatin'*! The South had the independent music game totally sewed up. From '97 all the way to 2003, man, them albums was sellin' all the way, until Robert and them decided to close down Southwest Wholesale and shut down the system here. We had radio, we had all them mom-and-pop stores. Man, when they began to make the smartphones and they could take the digital music, that's what hurt the South game."

Charlie Franks "You had so many independent record labels spawned offa that movement. I was an artist that came out of it. Steve with Perrion and E.S.G., you had Wreckshop, Jeriod, you had forty, fifty labels came outta that! And for a minute, for the longest, Screw was that underground medium, that underground platform where artists didn't have to go to the radio to get your record broke. He had enough power and enough people buyin' those tapes that your record would break in the underground! Off of the Screw tapes! And people would be like, *Man, you heard that song, that 'Goin' to the Kappa'? . . . Yeah, who was that boy?* And before you know it, you can break from the Screw medium, the underground. It was crazy just watchin' everything. Everything just kinda took a life of its own. Everything grew legs and started . . . the crazy part about it is like nobody really took care of they business, know what I'm sayin'? It just happened out of fun. Screw didn't take care of his business either, but shit . . . if he woulda *really* took care of his business, that man coulda been a billionaire like Jay-Z really, to be honest with you. It's just like an unfinished thing, or something. If he would have lived to venture into that CEO mind, that business-oriented mind . . . man!"

Shawn Brauch "I remember the shock and loss that was felt throughout the music community. There was almost a vacuum effect for a few weeks, then a surge. Posthumously, DJ Screw found new life with his slowed, smooth, syrupy sound. It seemed anyone on the fence about how popular it was was sold after his passing. He was a rather quiet guy, but he had the confidence in his craft that enabled him to expand other artists' music into a new genre. He reinvented their music into his own. Screw was a legacy in his own time, he experimented with technology and was never afraid to push it over the edge."

Kay-K "He just spread it out too wide, man. I can't think of nobody in Houston that spread it out that wide and not really be like . . . you know, like a Lil' J or somethin'. Lil' J spread out wide, but you know, most people scared of him. And ain't no one feared Screw."

Cl'Che (South Park Coalition) "Our music industry in Houston would be so different if Screw was still alive. We *need* him because of the energy, the love, and everything he had to bring to the table. I need that from Screw, and not just because he's DJ Screw and he can put us on and all that. Naw. He set a *tone* that we need in Houston right now, and I'm not even sayin' with just his music, but who he was *through* the music and what he brought to the table! Honestly, he made a lot of niggas calm down! He made 'em calm down. I can honestly say that. Not in a forceful way, like he checkin' somebody, but I'm sayin' they wanted to be around him and be connected to Screw so much that they was a part of that *tone*. They chilled in *his* zone. Screw stayed Screwed Up! He stayed in his space. He didn't let the world rush him."

Big Shasta (R&B singer, as told to Jason Culberson) "Seein' him as an entrepreneur, seein' him transition his music from a hustle to a business to a worldwide-known name in the industry that stained the whole world, that's very inspirational. So I just salute that hustle. I salute that grind. You know, strong hustlers always survive through adversity. It don't matter whatever adversity that the South has came through, we've always managed to survive, and that's actually an acronym for my name, Shasta: Strong Hustlers Always Survive Through Adversity. Real recognize real, the fake fade away."

E.S.G. "No matter what new artist come out right now—I hear 'em all the time—they try to differentiate theyself from the S.U.C. Like, *I'm not about the syrup, I'm not about the swangers.* It don't matter—*you're* gonna put a car or a slab or somethin' in the video, or you're gonna reference to it in your music eventually. 'Cuz I see it now! And I be wantin' to go back to the young cats who be brand new and I wanna be like, *Well you said you wasn't part of this Screwed Up Click thang! You sho' got a slab line in your video!*"

Big DeMo "I ain't got Screw to give me a stamp of approval now. I ain't got Screw to say, *Yeah, this my boy Lil' Flip.* You know, we ain't got that no more. We ain't got Screw sayin', *Yeah, that new Botany Boys—go get that C-Note.* We don't have that anymore. We gotta do that for ourselves. You know, there's people that never done shows without Screw. But guess what? You gotta do them without him now."

Hard Jarv (Black Hearted Records) "Screw was a child of God. You know, he had a love for the turntables, and that love got him caught up! He was for the underdogs, and the underdogs is the ones on top. Keke and Z-Ro. They was the have-nots. They was the ones with nothin'. They was the ones with dirty tennis shoes on. They was the ones with no-name jeans and no-name shirts on. And the ones that *had* the Jordans, that was ridin' up choppin' on blades and buttons, *those* are the ones down. They the ones that's down now in the game. And the have-nots—Screw made sure those was the ones on top. Screw gone, but the ones he put on top *still* on top!"

May 16, 2005—While driving late at night on a promotional trip through Richmond, Virginia, Orpheus "Justo" Faison falls asleep at the wheel of his car and crashes into a guardrail. He was pronounced dead at the scene. Justo was thirty-six years old and had been in his tenth year of promoting a movement that generously and selflessly connected people in the industry. His death was felt throughout the hip-hop community, with many wondering if the art of the mixtape would have evolved the way it had over the last decade without him.

Tytanic "I would never have known anything about DJ Screw if Justo had never honored these guys. Justo knew, and that was what made *him* special as a person, like a heartbreakin' thing. All these legends. If Justo didn't do these Mixtape Awards, who's to say mixtapes was gonna be this popular?"

IDA MAE

Screw's mother, Ida Mae Deary Davis, retired to a trailer about three miles south of Smithville on Zapalac Road with her boyfriend, PawPaw

Jack. If Smithville was the country, this was the *country*. Thick groves of oak dot the prairie land around freshwater ponds, cattle grazing between barbed wire fences and mailboxes on wooden poles off lonely roads so narrow they don't bother to paint a stripe down the middle.

In the years following her son's death, Ida was known to make multiple trips a day to his grave site, often taking her grandson (Screw's nephew Poppa, whom she called "Mr. P") with her, eventually teaching him how to drive her car. Poppa wasn't yet a teenager, and was barely big enough to see over the wheel of the Taurus Screw had bought for his mother, but he made the twenty-minute drive down those skinny roads, under the trees, across Highway 71, and into a forest in the middle of the countryside.

"I go out there every day, put flowers on his grave and talk to him," she told Michael Hall in 2001. To anyone visiting the cemetery, it was no surprise to see her there. Since Ida worked in the schools, everybody in town knew her, and they knew how proud she was of her son. And like him, she was a legend in Smithville.

Nikki "That's the family member that, to me, deserves all the praise. She's the one who made all the sacrifices."

Larry B "It's crazy because, you know, his mother used to say, *That's a perfect name, Screw, given that our whole family is screwed up.* She used to say that! I used to laugh at her, man. She was a character. I tell you. She was a character. I used to be around her a lot, and even when Screw had left, she would always come—I used to work in the grocery store in Smithville. She would always come in there, you know, and she *loved* liver. Hot liver. I love it, too, but it's just all in how you fry it. She fixed it with rice, gravy, you know, with onions cut up in it. Aw, man, it'd be *good*! [*laughs*] I don't know if Screw ever ate the liver."

Michelle "Red" Wheeler "The one thing that she could not break, and that was the drinking part. She just couldn't . . . and it was like, for the first two years in this house, and even when we were in the apartments, she would drink, but it was a stable drinker. She didn't get like just tore-up drunk where . . . we tried so hard. Screw and I tried everything. He would talk to her and I would talk to her and it just . . . that was her way of dealin' with a lot of things. And it just . . . I think what made her break the barrier, because even my auntie told me when she came to California, she didn't drink. She didn't drink out there, which was amazing, and then she came back here, and she didn't drink here—even when she came back in '91, it was probably maybe two years before she even started to even test liquor again, and then of course she started back drinkin', bein' a social drinker with PawPaw Jack, because they would always go out. They were, you know, young enough to go to the club! We had two clubs here, and they would go to the club, and of course you can't just sit in the club and drink soda water all night long, you know? And so PawPaw Jack, he was a drinker as well, but it just opened up the floodgates for my mama to start back drinkin' again, and then once she started, she didn't stop."

Poppa Davis "Those last few years when she was stayin' with us, my nanny was drinkin' up to a gallon of extra-dry gin a day. Like, we done cut the liquor store off and everything, and she'd go to another liquor store out of town! No mother wants to bury their son. No mother wants to do that, and it just tore my nanny up. It hurt me bad, but it hurt my nanny . . . drinking isn't what caused my nanny's death. My uncle's death is what caused her death, because that's the only way she could cope with it."

Ida Mae Deary Davis died on May 30, 2005, two and a half years after the death of her own mother, Jessie. Ida was fifty-six years old, survived by her daughter, Michelle; sister, Eula Mae; brothers Man and Robert; three grandchildren; and a still-growing brood of great-grandchildren. She was laid to rest in the same cemetery as her son, near where she went to visit him every day.

BOYS IN A DAZE

In March 2004, Swishahouse released a track called "Still Tippin'," featuring Northside Houston rappers Slim Thug, Mike Jones, and Chamillionaire on a beat made by Randy Jefferson, who went by Bigg Tyme and had worked on *The Day Hell Broke Loose* back in 1999. He also made records for many members of the Screwed Up Click along the way. That particular version of the song didn't do any better or worse than anything else circulating in the Houston underground at the time, but the remix was a different story. Chamillionaire and Mike Jones became estranged at some point, and so when Jones was preparing to put "Still Tippin'" on his album, he decided to boot Chamillionaire from the track and replace him with Paul Wall—from whom Chamillionaire was *also* estranged. So the move already stung twice, but the kicker was that the new version was a hit—beyond Houston—right out of the gate.

The new beat was produced by Salih Williams, Screw's cousin from Luling who had worked with Big Moe over at Wreckshop. Williams sampled the strings from Rossini's "William Tell Overture" and anchored them into an old-school drum pattern, cranking it down to where it gave off a feeling reminiscent of the dragging of a Screw tape. There was Screw's influence, breaking through to the mainstream, with room for the South to make a mark having been made years earlier by artists from Atlanta. "Still Tippin'" would be the H-Town catalyst.

The year 2005 was already shaping up to be a loaded one for Houston rap music. In the handful of years prior, UGK's collaborations with Three 6 Mafia ("Sippin' on Some Syrup") and Jay-Z ("Big Pimpin'") had been genuine megahits, and Houston artists were finding ways to get their music out into the world post–Southwest Wholesale and Pen & Pixel. All of them knew how to move units underground, but now they were having to pivot and adjust to the internet age, and bring their fans with them.

Hawk dropped a couple of albums around the millennium, making his biggest splash yet. Lil' Keke's *Platinum in Da Ghetto* was released in 2001, and even though *Don't Mess Wit Texas* had moved a lot of units, his new deal with Koch Records extended his reach and his peak on the charts. Big Moe's highest-charting album was *Purple World* from April of 2002, and then Pokey charted a few months later with *Da Sky's Da Limit* (both of them on Wreckshop). Lil' Flip, the first member of the Screwed Up Click to sign a major-label deal, had back-to-back platinum albums in 2002 and 2004—the latter coming in the same stretch of months in which Devin the Dude dropped *To Tha X-Treme* on Rap-A-Lot (his highest-charting album). So when Geto Boys released *The Foundation* in January of 2005—their first album in seven years—and it turned out Scarface, Willie D, and Bushwick Bill (who were a generation older than the artists in the S.U.C.) still had a lot to say, it was a harbinger.

That spring, while still in prison for a gun incident a month after Screw's death, Pimp C dropped *Sweet James Jones Stories*, his first solo album, and Z-Ro came out with *Let the Truth Be Told*, which opened with what would become his most famous freestyle, "Mo City Don" (the lyrics to which Houstonians have since memorized to shout back at him during concerts). Klondike Kat had released underground albums in consecutive years, and K-Rino had dropped two the previous year, with another on the way. A storm was gathering in Houston.

The first tremor was on April 19, when *Who Is Mike Jones?* debuted at no. 3 on the *Billboard* 200. The contract Jones signed with Swishahouse had a provision built in that would allow for his album to be upstreamed to Warner Bros., and as Jones established a new cult of personality, even including his phone number in advertisements (people *did* call him), that was exactly what happened. Paul Wall's Swishahouse deal had a similar agreement in place with Atlantic. Slim Thug had signed with Interscope, and his *Already Platinum* came out July 12. On it he showed the flexibility of Houston culture in reaching all the way across the South to Virginia, where he called on Pharrell Williams and Chad Hugo of the Neptunes to produce half of the album's tracks, with the rest produced by Houston stalwart Mr. Lee. It dropped at no. 2, and then Paul Wall came along two months later and released *The Peoples Champ*, which debuted at no. 1.

The leadoff single, "Sittin' Sidewayz," was released on August 20, 2005. One of its verses featured Big Pokey, and the hook was a sample of him from a Screw tape. Paul Wall is a Northsider, but he was a Screwhead back in the day and knows the tapes by heart. The song's refrain, "Sittin' sideways, boys in a daze," was sampled from Pokey's verse on *June 27th*, and with Wall rapping, "The trunks popped up, my music screwed and chopped," everything they were talking about was straight out of the culture chronicled on Screw tapes. *The Peoples Champ* served as a kind of table of contents of Houston rap music, a beginner's notebook that happened to be brilliantly produced (Mike Dean, Kanye West, Mr. Lee, among others) and was a career and creative accomplishment for the young rapper.

In September, Bun B shot a video for "Draped Up" featuring Slim Thug, Mike Jones, Paul Wall, and Lil' Keke, with Kanye West showing up to the shoot at Screwed Up Records & Tapes. And on October 18, when Bun dropped his first solo album, *Trill*, it hit at no. 6 on the *Billboard* 200. Chamillionaire's *The Sound of Revenge* came out on November 22 and debuted at no. 10. The albums by Paul Wall, Mike Jones, and Chamillionaire each went platinum, while Slim Thug, and Bun B went gold. The debut by Mike Jones ended up as one of the Top 40 best-selling albums of the year, and 2005 was the most lucrative year for Houston rap music ever. Houston even had a viral song that summer, with K-Otix's surprise hit "George Bush Doesn't Care about Black People" coming right after Hurricane Katrina. At the end of 2005, Beyoncé released a song with Slim Thug and Bun B, "Check On It," that went to no. 1 for weeks, and became one of the highest-charting songs of 2006. The bomb had truly gone off.

In April of 2006, *The Source* ran a twelve-page article on Houston, with profiles of Chamillionaire, Slim Thug, Mike Jones, Lil' Flip, Michael Watts, and Scarface. Matt Sonzala wrote the piece, and photographer Michael Blackwell came to J. Prince's ranch, where a who's who of Houston rappers lined up, twenty men standing side by side (Prince among them), for a shot that illustrated generations of rappers at work in Houston. It was the Swishahouse movement that burst the seams in 2004, no doubt, but the foundation had been laid years before.

Trae Tha Truth "When Houston was at the forefront of the music industry, it was based around Screw's sound. So by far I think it just would have been elevated ten times more than that if he actually woulda been here. Because that sound is *his* sound. Can't nobody tell you nothin' no different. That sound is owed to him. That sound was created by him."

K Dubb "You think about at the end, with the last people getting that shine, getting that push being Lil' Flip, Z-Ro, Trae. He had the ear to our streets. He had the ear! He knew what our city was about. And that's why, even during all the whole Northside-Southside wars and all this stuff, nobody can question the man's *ear*. When I think about Screw,

I think about how many layers of excellence people probably have over-looked over the years. He had a phenomenal ear and a phenomenal understanding of what drives the H-Town sound."

Michael "5000" Watts (as told to Chowtime TV) "I feel, honestly I feel like if it wasn't for Screw startin' this slowed-down music, you know . . . I don't even think that trap music would even exist right now, because all the music right now—all the music is produced right now at 60, 70 bpm! The majority of the hits right now! And while Screw was alive, right? Man, we didn't have music that slow! Honestly! Everything before Screw started slowin' down stuff, right—all I hear about was eighty beat per minute, to a hundred. Everything was eighty to a hundred, period, and at that point if your song was eighty beats per minute, it was considered being *slow!*"

Paul Wall "I'll see people on Twitter, like somebody says something about Screw and somebody will be like, *Oh, Screw wasn't a music, Screw was a man, that ain't Screw, there's only one Screw . . . Screw was a man, not a style of music.* There's a few people that feel like that, but I com-pletely disagree. I feel like DJ Screw was so much more than just a man. He *created* a style of music, and DJ Screw still is the heart and soul of this Texas music scene. Not even just Houston, but the whole state. DJ Screw stands for so much more. DJ Screw is an iconic figure, and he's so much more than just a person. He's not just a DJ, but DJ Screw represents the whole culture, the whole lifestyle we live, and man, the music in general. Because he had that kind of effect on the music, and all of the Texas music is kinda grouped in as 'Screw music,' and I think—I think, man . . . I'm proud of that. Some people would disagree, and some people feel like, *Man, Screw was a man, not a music,* but I'm proud that what became—what started off as just a man doin' mixtapes became so huge, to where Black Eyed Peas are puttin' it in their music. 50 Cent, Ciara, any artist you can think of—Ludacris, all these artists are integrating this type style of music into their music sometimes, shit . . . Justin Timberlake got a song with slowed-down music! So these are the biggest names in entertainment, and that's just to see how far one man started his legacy is so much more than just bein' just 'DJ Screw.' It's so much more than him bein' just a DJ, and him bein' a man. He's the man. He's the heart and soul of the Texas music scene, Texas music culture in general."

THE FIVE-STAR GENERAL

After Screw died, the void wasn't just that of a DJ who made mixtapes. For plenty of people, the loss was more acute because they'd lost a big-brother figure in Screw. Somebody had to pick up the slack, and that person was Big Hawk, whom everybody called the Five-Star General. Lots of younger artists came up with Hawk as a big brother, like the Grit Boys, and plenty of others who weren't artists at all.

Meshah Hawkins (from *Houston Rap Tapes*) "Everybody loved him and he was friends with them, and they always called him first for everything. And he was always there for them, and he was like a father figure to them. A lot of them would call him 'Daddy.' 'Cuz they know that he was gonna get on them if they were messin' up . . . you know, he wasn't gonna sugarcoat anything. He was gonna tell them real, straight up, and be honest with them."

At the beginning of 2006, a year or so after Houston had blown up, Big Hawk was still being pursued by major labels, but he was resistant to signing a deal. There he was in *Spin* magazine, accompanying Jon Caramanica's article "The Tippin' Point," about Houston's rise, and he was doing features on plenty of songs. But while Hawk's superstar qualities had him going for a music career, his business sense from working a straight job for all those years had him not going after bad paper.

Big Hawk (as told to *Game 101* magazine) "Even from my last album I had them comin' at me, but you know, I didn't hear what I liked, man. I been in the game for a long time—blood, sweat, and tears—and I just wasn't gonna take anything. But right now talk's goin' on, I'm gettin' a lil communication whereas I wasn't gettin' that communication too much from my last album. But just me takin' my break, I'ma always stay in the midst of thangs, you know, and keep Hawk ringin'. So, I'm just in the middle of somethin' right now and it's lookin' good. It's lookin' good. Real good. Might be in my favor, so y'all just pray for your boy."

Koldjak "Before the music or anything, man, I used to go pick up Hawk just to get him in the car, just to get him to *laugh*. I used to act so silly and stupid just to get Hawk to laugh! Man, Hawk had a *distinct laugh*, man. And you gon' start *dyin'* laughin' because he laughin' for real. But when Screw died, Hawk assumed that role with honor. It wasn't that he made people look at him like that. It was just awarded to him like that. Hawk gon' tell you what it is! Hawk ain't gon' sugarcoat nothin'. And you have to respect that from a person, from a *working*-level person. That's why I have respect for Hawk, because he was a hustler in the nature of hustling music, but before the music hustle, he was a nine-to-five guy, and he was cool with that!"

After dating for years, Hawk and his longtime girlfriend Meshah were married in March 2006. They already had two young boys together, and the marriage made their union official. But tragedy would befall the newly united family in just a matter of weeks. On the evening of May 1, 2006, as he was walking through a friend's yard in South Park to attend a domino game, Big Hawk was tragically shot and killed. He was thirty-six years old. His murderer has never been found.

Kay-K "There's certain people that we lost that really, really knocked a dent in our leader or figurehead, you know what I'm sayin'? When I left, it was a big dent. When Screw left, it was *definitely* a big dent. When Hawk left, you had nobody else . . . if you talk to Z-Ro, you talk to Trae, Lil' Flip, you talk to any of the people that came up . . . Hawk was the one to bring them along and to show them love. He was the last of that, and since he been gone there's not no togetherness, and I can't bring us together unless I got somethin' really goin' on. We can't make no music that's gonna blow up. We already *did* that. What we did is history already. It's just about how are we gonna play it out?"

SCREW'S HOUSE

July 20, 2006—For what would have been DJ Screw's thirty-fifth birthday, the *Houston Chronicle* publishes an article I wrote in advance of the very first Screwfest, held at the Pasadena Convention Center in Pasadena, Texas. Trae Tha Truth was on the bill with Botany Boys, Chingo Bling, and New Orleans bounce legend 5th Ward Weebie, who had relocated to Houston after Hurricane Katrina. Slim Thug and Grit Boys also performed on the indoor stage, while temperatures reached 109 degrees outside, breaking an all-time Houston record for DJ Screw's birthday.

The month before that, a documentary called *DJ Screw: The Untold Story* had been released, the first feature-length presentation on Screw since REL's *Soldiers United for Cash*. For *The Untold Story*, Reggie "Bird" Oliver was the man behind the camera, as he had been shooting for years while Screw was still alive, conducting interviews and gathering raw footage of the Click. The festival and documentary helped forge a healing moment in a community that still had pain surging through it from Hawk's murder just a couple of months earlier. And they would need it, as tragedy struck again in late 2007. Big Moe died on October 14, and Pimp C on December 4, both of their deaths stemming from different health issues complicated by consumption of codeine-promethazine.

D-Gotti "Pimp C was just a straight genius, man. I remember one night I'm in the studio and D-Reck and Pimp C, they was kinda goin' through a lil somethin', you know, behind some show business. So we in the studio—this how Pimp C made it right with D-Reck: he come to the studio with us one night and do *five songs* with me, man. I'm talkin' 'bout he freestyled every song, and it sound like a real record. Every time he come out the booth, my verse was wrote already, you know what I'm sayin'? He go in the booth and freestyle, the beat playin', while he freestylin' I'm writin'. He come out, I go in, drop my verse. I come out, he go in and freestyle. By the time he come out, my verse wrote. About the third time he come out, he say, *Oh, you the one over here can rap, huh? You really could rap!* We done some *records* that night, bro. We did some real records, but the boy freestyled every record. He picked up no pen, no paper, and you know it's real freestyle because he not . . . you know how new rappers do, they might go in the booth, do two bars, *Hey, hol' up—punch me back in!* No, no. I'm talkin' 'bout a straight sixteen. Straight genius, man. Pat, Mafio, 3-2, Keke, they do the same thing. I done seen 'em all in action, bro. They do the same thing. They don't write down nothin'. When they say it's freestyle, that was *freestyle*."

February 15, 2009—On his third mixtape, *So Far Gone*, the Canadian rapper Drake, then on the cusp of releasing his breakthrough hit, drops a tribute to *June 27th* with "November 18th." The title referred to the date the rapper first flew from Toronto to Houston to meet with Lil' Wayne after being discovered by James Prince's son Jas, and the whole thing was an ode to Screw's most infamous freestyle. "November 18th" used the same Jermaine Dupri beat that Screw put down for *June 27th*, in this context with DJ Screw listed as the producer because it was actually sampled from the Screw tape released thirteen years earlier. At the end of the track, which was a half hour shorter than the original, Drake spoke quietly through the slowed-down outro, much like the person he was talking about in the lyrics:

> *Candy paint switching colors in the light*
> *It's about like 11 p.m.*
> *Niggas just rolling through the city*
> *Bumping that Screw, Big Moe, UGK, Lil' Keke*

Across the border in Michigan, the electronic trio Salem were making their own kind of noise. It was pop music, not rap, with light-fisted electronic drums and hot synthesizers rattling under vocals that sounded like they floated up out of a car ashtray. The effect wasn't heavy like the fat beats on Screw tapes, but in exploring the high end, they gave a nod to Screw's pure rhythmic influence. Digitally rather than via analog, and without any of the same tools, Salem managed to find footholds in the same typhoon of sound as Screw.

Robert Disaro's Houston-based experimental label released two early CDRs by Salem in 2007 and 2008, helping plant the seeds for a movement that became known as "witch house." Because Salem championed the influence of DJ Screw, the cadre of bands that emerged with an association to the genre by default referenced Screw. In the years following, witch house became less about Salem, their aesthetic, or even a particular sound. There were subgenres that branched off, perhaps deriving less from Screw than from witch house but nonetheless inspired by a sound that wouldn't have happened without him.

On the tenth anniversary of his death, Screw's sound reverberated through waves of musical genres, and his legacy was celebrated around the world. There were articles in the UK's *Guardian*, the *New York Times*, and hip-hop publications of all stripes. In the pages of *Frieze* magazine, Jace Clayton (a.k.a. DJ Rupture) wrote that "DJ Screw's swamp gospel continues to spread." The Swedish rapper Yung Lean debuted a couple of years later, and would go on to credit Houston as his inspiration. Long after Screw had passed, it was impossible to ignore the effect he had on music everywhere.

Poppy (10201, as told to Jon Caramanica) "He would always say, *I'm going to Screw the world*, and it's crazy, because the man Screwed the world."

UNIVERSITY OF HOUSTON

March 28, 2012—In an all-day series of panel discussions at the University of Houston, Screw's legacy is discussed in an academic setting for the first time. UH Special Collections librarian Julie Grob, who grew up booking and promoting shows in Houston's punk scene at the legendary east downtown venue the Axiom, spearheaded the organization of an event called "Awready! The Houston Hip Hop Conference," held in the grand Houston Room at the university's main campus in Third Ward.

Julie Grob "One thing I will never forget is walking into the space before the event started. I'd had oversize posters of five of the soldiers who had passed away printed and set up on the stage—DJ Screw, Fat Pat, Big Hawk, Big Moe, and Pimp C. I walked into this large event space, with their faces larger than life, and the first track from the DJ Screw tape *Endonesia* started playing 'One Day' by UGK, which is a song about losing loved ones. It was a moment that gave me chills."

In front of a few hundred folks who came out early on a Wednesday morning, E.S.G. warmed up the room with a freestyle wherein he found rhymes all around the big auditorium—shirts, hats, hair, glasses, beards—anything he could see was fair game on which to riff. He is a master of the art form. Grob introduced the conference, and then writers Maco Faniel (joined by K-Rino, Willie D, Steve Fournier, and Rick Royal of Royal Flush) and Langston Collin Wilkins (with E.S.G., Lil' Randy, and car customizer Eddie Kennedy) each moderated panels oriented around Houston hip-hop culture and history. I was on the first of two panels specifically talking about Screw. Our session was called "DJ Screw and the Screwed Up Click," and onstage with me were E.S.G., Big Pokey, Shorty Mac, Meshah Hawkins, and Lil' Keke, all of them just sitting around telling stories for an hour. The *Houston Chronicle* would later write that it was like the Houston Room was their living room that day.

Dr. Ronald Peters stepped up to talk about codeine-promethazine, and he was followed by the second Screw session, in which Matt Sonzala spoke with Bun B, Paul Wall, OG Ron C, and Chingo Bling on a panel called "The Legacy of DJ Screw." I was seated off to the side in a section next to the stage, and at one point during Sonzala's panel, MC Wickett Crickett leaned over to me and said, "I booked DJ Screw's first gig." Seconds later, a hundred yards away and impossibly out of earshot, Bun B looked over in our direction and said, "I also want to point out that my man Wickett Crickett gave Screw his first DJ gig!" Crickett slapped my shoulder and we nearly fell out of our seats.

In attendance were plenty of people written about in this book—Big Bubb, Al-D, DJ Gold, D-Red, Double D, Lil' D, DJ DMD, Jhiame Bradshaw, Poppy, Lump, Grit Boys—as well as Poppa Screw and Pimp C's mother, Mama Wes. The event coincided with the opening phase of the DJ Screw Papers and an exhibition of materials from the UH collections, *DJ Screw and the Rise of Houston Hip Hop*, which ran until September of that year. The collection contains 1,500 of the vinyl records Screw used to make his mixtapes, along with his papers, flyers, receipts, and other items donated to the UH Libraries. Grob's background in punk rock—in which ephemera such as liner notes and flyers are revered—helped her in cataloging Screw's collection. All items displayed in the exhibition are housed at the University of Houston Libraries and are accessible to anyone—including a large selection of photographs by Peter Beste and transcripts and audio recordings of interviews I conducted over the years.

Julie Grob "I think the Screwed Up History event in particular was the Libraries' attempt to show that we were serious about documenting Houston hip-hop, that we respected the voices of those who had been there, and that we wanted to be welcoming to the hip-hop community and general public. It was really important to me that the speakers and panelists be a mix of not only scholars and journalists but rappers, DJs, and others who were active in the hip-hop community and knew DJ Screw. We wanted to provide a platform for them to share their experiences and knowledge about making music and creating culture."

SCREWED UP HEADQUARTERS

Al-D "I'ma tell you one person that was there, and that was Big Bubb. Through *everything*. Ups, downs—*everything*. Bubb was there, man. And I respect Bubb so fucking much, man. For real."

The shop remained open after Screw's death. Shorty Mac worked there for a while, but he eventually moved back to Austin. It was Screw's cousin Big Bubb who took over operations, outlasting everyone else who worked there while adapting to the changes in the music industry that made it difficult for a retail record store to survive.

Big Bubb "Everything I do for Screw is from the heart, man. You feel me? That's how *he* did it. I mean, this whole creation was his. It's his work. He put his heart into it, each one of them mixtapes. That's why it's just phenomenal, man. I don't know no artist right now that, you done played one of they mixtapes and heard it over and over again and just chill out for a month or two, not listen to it. And you could come back and jam it right now like it's brand new. Who? Where? There's not another one. That's 'cuz it's straight from the heart. You not supposed to deal with business and emotions . . . how they say that? It's not supposed to be no emotions in business, but with *this*? If you ain't emotional about it, you in the wrong place! You in the wrong place."

The business model has changed, as the operation moved away from cassettes, releasing old Screws on CD through the "Diary of the Originator" series (Screw tapes take up two CDs), but Houstonians have continued to shop at Screwed Up Records & Tapes. Archived recordings occasionally surface, recorded into Pro Tools and then pressed up, their names scribbled on the whiteboard in the shop that has a list of all the chapters.

Over the years, other locations have popped up with different proprietors. A Screw shop opened on Lawndale on the Eastside, and another at Eisenhauer Flea Market in San Antonio. Then there was one in the Dallas–Fort Worth area, and one in Austin. The original location on Cullen outlasted all of those, but it wasn't immune to change. In 2011, the owner of the strip center at 7717 Cullen decided he wanted the space back, and for a spell, the shop had no home. Big Bubb pressed on, though, and finally found them another storefront about thirty minutes away from South Park. It was a trek for those who lived near the original location, but Bubb had to go with his feeling that people would come to the shop no matter where it was located.

He was right. In 2012, Screwed Up Records & Tapes II opened up at 3538 West Fuqua, right where Buffalo Speedway dead-ends in Hiram Clarke, across the street from an empty lot and sandwiched between a tire shop and a Tejano nightclub. It's a much bigger space, where accommodating dozens of people as opposed to just a handful allows more room for titles and stock. They have DJ Screw T-shirts and hoodies, and there's even a studio in the back for live broadcasts and freestyles. Video shoots and radio shows frequently occur there, with block parties in the parking lot on Screw holidays.

Much like in the old shop, the Screws are kept behind a window. Big stacks of them line the wall all the way up to the ceiling, and Big Bubb and his partner Big A hold it all down, sorting mail orders for CDs and shirts, running to the post office to send out packages every day. People call and Bubb answers it on speaker, the sound of DJ Screw's music swallowing up all the atmosphere around him. He's used to the noise, as is anyone who calls, and he understands every word and answers all of the questions. People flow in and out of the shop all day, and members of the Screwed Up Click are a common sight.

THE SLAB

In 2013, Smithville native Jason Culberson (a.k.a. K.i.d) started work on a documentary project called *Screwville*, conducting interviews with a range of Screw's relatives and friends that focused on his time in the country in the mid-'80s. The project brought a lot of people out of the woodwork who hadn't been interviewed before, like Screw's cousins D-Ray and Lil' Doug (Culberson generously allowed sections of those archived interviews to be quoted in this book). But the most significant breaking of silence as a result of that project was of Screw's sister, Michelle "Red" Wheeler.

Over the years, Red largely stayed away from the commotion that followed Screw around. She did live at Broadway and at Greenstone in the early days, and sent her kids to stay with their Uncle Earl for months each summer, but when she and Screw spent time together, it was usually just the two of them alone. Robert Earl wanted his sister to himself.

So it took a lot for Red to come out and finally begin to appear publicly as a family member, the blood sibling with whom Screw grew up, the big sister of the house, the one who knew him like no one else possibly could. And when Trae Tha Truth invited her to speak on behalf of her brother at his annual outdoor celebration, thousands in the crowd that day saw reflected in her face *their* connection to Robert Earl Davis Jr.

Michelle "Red" Wheeler "I said, *Okay, I can't fill the shoes, but I'ma put my feet in 'em, and I'ma do my best.* And that's where I'm at with it. I'm gonna do whatever it takes to keep that name goin', I'm gonna do whatever it takes to make sure nobody forgets about him—which I'm quite sure nobody will, but you know, I just . . . from here on out I wanna be part of that legacy, because that was my brother. That was my baby brother, and we were kinda like two peas in a pod."

Red appeared in *Screwville* and eventually formed a partnership with K.i.d with the goal of fixing up Screw's grave site, which had so many regular visitors that a more dependable structure was needed around it. So they started selling shirts to finance a concrete slab to go on top. They crowdfunded part of it, and Houston artist Donkeeboy and 8th Wonder

Brewery in Third Ward also stepped up, but the last part of the money came from a source close to Screw.

Jason Culberson "I had ended up doin' an interview with Trae, and he was askin' me, *What's all this for? What's this interview for, what y'all tryin' to do?* And we were like, *Well, we're tryin' to put out a documentary about Screw and his last days, and then we tryin' to fix up the grave. That's why we usin' everybody as awareness.* And he was like, *Oh, y'all tryin' to fix up the grave? Well what y'all doin'?* And we like, *Well, we been online sellin' shirts,* and he was like, *Well, how much do y'all owe on it?* And we told him how much we owed, and he said, *Man, I'm fittin' to go on tour, and when I get back from tour, I'ma give y'all the rest of the money to finish that grave.* And we were like, *That's cool!* So I'm talkin' about two or three days after he came back from tour, he had a show in Austin, so he invited us. And we really had forgot about the money. We just thought he was just invitin' us out to the show, and then at the end of the show, he ended up just comin' up to us and givin' us the money for the grave. He paid the rest of it. He got that heart like Screw had."

BOW DOWN
March 18, 2013—Native Houstonian megastar Beyoncé Knowles-Carter releases "Bow Down / I Been On," a one-off single between her fourth and fifth albums with distinct references to Houston rap culture:

> *I'm out that H-town*
> *Coming, coming down*
> *I'm coming down dripping candy on the ground*

Bow Down was also the name of a Screw tape from 1997. For the song's outro (which appears as the epigraph for *Houston Rap Tapes*), she slowed things down to talk about Houston culture, about Frenchy's, about appearing in a Willie D video, about growing up listening to UGK. And then on December 13, eight years to the day since the release of "Check On It" with Bun B and Slim Thug, her video for "No Angel" dropped. Filmed primarily on the streets of Third Ward and Fourth Ward, it was a fully realized visual tribute to Houston, focusing on the neighborhoods and the people living there while still taking time to squeeze in Bun B, Willie D, Lil' Keke, Scarface, Slim Thug, Trae Tha Truth, Paul Wall, and Z-Ro, with a mural of Screw in there, too. A lot of new people learned about DJ Screw in 2013.

March 25, 2014—A whole posse's worth of S.U.C. rappers collaborate under the name Original Screwed Up Click to release a full-length called *The Take Over*. The album by no means featured a complete Screwed Up Click, but it was as near a full sampling as was possible at the time: Mike-D, Mr. 3-2, Z-Ro, Trae Tha Truth, Lil' Keke, Lil' Flip, Chris Ward, Will-Lean, Big Pokey, Lil' O, Billy Cook, E.S.G., Clay-Doe, and Macc Grace, with posthumous contributions from Fat Pat, Hawk, Big Moe, and DJ Screw himself. Most any album by an S.U.C. artist is a tribute in some form, but this would be the last big gathering before more voices were lost.

Lil' Flip "He put us all together to form a brotherhood and we still here helpin' each other. I got different people I still deal with in the Screwed Up Click. C-Note, Mike-D, Z-Ro. Those are the people I'm close with. D-Red. Me and Keke cooler than we ever been. Me and Pokey always been cool. I was in Al-D video three months ago. The legacy that Screw left, puttin' us together, it's up to us to figure out what we do next. It's up to us to look out for each other, and keep his name alive."

Lil' O (as told to Jason Culberson) "What would I say? Thank you. God bless you. Thank you. Thank you for changing my life. Thank you for giving me an opportunity. Thank you for giving me a microphone. Thank you for giving me an introduction to the world. I will forever be grateful."

November 23, 2015—MC Wickett Crickett dies of complications from lung cancer. He was fifty-six years old and had been celebrated for decades throughout the city for his work with up-and-coming artists. Crickett was a constant presence in Houston clubs through the years, and his mentoring had a lasting effect on the lives of generations of young Houstonians, culminating in an outpouring of citywide support for him before he died. Born in New York and living in Houston as hip-hop was coming alive, he was beloved by the people of his adopted city.

November 10, 2016—Christopher Barriere, Mr. 3-2, is riding through Hiram Clarke late on a Thursday night in a car with three other men when an argument breaks out among them. They pulled into a gas station at Beltway 8 and Rockwell Boulevard, and all of them got out of the car except for the driver, thirty-nine-year-old Vincent Depaul Stredic, who lagged behind as they walked toward the store.

Ronald Bob (producer, manager) "That night they were all smokin' and drinkin', four guys, and they decided to get in the car to go somewhere. And I don't know where they were goin', but the guy that was driving had too much to drink and smoke. And so he was driving radically, and 3-2 told him, *Man, pull this car over,* you know. *You gonna get us all killed in this car.* And the guy pulled over. He was pissed off but he pulled over anyway at the gas station, and pretended to pump gas in the car. And 3-2 was goin' inside the store to get some cigarettes or somethin', and he just ran up behind him and shot him in the back of the head."

Stredic fled the scene, and 3-2 was pronounced dead when paramedics arrived. That next day the entire Southside was put on notice, looking for his killer, and working from a tip from within the community, Houston police apprehended Stredic within days. Barriere's funeral services were held nine days later at Houston Memorial Gardens in Pearland. Stredic was later convicted of the crime and sentenced to thirty years in prison.

Mr. 3-2 (as told to Polow's Mob TV) "Shit need to be different. All that plex ain't all it's cracked up to be. Stop the violence, like KRS say, and do your thang! Try to get some motherfuckin' money, you know what I'm sayin', 'cuz you gotta feed your family or so have you. At the end of the day, so all that plexin' ain't necessary. You can't make no money makin' no plex. All you can make is problems. A nigga ain't tryin' to make problems. A nigga tryin' to make some peace and playerism around here, move on to somethin' bigger, see somethin' better. Straight up."

August 10, 2017—Screwed Up Click rapper Macc Grace is vacationing in South Padre Island, Texas, when he suffers a stroke in his hotel room after an early morning run on the beach. Only a few months before that, Grace and I had done an interview over the phone. After years of he and I writing letters back and forth to one another while he was in prison, it was the last time we would speak. Almost seventeen years later, Screw was still heavy in his life.

Macc Grace "I wanna do shit for my family, but you know the reason why I won't stop? I got a day job now, but I'll never stop rappin', tryin' to reach that pinnacle, that lil status. It's because of Screw! From way back in the gap he saw something in me that I didn't even see in me. You know, he would tell me, *Man, you cold.* He basically *made* me, you see what I'm sayin'? He built my confidence up, helped me around the environment, and allowed the proper tutelage to where I could really take off. And back then, it was against the grain, because you gotta remember—all them guys, they was from down South Park, Third Ward, you know, out there, Dead End. The Deep South. I was from the West. There was no one ever—there wasn't no Z-Ros, there wasn't no Lil' Os. There was no one. There was just Southside, and then this lil nigga Screw bringin' from the West. That's what I was! Because Screw, who he was, it would be kinda like showin' the way, but it allowed some people to kinda turn they nose up to me and shit, you know what I'm sayin'. It was a big deal for him to jump off—he said I was his Tupac! That's a fuckin' hell of a compliment, right? That nigga saw somethin' in me that I *still* don't really see in me, but because he saw it I just . . . it's *there.* I just gotta keep fightin' and get it out, bring it to the world. Because I wanna do that for him, and for my family and shit, but that's the *main* main fuckin' reason. Because I coulda *been* said, *You know what, man? Fuck this shit,* just fell back and did some other shit. You know, I got a job and I'm doin' other stuff, but I'll never stop tryin' to prove to the world what he saw in me."

LOS "The most fucked-up part is I couldn't even—my wife had to call and tell my parents. Everybody'll tell you how tight we was. My brother was my everything—my idol, my everything. Everything I do, I did because of him. He played basketball, I wanted to play. He played football, I wanted to play. He played baseball, I wanted to play. He rapped, I wanted to rap. Everything he did, I did. Him and my pops and my grandfather. I looked up to them. Family's all I know. I be tryin' to get through that shit, but it be rough, man."

May 7, 2018—Terence "Big T" Prejean, whose voice appeared on a number of S.U.C. recordings and the hook for the national hit "Wanna Be a Baller," dies of an apparent heart attack. Of the five voices (Lil' Troy only appears as producer) heard on that song—Yungstar, Fat Pat, Hawk, Lil' Will, and Big T—only Yungstar is still living.

August 3, 2018—Travis Scott (born Jacques Webster, raised in Missouri City) releases his long-awaited third studio album, *Astroworld*, named after the Houston theme park across the freeway from the Dome that was shut down and bulldozed in 2005, when he was thirteen years old. The album featured a host of songs in tribute to DJ Screw, the most direct of which being "R.I.P. Screw," where the first voice you hear is Screw's, saying "Southside," sampled from his interview with Houston television station ABC 13 twenty years earlier. In the refrain, Scott makes known his feelings:

> *Rest in peace to Screw, tonight we take it slowly*
> *Oh, my God, I just can feel the love*
> *Drop-top with the windows up*
> *Jump inside, oh, won't you roll with us?*

Astroworld debuted at no. 1 on the *Billboard* 200. "R.I.P. Screw" was never released as a single, but when it came time for Scott to shoot the video for "Sicko Mode," the album's biggest hit, he did so outside of Screwed Up Records & Tapes II, in the parking lot, with the shop's iconic sign plainly visible in the background. When he performed on *Saturday Night Live* that fall, video of Screw was projected onto the wall behind Scott on the stage—and right into America's living rooms. The album also kindled a resurgence of interest in other members of the S.U.C., as

Scott referenced Big Moe ("Sippin' on purp', feelin' like the Barre Baby") and sampled Fat Pat (I'ma swang, and a-swang, and a-swang to the left / Pop-pop my trunk / Dip-dip-dip-dip"). But the brightest light was shone on Big Hawk, whose refrain from the "Come and Take a Ride" freestyle that Screw featured on his 5:00 AM tape ("To win the retreat / we all in too deep / playin' for keeps / don't play us for weak") was sampled for "Sicko Mode." So nearly twenty-five years after that tape's release, with Scott on-stage at the Super Bowl in 2019, Big Hawk's voice went booming out into the stadium in Atlanta and into the homes of almost one hundred million people, probably much like the late rapper believed it one day would.

March 1, 2019—Just a few weeks later, Screw's legacy is given another high-profile nod when Solange Knowles releases her fourth album, *When I Get Home*. Solange was already a supporter of Houston rap, bringing Yungstar up onstage a couple of years before on the eve of the Super Bowl in Houston to perform his seventeen-year-old hit "Knocking Pictures Off Da Wall" while she and her band backed him up live. She had also filmed a video at King's Flea Market years earlier. But on *When I Get Home*, she was honoring her hometown neighborhoods, specifically the Southside of Houston, and more specifically Houston *women*, referencing Third Ward natives Phylicia Rashad and her sister, Debbie Allen, who grew up on South MacGregor (right near the park) before going on to acting careers, and the LGBTQ poet Pat Parker, who was raised in Third Ward and Sunnyside but moved to California as a teenager and wrote about her life experience in the influential collection *Movement in Black* before her death in 1989.

Screw's sound and sensibility were all over the album, perhaps no-where more profoundly than on "Almeda," the title of which no doubt refers to the Third Ward thoroughfare, but also happened to be the name of the skating rink where Screw got his first job. The lyrics come from the culture, "Pour my drank, drank / Sip, sip, sip, sip, sip," and the feel of the Solange and Pharrell–produced beat hints at slowing and chopping, without actually doing so, finding new ways to illustrate the inspiration of Screw's work. A generation later (Solange was born the year Screw moved to Houston), you can hear DJ Screw at Almeda Skating Rink in the rhythms of her album, tugging back and forth in a big circle like roller skates on the hardwood.

When I Get Home also made a contribution to Screw's legacy by pouring cement over the distinction of what is and isn't Screw music through the voice of none other than Scarface, by far the best known rapper from Houston and also a supporter of Screw—even if he never did appear on a tape. On an interlude of *When I Get Home*, he draws the line in the sand when it comes to the subject of slow music that Screw's hands never touched: "It's *not Screwed!*"

POPPA SCREW

June 16, 2019—On Father's Day, Red invites me to come with her to visit her and Screw's dad, Robert Earl Davis Sr., where he was living in East Houston. She brought along her best friend since childhood, Angela, and later on Screw's older brother, Charles, showed up, too. Robert had been living for the last several years in an assisted living facility called Bridgecrest, and everybody there knew him well. One nurse came by and told a story about when Robert got into a fight with another man at the facility—both of them seated in wheelchairs.

Far removed from the sweaty pool halls and beer joints I remember meeting him in years earlier, Robert's room at Bridgecrest was tidy and quiet on a Sunday afternoon, and he was at peace. It wasn't hospice care, but he wasn't up and around, either. Robert was suffering from bone cancer, and both of his legs had been amputated beneath the knee from diabetes, so he lay on his back with his head tilted to one side for most of the afternoon. Red brought him some boudin and strawberry soda, and fed him as she stroked his head and talked to him all day. Even with those eyes closed, Red could read his face, and we all sat and talked while she held his hand and Charles told him stories of things he got himself into in his days of running around, often addressing his father, "Young *man!* Remember that time you . . . ?" There was always a story.

Robert soaked up the energy in the room. Red has a rich sense of humor and an infectious laugh, while Charles and Angela are famously at odds (by design) and fought genially all afternoon, so there was plenty of laughter circulating around the seventy-five-year-old. It was one of the last times those three faces sharing Screw's features would be in a room together. Robert Earl Davis Sr. died a few months later on September 3, almost nineteen years after the death of his youngest child.

DJ SCREW DAY

January 24, 2020—In the first month of the twentieth-anniversary year of Screw's death, he is awarded an honor bestowed on only a handful of Houstonians. As had been done with other Houston artists—Jazzie Redd (April 14), Big Hawk (May 8), Trae (June 22), Scarface (June 26), and OG Ron C (September 4)—on this balmy Thursday morning DJ Screw was honored with his own "DJ Screw Day" by the City of Houston. Mayor Sylvester Turner's daughter Ashley presented Red with the award on live television, with Lil' Keke and D-Reck standing right alongside her. Also with them was Houston producer and filmmaker Isaac "Chill" Yowman, who had announced that week that he and Red had partnered with D-Reck to create a live-action production about Screw called *All Screwed Up*.

On its face, the event was a ceremony for DJ Screw Day, but nobody had advance notice that the city had planned that, and the date didn't have any real significance in Screw's life, for that matter. What had actually happened was that Chill had been working on a visual tribute to Screw, for which he sent around a private link to a few prospective industry folks, and somebody leaked the video. It wasn't supposed to be something the public got to see, more like a preview reel, but everybody saw it anyway, and the internet did its thing—in the process showing that the world really wanted to see a movie about DJ Screw.

Isaac "Chill" Yowman "I wanted to do it as a short, as a tribute for the twenty-year anniversary. We probably had seven minutes of footage, just some vignettes. It wasn't even like a finished thing. One day I woke up and Keke was on my line, *Bro, what the hell?* I was crushed when that first trailer leaked, because I hadn't got a chance to talk to everybody I wanted to yet, so there were lots of hurt feelings. But in the same moment, I was getting calls like crazy, *Yo! What is this? We wanna buy this, we wanna partner up.* It was one of the most overwhelming moments of my professional career. By the time I looked up on the first day, that shit had like seven million views. We did the press conference, we ended up doin' the Deborah Duncan show. I had everybody in my ear. It was so many emotions."

FLOYD

> *It's Big Floyd, and you know I like to smoke skunk*
> *If I see the hatin' laws, I'ma still pop trunk*
> —*Tre World* freestyle

May 25, 2020—As Houston celebrates the return of slab icon Corey Blount from prison, another one of its own, George Perry Floyd, a.k.a. Big Floyd from Cuney Homes, is murdered by a Minneapolis police officer in broad daylight. The protracted Memorial Day incident, which ended with the officer kneeling on Floyd's neck for over nine minutes while he lay handcuffed in the street, was recorded on video by witnesses and quickly spread online, lighting up protests around the world, with the Black Lives Matter movement mobilizing young and old together.

George Floyd (from a video he posted to social media) "Our generation is clearly lost, man. Clearly lost, man, like . . . I don't even know what to say no more, man, like . . . you youngstas just goin' around, bustin' guns in crowds, kids gettin' killed. And it's clearly the generation after us, man, that's so lost, man. You know, man, I came back to Houston and a nigga told me, *Yeah, Floyd, that young nigga the truth right there!* Because he can bust a *gun?* Man, I *knew* it was crazy then, a nigga *my* age sayin' this shit here, mane. You know what I'm sayin'? And *condonin'* this shit, bro—you know what I'm sayin'? And you know, like half them young niggas shootin' them guns go home and they knees shakin' at night. They don't show it to nobody because, you know, they ain't tough then! Hey man, come on home, man. One day it's gonna be you and God. You goin' up or you goin' down?"

Cal Wayne (Cuney Homes) "He saw all the robbin' and jackin' out there! He *understood* the street, but that was never his thang. George never had the heart for the streets. He really didn't. He never had the heart for the streets. He wasn't no normal dude, you know what I'm sayin'? All the stuff they were doin', marching, protesting, he deserved it. He deserved all the support. He deserved it to be worldwide. He was that type of dude. Floyd, man, a really good man. *Really* good man. That was like my big brother. Big ol' gentle giant, know what I'm sayin'? That's the truth. He really was."

George Floyd (from a video he posted to social media) "People quick to count you out, man, but just so strict on countin' you *in*. One thing about old Floyd, man—I love the world. I ain't puttin' on! Ask anybody that know me—and they *know* me. You know, 'cuz like . . . people be actin' like they be *scared* to embrace God, worryin' about what the next man gon' say and all that. Man, you better get down!"

George Floyd's death became a flash point, drawing global attention to systemic racism in aggressive policing across the United States. Floyd had left Houston for a fresh start in Minneapolis years earlier, working in the city's nightclubs, crossing paths with some of the cops he'd run into on the street that Memorial Day, and for going out on a holiday to purchase a pack of cigarettes at the corner store with an allegedly counterfeit twenty-dollar bill, he was met with lethal force. His murder sent a shock wave through Houston like nowhere else because he was part of both Cuney Homes and the Screwed Up Click. Everyone in this book is connected to George Floyd in some way. This wasn't the first such injustice, and history says it won't be the last.

On April 20, 2021, Minneapolis police officer Derek Chauvin was convicted on all three counts against him in Floyd's murder, and later sentenced to 22½ years in prison. Floyd's family called it what it was: a down payment on justice. His memory will live on in Houston and beyond.

Man Poo "Floyd was always positive. That's why they called him the 'Big Friendly Giant.' He did not deserve to die like that. On national TV? *Come on*, man . . . the paramedics told the law to get up off of him. He was already dead! He was already dead. I know the Lord wouldn't let him go out like that, man. God don't throw no incomplete passes."

SCREW LUV

In his final resting place, Robert Earl Davis Jr. is surrounded by the shade of a wall of trees, in a cemetery at the end of a grassy road through the pastures near his father's hometown of Winchester. Sunlight drops down through a green canopy into thick grass where cars pull up alongside headstones scattered around like natural rock formations. As their mother used to do, Michelle still stops by regularly and clears the grave site. A recent visit there turned up candles, a lighter, a few quarters, a bag of Ninja Turtle gummy candies, loose cigarettes, and of course plenty of CDs (even if that wasn't Screw's preferred format). There were baseball hats, a towel Michelle believed Al-D had left, and a bullet, likely set there for protection, knowing the way people felt about Screw. Michelle read one of the letters left for him: "It says, *To DJ Screw, from Paul and Sherry. I would have left you a blunt, but I smoked it on the way here. Wish you were still alive. Would travel far to see you.* That is so nice! And they were just here, April the twenty-ninth."

In 2019, a new photo of Screw was put on the headstone, and in early 2020, Michelle's vision for the grave site finally came to fruition when a trench filled with blue stones was added around the perimeter. The inscription on the slab Trae Tha Truth helped them get reads:

Legend

ROBERT EARL DAVIS, JR.

IF TEARS COULD BUILD A STAIRWAY AND MEMORIES A LANE,
I'D WALK RIGHT UP TO HEAVEN AND BRING YOU HOME AGAIN.

DJ SCREW

SCREWED UP TEXAS

HIS GREATEST LOVE,

Family

DJ Screw (as told to Daika Bray) "Like I said in 1990, I'm gonna Screw the world up. It's Screwed up, but it ain't finished. I'm gonna keep on squaggin', go to Japan, Tokyo. A lotta people don't know this underground, it's really worldwide. I have people from all over the world comin', getting these tapes. Somebody come down from Dallas, get a tape, take it back. They got a cousin from Tennessee, dub that tape, take it there, they got a cousin . . . it just go on and on and on. Stay up, stay real, and we'll be Screwed for life."

Charles Oliver "Man, I'm so proud of him. Who could imagine a little kid, a young man from the country doin' what he did? Like the country, man . . . people don't expect for nobody to get out of there, make it big. You might get out of there and go get a good job, you know, take care of your family, this and that, but I don't know nobody that came out of Smithville that's made it *worldwide*, you know—everybody know him. I just wish he was still here to keep doin' what he been doin'.'"

Ida Mae (as recorded by Ariel Santschi at Screw's funeral in Smithville) "I love you, Screw. You know I love you, man. I always have, I always will. Man, you know, always. You'll be in my heart, man. Thank you for everything you taught me, man. I was so proud that he was my son. So proud."

Shimeka "Sometimes . . . he could be on the phone, right? Like whoever he was talking to had him cracking up. He had the silliest, goofiest smile. You don't know what he's laughin' at, but you're laughin' at *him* because of the way he laughs. It'll have your stomach hurtin' because you're like, *This is so funny!* But yeah, things like that. I just have nothin' but good memories of my uncle, just the good-hearted person he was. Everything. I just . . . I miss him. So much."

Big Bubb "We would call each other on the phone, man, and we'd just *rank*. We'll just rank on the phone for goddamn thirty, forty-five minutes straight. Just from the time you answer that motherfucker, we goin' *in*. We had another cousin, Chris Cooley—we'd call each other, man, we couldn't even *talk*. With Chris on the phone? Aw, man. That forty-five minutes was pro'ly like an *hour* or more. We just rankin' from the time you answer the phone! We *dyin'*, man. Screw might get on Chris and we laughin' and both of 'em get on me, then me and Chris might get on Screw. You never knew who was gonna get in!"

Michelle "Red" Wheeler "I don't know and I'll probably never understand why, but he would call us around three o'clock in the morning. He would call me first, and his words were, *What are you doin', fat ass?* And I'd be like, *I'm 'sleep! Call your mama! 'Cuz she waitin' on the phone call.* And he'd chuckle a lil bit and then he'd say, *Alright, I'll talk to you tomorrow, fat ass.* And I was like, *Alright, bye.* And my mom was faithfully waiting on that 3 a.m. phone call."

Ida Mae (as told to Matt Sonzala) "I miss him. There's not a night I sleep past three in the morning. 'Cuz that's when he used to call me. It's be two forty-five and he'd say, *Mama, what you doing?* And I'd say, *I was sleeping, boy!* But there's not a night since that boy been dead that I can sleep past three o'clock. I cannot sleep. At two forty-five I'm wide awake."

Poppa Davis "When he said, *The world is gonna feel me,* he *meant* that. The good die young, man. My uncle was a good man. He was an entrepreneur, he was a leader in a positive way that a lot of people followed in a positive way. Not sayin' he was on some *Be a leader, not a follower* type shit. Everything wasn't because *I'm better than you.* Naw, *I want you up here* with *me. If I got a hundred thousand, I want* you *to have a hundred thousand.* He had a real big heart, and he would always give you the shirt off his back. It was real hard for him to say no, especially if you know he had it—and even if he didn't have it, he'll still pro'ly tell you, *Yeah, go get it.* And I just wish that I was able to spend more time with him, just vibe with him even more. Because I sit back every day and wonder, *What would I be doin' right now if my uncle was still alive?* Would I have kept on pursuing, wanting to be like him and be deejayin' right beside him? Would I be rappin', would I just be there in the background? And what would he be like? He'd have some gray in him! Would Smithville be the same? Would Houston be the same? What would the family be like? Would my nanny still be here?"

Michelle "Red" Wheeler "When Screw first passed—I believe in spirits—
and Screw had talked to everybody except for Pam, and that just broke
her heart. She was like, *I don't know why I can't see him! I don't know.* And
I said, *Honey, when it's time for him to talk to you, you'll know it. He knows
you the scary one of the bunch! It'll happen.* And I guess probably 2004,
Screw finally came to her. She said she was 'sleep, and she felt somebody
sit down at the foot of her bed, in front of her, and she just kinda—you
know how you kick your feet to see if somebody is there? But of course,
it's a spirit, so you kickin' *through* him. You not kickin' *him.* But she could
still feel that pressure, and so she just kinda raised up and looked and he
was sittin' there with a smile on his face. She could see him! And he told
her, he says, *Pam—Uncle loves you.* He says, *That baby girl you packin'?
She's gonna be beautiful.* She just kinda looked, and of course immediately
she started cryin', beatin' poor Oscar to death, you know, tryin' to wake
him up. And of course, he's not seein' what she's seein', 'cuz it's only
meant for *you!* She's still seein' him sittin' there, and he's talkin' to her
and he's tellin' her, *I love you,* and he says, *Tell your mom to be patient.
Her day is comin'.*"

Pamela Davis "It felt like a dream. He was sitting at the end of my bed
and he had on all-white Dickies suit, and he had on a white hat with it to
the back, you know, how he always used to wear his hat to the back. And
I wasn't scared . . . like, I don't know. Maybe because I knew he wouldn't
harm me in any kinda way, so I wasn't scared, but I was just kinda like
. . . I felt like I was dreaming."

Nikki (as told to Jason Culberson) "Well, he was a ghost. He came to me
dressed in all white. All-white Dickies, at my grandmother's house. I'll
never forget that. If I could take two minutes out, and just talk to him,
and just tell him I appreciate him. I appreciate him introducin' me to
love. To introducing me to *life.* Just saying *thank you.* If it wasn't for him,
I probably wouldn't—and I *love* music. I love music with all my heart.
I listen to so much old stuff it's not even funny. But he introduced me to
music—the passion for it."

Al-D "I know he smilin' right now. Funny how my doors opened up and all kinda shit happens on his birthday. I had two jobs on his birthday, I went to court twice on his birthday, and I was freed two times on his birthday. Well, on the day that he passed. I got my job that I'm workin' at now, November the sixteenth. People do not fuckin' know, man. You know, I think the spirit is just tellin' me the day that you lost is the day that you win from now on, you know what I'm sayin'?"

Michelle "Red" Wheeler "My sister-in-law tells me all the time, *It's in Screw's time. He didn't do anything fast.* And I can laugh about it now—I couldn't laugh about it a few years ago—but even when he passed and they were tryin' to . . . you know, the ground was so soft his casket wouldn't go in the ground, and I told them, *Wait a minute.* I say, *Y'all need to get out of there and quit tryin' to rush him in the ground.* I said, *My brother did nothing fast. Everything he did, he did it slow.* I said, *If y'all stand back, and just let him have his way . . .* And everybody got out the grave. Shorty Mac got out the grave, everybody got out the grave, and then about maybe five minutes later, the little conveyor belt just started rollin' down by itself. I said, *Baby, you can't rush perfection! You gotta let perfection happen on its own.* That's what I told them! You cannot rush perfection. That's the way I feel. Everything happens in Screw's time. That's one thing that he used to tell me all the time. After he passed, he came to me and he told me, he said, *Don't you worry about nothin'.* He say, *When it's your time, you'll know it.* And that's the reason I didn't . . . I didn't worry about what was goin' on back then. I just worried about my mother, to make sure she was gonna be okay, and once she passed, I just left it alone. I didn't have to worry about her anymore, because the both of them, they made me a very strong woman, and so I didn't worry anymore. *Well, I guess it's my time, because* you *came to me, and I agreed.* That was the one thing Screw told me, he said, *You don't worry about nothin'.* He said, *Sister, when it's* your *time, you will* know *it.* That was the last conversation we had, and he was in spirit. I'll never forget that night. He was in all white, and he sat at the foot of my bed and told me that. And I never worried about anything else."

Robert Earl "DJ Screw" Davis Jr.   (1971-2000)
Ida Mae "Mama Screw" Deary Davis   (1949-2005)
Robert Earl "Poppa Screw" Davis Sr.   (1944-2019)
Jessie M. "Gessie" Deary   (1915-2002)
Jack "PawPaw Jack" Thompson   (1934-2014)
Tammy Gayton   (1968-2015)
Patrick "Fat Pat" Hawkins   (1970-1998)
John "Big Hawk" Hawkins   (1969-2006)
Kenneth "Big Moe" Moore   (1974-2007)
Chad "Pimp C" Butler   (1973-2007)
Darrell "MC Wickett Crickett" Veal   (1959-2015)
Christopher "Mr. 3-2" Barriere   (1972-2016)
Charles "Macc" Grace   (1973-2017)
Eric "O.G. Style" Woods   (1970-2008)
Andrew "D Drew" Lewis   (1981-2008)
Curtis "Big Mello" Davis   (1968-2002)
Robert "Big Rue" Jackson   (1975-1999)
Richard "Bushwick Bill" Shaw   (1966-2019)
Steven "Granpappy Mafioso" Eduok   (1974-1999)
James "Big Chance / King James" Hughes   (1973-2020)
Jerome "5th Ward Weebie" Cosey   (1978-2020)
Danta "B.G. Gator" Smith   (1977-1999)
Terence "Big T" Prejean   (1966-2018)
Will "Lil' Will" Anderson   (1979-2016)
Keenan "Maestro" Lyles   (1958-2010)
Marvin "Bird" Driver   (1974-2020)
Patrick Lemon   (1969-1997)
Michael Price   (1971-1993)
Ray Barnett   (1931-2012)
Skipper Lee Frazier   (1927-2016)
George Perry Floyd   (1973-2020)

Acknowledgments

The people who were close to DJ Screw will tell you that it took a village to make his world come alive. Well, it took a village to make this book happen, too. I want to thank sincerely the big family who let me into their lives in varying degrees over the course of untold years of research: Red, Nikki, Charles, Shimeka, Pam, Pop, Poppa Screw, Bubb, Chris Cooley, Shorty Mac, Larry, Al, ACT, Doug, D-Ray, Zo . . . I hope I did the family history justice in this book.

I also want to thank members of the Screwed Up Click family for their generosity of spirit and time. For helping me make connections beyond the world I had within reach, I want to extend a special thank you to Orian "Lump" Lumpkin, Sean Solo, Darryl Scott, Mike-D, Den Den, Kyu-Boi, E.S.G., ACT, Mike Frost, MC Wickett Crickett (RIP), Sean Solo, Man Poo, Madd Mack, Stick 1, Spider, Showtyme, Big A, DJ Chill, DJ Domo, Sherall Jack, Charlie Franks, Dominique Turner, Nancy Byron, DJ Gold, Reggie "Bird" Oliver, Bamino, Bun B, and Jugg Mugg of Coughee Brothaz.

This book also could not have worked without the detail afforded by the interviews, videos, and photographs from the archives of other writers, filmmakers, and artists who have covered Screw over the years: Jason Culberson, Matt Sonzala, Daika Bray, Ariel Santschi (*Pitch Control*), Michael Hall, Chris Cooley, James Bland, Deron Neblett, Ben Tecumseh DeSoto, Bilal Allah, Cheryl Smith, Desmond Lewis, Insanul Ahmed,

Cheryl K. Brown, Mr. Nike and J Daniels with Game 101, Polow (Mob TV), Kyu Boi, Douglas Doneson, and Donnie Houston.

Thanks to the institutions and organizations that have hosted me over the years: Texas Book Festival, Houston History Alliance, Association for Recorded Sound Collections (ARSC), Houston Public Media, Red Bull Music Academy, Contemporary Arts Museum Houston, Julie Grob and University of Houston Libraries, John Guess and Houston Museum of African American Culture, Sean Ripple and the Contemporary Austin, Jason Mellard and Alan Schaefer at Texas State University (San Marcos), Catherine Olien at the American Library in Paris, Adam Silverstein and Rocky Bucano with the Universal Hip Hop Museum (Bronx), Matt Carter and Dennis Brandner with CUNY City College (New York), Boo-Hooray (New York), Powerhouse Arena (Brooklyn), McNally Jackson (Brooklyn), Oren Bloedow and the Owl Music Parlor (Brooklyn), Record Grouch (Brooklyn), Rough Trade (Brooklyn), Rough Trade East (London), NTS Radio (London), FM4 (Austria), UGS Radio (France), Type Books (Toronto), Unitarian House (Ottawa), Joint Custody (Washington, DC), Red Emma's (Baltimore), UGHH (Boston), the Last Bookstore (LA), Deep Vellum Books (Dallas), Piranha Records (Round Rock), Complete Culture (Austin), Farewell Books (Austin), KUTX (Austin), Hi-Tones and Ghostpizza (San Antonio), Friends of Sound (San Antonio), Brazos Bookstore (Houston), Sig's Lagoon (Houston), Screwed Up Records & Tapes (Houston), Cactus Music (Houston), Sunrise Records (Beaumont), Galveston Bookshop, El Dusty and PRODUCE® (Corpus Christi), Crowley Theater (Marfa), Tim Johnson and Marfa Book Co.

For additional support I want to thank Peter Beste, Jessica Hopper, DaLyah Jones, Tyina Steptoe, Carla Valencia, Maco L. Faniel, Todd Burns, Shea Serrano, Donnie Houston, Brad Tyer, Joan LeMay, Rocky Rockett, Kurtis Blow, Nardwuar, Bepi, Beyoncé Knowles-Carter, Charlie Braxton, Gabriel Szatan, DJ BenHaMeen, Alex La Rotta, Diana Nguyen, DeVaughn Douglas, Kiana Fitzgerald, Jay Shelowitz, Patricia Restrepo, Mickael Sinixta Cather (France), Felix Diewald (Austria), William McKenna (BBC News), Bobby Phats and K. Dubb (KPFT), Murdoq, Jazzie Redd, John Nova Lomax, Keith Venable, Anders Firing Lunde, Craig Lindsey, Scotty Hard, Grant Brydon (UK), Jay Green, Stefanie Sobelle, Jeff Salamon, Rad Richard, Bucky Thuerwachter, Russell Etchen, Emma Schkloven, Craig

Mathis, Jon Caramanica, boice-Terrel Allen, Taylor Crumpton, Sama'an Ashrawi, Tom Sachs, Marco Torres, David Gutowski, Christina Dias, Darby Wheeler, Felice Cleveland, Buffalo Sean, Magus Magnus, Mary Manning, Reggie Harris, Darron Henderson, Tosin Nisot, Rodrigo Bascunan, Shara Morris, Jacques Morel, Brett Koshkin, James H. Williams, Pam Mitchell, Michael Hagerty, Vera Beren, Rashad Al-Amin, Fresh and the Breaks, Isaac Yowman, Sidney Walker, Randy Haaga and SoSouth, Chal Ravens (UK), Paul Wallfisch, Leor Galil, Jonathan Williamson, Casey Cheek, Bill Morrison, Wells Dunbar, Art Levy, Victoria Bartlett, Will Cameron, Nathan Smith, Skinny Friedman, Shenequa Golding, Jamie Saft, Tristan Jones, Langston Collin Wilkins, Lucy Gunter, Vance Muse, Bryan Hahn, Prince Paul, Katharine Sawchuk, Padraigh Perkins-Edge, Despot, Oscar Boyson, Samuel Strang, Eothen Alapatt, Y. E. Torres, Rocky Rockett, Yeiry Guevara, Tuck, Elijah C. Watson, Rob Pursey (UK), Aaron Thompson, Eddy Machtinger, Seba Suber, Austin Brown, Matt Goodman, Alexandra Wagner, Will Evans, David Pulido, Lauren Eddy, Charles Eddy, Amy Müller, Mathew Petronelli, Michael Hudson, Flynn Donovan, Elliott Goldkind, Andy Beta, Shawna Kenney, Avi Friedman, Kalpna Patel, Bobby Ramirez, Christopher Rosales, Sharan Zwick, Paul Randall, Shawn Duranni, Brandon Becker, Quincy Flowers, Meshah Hawkins, DJ Lil' King, Stephanie Phillips, Avery Zaddieus, JGTheengineer, Flash Gordon Parks, BBoy Craig, Gonzo, Mark Waldo Ward, Tomas Escalante, Chris Gray, Kasia McNeilly, Will Chase, Verda Carr, Brian Coleman, Lawrence Burney, Rachel Monroe, Michael LaCour, Cameron Ludwick, Optimo Ram, Sam Reis, Dave Tompkins, Lauren Martin, David Drake, Jayson Greene, Tamara Roper, Dan Sharber, Gary Suarez, Harley Brown, Shawn Setaro, Jordan Sowunmi, Quinn Bishop, Dana Scott, Tod A, Will Bundy, Bryan Hahn, Johan Kugelberg, Paula Mejia, Michael Tedder, Helen McCuaig, Grandma Lois, Camilo Smith, Anthony Rathbun, Katy Vine, Jeff Weiss, Brian Gempp, Torii MacAdams, Jay Van Hoy, Terence Nance, Naima Ramos-Chapman, Michael Azerrad, Andrew Dansby, Derek George, Angelica Lopez-Torres, Lynne Ferguson, Abby Webber, Kate Shannon, Bailey Morrison, Cameron Ludwick, Demi Marshall, Joel Pinckney, Dawn Bishop, Casey Kittrell, Roger Wood, and Jennifer Charles.

Oral History Guide

ACT Screw's cousin Adrian Washington from Smithville, rapper also known as ACTION

Al-D South Park rapper and friend of Screw's from high school whom he called his little brother

Ariel Santschi *Pitch Control* videographer who filmed and released Screw's last interview

Ben Tecumseh DeSoto longtime *Houston Chronicle* photographer, homelessness activist

Bernard Barnes neighbor from Quail Meadows, part of group 10201, "I Love These Streets"

Big Bubb cousin of Screw's whose father is Screw's dad's brother, runs Screwed Up Records & Tapes

Big DeMo rapper from South Park's Long Drive with the most famous Screw birthday tape

Big Hawk original S.U.C., brother of Fat Pat, husband of Meshah, father of Lil' Hawk

Big Jut barber and friend of Screw's who was later imprisoned for murder

Big Moe Third Ward singer whose voice became the soul of the S.U.C., brother of K-Luv, close with Big Toon

Big Pokey Yellowstone rapper and high school footballer, part of the
S.U.C. starting five

Big Shasta R&B singer, Lil' Flip's cousin, grew up on Teton (same cross
street as original Screw shop)

Big Swift producer who worked with Southside Playaz, E.S.G., K-Rino,
Big Mello

Big T singer/collaborator of E.S.G., Lil' Flip, C-Note, sang E's hook for
"Wanna Be a Baller"

Bun B Port Arthur rapper, radio host, and college professor, original
member of UGK

Cal Wayne Cuney Homes rapper, childhood friend and later roommate
of George Floyd's

Charles Oliver older brother of DJ Screw, eldest son of Robert Earl
Davis Sr.

Charles Washington producer/promoter, architect of some of Screw's
early career moves

Charlie Franks S.A. Fools producer, South Acres Crime Family, old
friend of Scarface

Chris Cooley cousin of Screw's from San Antonio, produced for Al-D,
stayed at Greenstone

Chris Ward rapper from Yellowstone, came up under Big Pokey, met
Screw as a high schooler

Cl'Che S.P.C. rapper/mother/activist, S.H.E. Movement, freestyled on
Southside Still Holdin' tape

C-Note Cloverland, Botany Boys, Big Shot Records, first rapper to freestyle on a Screw tape

Cory Nelson white-boy next-door neighbor of Screw's from his house
in Sugar Land

Crazy C producer who engineered Screw's '99 album *All Work, No Play*
for Jam Down

Daika Bray writer (*XXL*, *Murder Dog*, *Dialect*) who interviewed Screw,
sister of DJ BenHaMeen

Darryl Scott legendary mixtape/club DJ whose slowed-down mixes
influenced Screw

Daryal Butts Smithville native who let a young DJ Screw use his
records and turntables

Den Den rapper and CEO of Straight Profit Records, released Yungstar's first records

Derrick "D-Reck" Dixon CEO of Wreckshop Records, producer of *The Dirty 3rd: The Movie*

Desmond Lewis dean/writer/professor, enlisted Screw to write for *Platinum* magazine

Devin the Dude rapper/producer, Odd Squad / Coughee Brothaz, marijuana enthusiast

D-Gotti rapper from Herschelwood who recorded for Wreckshop, freestyled on Screw tapes

Disco Dave Miami producer who made slowed-down tapes years before fellow Floridians Jam Pony Express

DJ Big Baby Screw's younger cousin from Smithville, recorded new "Screws" after he passed

DJ Chill early DJ gigs with Screw, KBXX, *Damage Control* radio (KPFT) with Matt Sonzala

DJ Cipher Otha Baker, DJ/producer/skater, worked at Blast Records & Tapes in late '80s

DJ DMD Port Arthur producer/rapper who crafted S.U.C. songs "So Real" and "25 Lighters"

DJ Gold Sunnyside DJ who worked with Keke and Al-D, sold tapes for Screw at shows

DJ Kay Slay New York City DJ/producer, won multiple Justos around the time Screw was honored with his award

DJ Screw the Texas turntablist who slowed down the world, a.k.a. Screw Zoo, born Robert Earl Davis Jr.

DJ Zo Tha Affiliate cousin of Screw and Chris Cooley from Houston, FreshPack DJs

Double D Wreckshop / Platinum Soul producer of Herschelwood Hardheadz, Keke's "Southside"

D-Ray cousin of Screw's from Smithville, brother of Lil' Doug, worked at Screw shop in mid-2000s

D-Red Cloverland rapper/producer, Botany Boys, produced for Godfather, 2 Real, Mass 187

Duke Herschelwood Hardheadz rapper who started coming to Screw's house in early '94

D.W. Sound Texas Hill Country DJ who brought tapes of *Kidz Jamm* back home to Screw in Smithville

Enjoli one of the few female rappers (along with Sherro) on Screw tapes, close with Al-D

E.S.G. Louisiana-born freestyle specialist and hitmaker, a.k.a. E, heard on countless Screw tapes

Fat Pat Dead End rapper whose swagger and slang set the tone for Screw tapes in the very beginning

Frank Popa Watts rapper from Quail Meadows, 3-4 Action, Herschelwood, cousin of Poppy

George Floyd Yates football player who grew up in Cuney Homes, freestyled on several tapes

Great Black Shark Sterling High School rapper/producer from Screw's group IMG/Nation

Hard Jarv from Sunnyside, longtime friend of Mike-D, E.S.G., ran Black Hearted Records

Head Napoleon Head Randle, Cloverland rapper and extended Botany Boys family

Heat Houston Quail Meadows resident, grew up going to see Screw spin at the skating rink

Ida Mae Deary Davis mother of DJ Screw and Michelle "Red" Wheeler, Screw's biggest fan

Isaac "Chill" Yowman filmmaker/rapper/producer helming DJ Screw biopic *All Screwed Up*

Jason Culberson a.k.a. K.i.d, filmmaker/director of *Screwville off Harris* and *The DJ Screw Story*

Jhiame Bradshaw R&B singer/producer, moved from Memphis, TN, to Acres Homes in '81

Julie Grob librarian and archivist, DJ Screw archive at University of Houston Libraries

Justo Faison promoter whose Mixtape Awards show presented Screw with top honors in '99

Kay-K South Park rapper, grew up with Fat Pat and Hawk, only living member of D.E.A.

K Dubb producer, promoter, radio host (KPFT's *The Groove*), son of Astros great Bob Watson

Key-C rapper from South Park's Long Drive, close with Big DeMo and Yungstar

King Bo friend and neighbor of Screw's from Gulf Meadows, where Screw lived in the late '80s

Kiwi grew up in Dead End with Fat Pat, met Screw at Broadway, made tapes with Big Hawk

Klondike Kat South Park Coalition rapper/producer, taught Screw beat making with Icey Hott

Knock Herschelwood Hardheadz rapper who met Screw at Quail Meadows, brother of Duke

Koldjak a.k.a. Runn G, Dead End Records, who picked up the Dead End Alliance project when Kay-K was locked up

K-Rino South Park Coalition rapper/writer/founder, went to Sterling High School with Screw and Al-D

Kurtis Blow New York legend who was the first touring rap artist to come through Houston

Larry B schoolmate of Screw's from Smithville and member of his first group, Z Force Crew

Lester "Sir" Pace Houston radio legend who started on *Kidz Jamm* and now owns his own station in New York

Lil' Doug cousin of Screw's from Smithville, came to Houston in late '90s to live with him, brother of D-Ray

Lil' Flip platinum-selling Cloverland rapper whom Screw dubbed the "Freestyle King"

Lil' Keke Don Ke of Herschelwood, early Screw tape favorite who went on to a powerhouse career

Lil' O rapper who came up in southwest Houston, early on collaborated with Destiny's Child

Lil' Randy Southside DJ who spoke on the mic with Screw on the tapes, brother of Ron-O

Lil' Rick big-voiced rapper from DSD1, friend of Michael Price, met Screw with him in late '92

Lil' Sock producer and part of DSD1, a.k.a. Sock-a-lock

Lil' Troy Short Stop Records rapper/producer who got S.U.C. rappers to appear on "Wanna Be a Baller"

LOS a.k.a. L.O.S. or Los Grace, younger brother of Macc Grace, appeared on *Killuminati* tape

Macc Grace Dat Boy Grace, brother of LOS, a favorite of Pimp C's when UGK was in town

Man Poo Man Phoo, Man Pooh, Poopac, friend of George Floyd whose name was also the title of a Screw tape

MC Wickett Crickett NYC native who moved to Houston in the late '70s, nightlife pioneer

Meshah Hawkins activist, widow of Big Hawk and mother of his two sons, runs his label

Michael "5000" Watts Northside DJ whose slow Swishahouse mixes irritated Southsiders when they first came out

Michelle "Red" Wheeler DJ Screw's older sister, daughter of Ida Mae Deary Davis, mother of Shimeka, Pam, and Mr. P

Mike-D Southside Playaz / A.N.M. / S.U.C. rapper, brother of Bamino of BAM's car shop in South Park

MoMo Nikki's friend Monique, who worked with her at Screwed Up Records & Tapes

Morna Gonsoulin medical examiner who wrote up autopsy of Robert Earl "DJ Screw" Davis Jr.

Mr. 3-2 of Convicts, Blac Monks, Southside Playaz, whose style influenced S.U.C. and Snoop Dogg

Ms. Patricia Al-D's mother, fed Screw in the 10201 days when his dad was away at work

Nikki Williams Screw's longtime girlfriend, played a huge role in his artistic development and getting the shop running

Noke D Wreckshop producer Screw encouraged to get Big Moe's recording career underway

OG Ron C Swishahouse producer and Chopstars DJ, calls his style "chopped not slopped"

Orian "Lump" Lumpkin producer, promoter, photographer with On the Level promotions

Pamela Davis Screw's niece, spent summers at Uncle Earl's in Houston with her siblings

Patrick Lewis owner of Jam Down label, which produced the first official release in which DJ Screw appeared

Paul Wall Northside rapper and Screwhead, came up as part of the Swishahouse movement

Poppa Davis Screw's nephew from Smithville, a.k.a. Mr. P, played young Screw in *Soldiers United for Cash*

Poppy Quail Meadows / 10201 / 3-4 Action, early supporter and close friend of Screw, Action Smoke Shop

PSK-13 South Park Coalition rapper, Wreckless Klan, appears on *All Screwed Up, 3 'N the Mornin'*

Quincy "QDOGG" Evans early slab pioneer, friend of Scarface, brother of Toast, Quanell X

Ray Holmes III younger neighbor of Screw's at Quail Meadows in the late '80s

Reggie "Bird" Oliver rapper and videographer who shot shot Cliff Mack's documentary *The Untold Story* with Hank Bell and Shaka Sulaman

Robert Earl Davis Jr. *see* DJ Screw

Robert Earl Davis Sr. Poppa Screw, father of DJ Screw, from Winchester, Texas

Robert Guillerman Southwest Wholesale mastermind of local rap production/distribution

Rob Quest rapper and producer from Odd Squad / Coughee Brothaz who met Screw in '93

Ronald Bob producer/manager, worked with Mr. 3-2, Scarface, and many Houston zydeco artists

Ronnie Spencer singer and DJ who got Screw his first real DJ gig at Almeda Skating Rink

Russell Washington BigTyme Recordz CEO who was briefly a roommate of Screw's in '86

Scarface rapper/producer/author from South Acres, Geto Boys, Facemob, Houston's rap king

Sean "Solo" Jemison producer, worked with E.S.G. early and later countless S.U.C. artists

Shawn Brauch head of Pen & Pixel, the company that designed myriad '90s Houston rap album covers

Shimeka Screw's niece, six months old when he left Smithville, later worked at Screwed Up Records & Tapes

Shorty Mac Screw's cousin Trey Adkins from Smithville, his partner in discovering hip-hop, Z Force Crew

South Park Mexican rapper/producer/founder of Dope House, in prison for sexual assault since 2002

Spice 1 Bay Area rapper with family in Houston who freestyled on a tape at Screw's house

Stick 1 rapper from South Park's Dead End, grew up with Fat Pat, later became a minister

Toe neighbor of Screw's at Quail Meadows who was the first to offer to buy a tape from him

Tommie Langston Stickhorse Records, music industry mainstay, helped road manage Screw

Trae Tha Truth met Screw in the late '90s, Guerilla Maab / A.B.N. / S.U.C., rapper/philanthropist/activist

Trouble House rapper from the group Legion of Doom, which became IMG/Nation

Tyrone from Herschelwood, hustled close to Screw's window at Quail Meadows so he could hear him mix, early Screw tape customer

Tytanic NYC producer/DJ Ty Hendrix, close to Justo Faison and helped with the Mixtape Awards

Warren Lee brother of Scarface from South Acres, close with DJ Domo of Geto Boys

Will-Lean Cloverland rapper from Botany Boys who met Screw in the Broadway Square days

Wood Third Ward rapper, late '90s wave of new S.U.C. artists, the Half Dead Organization

Yungstar "Wanna Be a Baller" rapper whose first time recording with DJ Screw was June 27, 1996

Z-Ro a.k.a. Mo City Don / King of the Ghetto, from Ridgemont, in Guerilla Maab, A.B.N.

Bibliography

BOOKS AND MAGAZINES

Ahmed, Insanul. "Scarface Breaks Down His 25 Most Essential Songs." *Complex*, January 31, 2013.

Allah, Bilal. "DJ Screw: Givin' It to Ya Slow." *Rap Pages*, July 1995.

Baker, Soren. "Rappers Salute DJ Screw, Known for 'Screwing' Hit Songs." MTV.com, August 22, 2001.

Barr, Alwyn. *Black Texans: A History of African Americans in Texas, 1528–1995*. Norman: University of Oklahoma Press, 1996.

Beverly, Julia. *Sweet Jones: Pimp C's Trill Life Story*. Atlanta: Shreveport Ave Inc, 2015.

Black Dog Bone, and Paul Stewart, eds. *Murder Dog: The Interviews, Vol. 1*. Los Angeles: Over the Edge Books, 2015.

Bradley, Regina N. *Chronicling Stankonia: The Rise of the Hip-Hop South*. Chapel Hill: University of North Carolina Press, 2021.

Bray, Daika. "Slow and Low." *XXL*, August 1999.

Bullard, Robert D. *Invisible Houston: The Black Experience in Boom and Bust*. College Station: Texas A&M University Press, 1987.

Brown, Cheryl K. "All Screw No Play." *Platinum*, May 2000.

Byrd, Sigmund. *Sig Byrd's Houston*. New York: Viking Press, 1955.

Caldwell, Brandon. "Remembering George Floyd's Life and Legacy in the Houston Hip-Hop Scene." *Pitchfork*, June 5, 2020.

Caramanica, Jon. "DJ Screw's Legacy: Seeping Out of Houston Slowly." *New York Times*, November 7, 2010.

———. "The Tipping Point." *Spin*, September 2005.

Chang, Jeff. *Can't Stop Won't Stop: A History of the Hip-Hop Generation*. New York: Picador, 2005.

Clayton, Jace. "The Slowed-Down Tempos of Screw and Its Influence on Contemporary Bands." *Frieze*, November 1, 2010.

Cole, Thomas R. *No Color Is My Kind:*

The Life of Eldrewey Stearns and the Integration of Houston. Austin: University of Texas Press, 1997.

Cuney Hare, Maud. *Norris Wright Cuney: A Tribune of the Black People.* New York: The Crisis Publishing Company, 1913.

Dansby, Andrew. "Conference Puts Houston Hip-Hop in Scholarly Setting." *Houston Chronicle,* March 28, 2012.

DJ Screw. "What's Dirty Down South." *Platinum,* May 2000.

Doneson, Douglas. "The Golden Boy of Screw: A Conversation with Lil' Keke." *Vice,* January 22, 2014.

Faniel, Maco L. *Hip-Hop in Houston: The Origin and the Legacy.* Charleston: History Press, 2013.

Frazier, Skipper Lee. *Tighten Up: The Autobiography of a Houston Disc Jockey.* Victoria, BC: Trafford, 2006.

George, Nelson. *Hip Hop America.* New York: Penguin Books, 2005.

Gunderson, Bill. "Actavis Continues Pharmaceuticals Dominance." *MarketWatch,* January 16, 2014.

Hall, Michael. "The Fast Life and Slow Death of DJ Screw." *Texas Monthly,* April 2001.

Hales, Douglas. *A Southern Family in White and Black: The Cuneys of Texas.* College Station: Texas A&M University Press, 2003.

Jones, DaLyah. "Solange's 'When I Get Home' Pays Homage to the Black Rural South." *Texas Monthly,* March 13, 2019.

Jordan, Brad. *Diary of a Madman: The Geto Boys, Life, Death, and the Roots of Southern Rap.* New York: Dey Street Books, 2016.

Klineberg, Stephen L. *Prophetic City: Houston on the Cusp of a Changing America.* New York: Avid Reader Press, 2020.

McComb, David G. *Houston: A History.* Austin: University of Texas Press, 1981.

Nosnitsky, Andrew. "Gray Matters." *Pitchfork,* March 4, 2013.

O'Brien, Timothy J., and David Ensminger. *Mojo Hand: The Life and Music of Lightnin' Hopkins.* Austin: University of Texas Press, 2014.

Prince, James, with Jasmine D. Waters. *The Art and Science of Respect: A Memoir by James Prince.* Houston: N-The-Water Publishing, 2018.

Roth, Mitchel P., and Tom Kennedy. *Houston Blue: The Story of the Houston Police Department.* Denton: University of North Texas Press, 2012.

Sarig, Roni. *Third Coast: Outkast, Timbaland, and How Hip-Hop Became a Southern Thing.* New York: Hachette Books, 2007.

Serwer, Jesse. "DJ Screw: From Cough Syrup to Full-Blown Fever." *Guardian,* November 11, 2010.

Shelton, Kyle. *Power Moves: Transportation, Politics, and Development in Houston.* Austin: University of Texas Press, 2017.

Smith, Camilo H. "Swedish Rapper Credits H-Town as Inspiration." *Houston Chronicle,* June 1, 2016.

Smith, Cheryl. "Have You Been Screwed Lately?" *The Source,* July 1995.

Sonzala, Matt. "Interview with DJ Screw's Mother." *Murder Dog* 9, no. 3 (2002).

Steptoe, Tyina L. *Houston Bound: Culture and Color in a Jim Crow City.* Berkeley: University of California Press, 2015.

Strauss, Neil. "Rap Is Slower Around Houston." *New York Times*, November 23, 2000.

Watson, Dwight. *Race and the Houston Police Department, 1930–1990: A Change Did Come*. College Station: Texas A&M University Press, 2005.

Wood, Roger. *Down in Houston: Bayou City Blues*. Austin: University of Texas Press, 2003.

Wood, Roger. *Texas Zydeco*. Austin: University of Texas Press, 2006.

MULTIMEDIA

"Big Hawk - Screwed Up Click Interview." YouTube video, 9:12. Posted by Presidential Records Inc. November 1, 2019.

"Big Tee The Million Dollar Hookman Says Houston Rappers Need To Stop Tripping." YouTube video, 8:49. Posted by Stric Hustle TV, April 4, 2017.

The Dirty 3rd: The Movie. DVD. Directed by Henry LeBlanc. Houston: Wreckshop Films, 2000.

DJ Screw: The Untold Story. DVD. Directed by Cliff Mack. Houston: Come Fly With Me Films, 2012.

The DJ Screw Story. DVD. Directed by Jason Culberson. Houston: Screwville, 2016.

Game 101 S.U.C. H.A.W.K. Lil Keke E.S.G. DVD. Directed by Game 101. Houston: Oarfin Distribution, 2007.

"George Floyd pleaded for young people to end gun violence in resurfaced video." YouTube video, 0:53. Posted by The Independent, May 28, 2020.

Ghetto Dreams. DVD. Directed by Derrick "D-Reck" Dixon. Houston: Wreckshop Records, 1999.

The Houston Hard Hitters, Vol. 2. DVD. Directed by Jose "Pepe" Ortiz. Houston: Paid In Full Entertainment, 2004.

Lewis, Desmond, and Albert Driver (Al-D). *Unconditional Luv—A Memorial to DJ Screw*. CD. Recorded 2000. Power House Records / Fukusumi Music Group, 2002.

Mann! The Movie. DVD. Directed by Derrick "D-Reck" Dixon. Houston: Wreckshop Records, 2000.

"Michael Watts Sets the Records Straight about Screw," YouTube video, 10:59. Posted by Chowtime TV, August 3, 2017.

Murda the DVD Magazine: Kappa Beach Party. DVD. Directed by DJ Jimmy D. Houston: Red Light District, 2004.

"Polow's Mob Tv Presents Exclusive Mr 32 Interview With Mob Tv." YouTube video, 39:14. Posted by polow mobtv, May 26, 2011.

Scarface. *The World Is Yours*. CD. Recorded 1993. Rap-A-Lot, 1993.

Solange. *When I Get Home*. CD. Recorded 2018. Columbia, 2019.

Soldiers United for Cash. DVD. Directed by Ariel Santschi. Houston: REL Entertainment, 2004.

ORAL HISTORIES
INTERVIEWS BY THE AUTHOR
ACT, 2016
Al-D, 2008–2019
Ariel Santschi, 2015
Bamino, 2012–2019
Ben Tecumseh DeSoto, 2012
Bernard Barnes, 2017
Big A, 2013–2019
Big Bubb, 2005–2021
Big DeMo, 2011

Big Dogg, 2011
Big Pokey, 2012
Bun B, 2005–2019
Cal Wayne, 2017–2021
Captain Jack, 2007
Carlos "DJ Styles" Garza, 2015
Charles Washington, 2019–2020
Charlie Franks, 2019
Chris Cooley, 2016–2019
Chris Ward, 2012
Clay-Doe, 2005
Cl'Che, 2005–2017
C-Note, 2015–2019
Cory Nelson, 2019
Crazy C, 2020
Daika Bray, 2019
Darrell Nixson, 2020
Darryl Scott, 2006–2021
Daryal Butts, 2019
Def Jam Blaster, 2016
Den Den, 2016
Deron Neblett, 2016
Derrick "D-Reck" Dixon, 2013–2020
Desmond Lewis, 2019–2021
Devin the Dude, 2006–2020
D-Gotti, 2005–2019
Disco Dave, 2020
DJ Big Baby, 2017
DJ Chill, 2007–2019
DJ Cipher, 2016
DJ Domination, 2019
DJ Gold, 2017
DJ Grayface, 2012
DJ Oakcliff, 2012
DJ Red, 2013–2020
DJ Zo Tha Affiliate, 2019
Dominique Turner, 2005–2017
Dope E., 2005–2018
Double D, 2020
D-Red, 2010–2020
D Solo, 2019
Duce, 2019
Duke, 2019

D.W. Sound, 2019
Enjoli, 2012
E.S.G., 2017–2020
Fly T, 2020
Frank Popa Watts, 2019
Freddie McFly, 2019
G-Dash, 2006
Great Black Shark, 2020
Hard Jarv, 2016
Head, 2019
Heat Houston, 2019
Icey Hott, 2019
Jason Culberson, 2013–2021
Jazzie Redd, 2019
Jhiame Bradshaw, 2019
Jude Auzenne, 2016
Jugg Mugg, 2008–2020
Kay-K, 2008–2019
Kay Slay, 2020
K Dubb, 2020
Key-C, 2019
Killahoe (20-2-Life), 2014
King Bo, 2019
Kiwi, 2016
Klondike Kat, 2017
Knock, 2020
Koldjak, 2020
K-Rino, 2005–2006
Kyu-Boi, 2006–2019
Larry B, 2017
Lester "Sir" Pace, 2019
Lil' Doug, 2017
Lil' Flip, 2021
Lil' Keke, 2005–2017
Lil' O, 2005
Lil' Randy, 2012
Lil' Rick, 2019
Lil' Sock, 2019
Lil' Troy, 2005–2017
LOS, 2016–2020
Macc Grace, 2017
Madd Mack, 2019
Manny Bezza, 2019

Man Poo, 2019–2020
Matt Sonzala, 2004–2021
MC Wickett Crickett, 2010–2011
Mean Green, 2010
Meshah Hawkins, 2011–2012
Michael "5000" Watts, 2006
Michelle "Red" Wheeler, 2016–2021
Mike Frost, 2006–2020
Mike-D, 2006–2019
MoMo, 2017
Money G, 2012
Mr. 3-2, 2005–2013
Ms. Patricia, 2005
Nikki Williams, 2012–2021
Noke D, 2019
OG Ron C, 2020
Orian "Lump" Lumpkin, 2017–2021
OZ, 2019
Pamela Davis, 2019
Patrick Lewis, 2020
Quincy "QDOGG" Evans, 2017
Poppa Davis, 2020
Poppa Screw, 2005–2019
PSK-13, 2021
Ray Holmes III, 2017
Reggie "Bird" Oliver, 2017–2020
Ricky Royal, 2008–2018
Robert Guillerman, 2020
Robot, 2019
Rob Quest, 2017
Ronald Bob, 2016
Ronnie Spencer, 2019
Russel "The ARE" Gonzalez, 2012
Scarface, 2017
Sean "Solo" Jemison, 2008–2021
Shawn Brauch, 2020
Sherall Jack, 2017
Shimeka Johnson, 2020
Shorty Mac, 2007–2021
Showtyme, 2006–2019
Sire Jukebox, 2016
South Park Mexican, 2019
Spice 1, 2019

Spider, 2019
Stick 1, 2019
Steve Fournier, 2016
SUC Den Den, 2019
T Farris, 2005
Toe, 2017
Tommie Langston, 2017
Trae Tha Truth, 2011
Tytanic, 2020
Tyrone, 2020
Warren Lee, 2019
Will-Lean, 2015–2019
Wood, 2008–2017
Yungstar, 2019
Z-Ro, 2011

OTHER INTERVIEWS
Al-D, interview by Jason Culberson, 2013
Big Hawk, interview by Presidential
    Records, accessed via YouTube,
    November 1, 2019
Big Jut, interview by Jason Culberson,
    2013
Big Pokey, interview by Jason Culber-
    son, 2013
Big Shasta, interview by Jason Culber-
    son, 2013
Big Swift, interview by Donnie Houston,
    2020
Big T, interview by Stric Hustle TV,
    accessed via YouTube, April 4, 2017
DJ Screw, interview by Ariel Santschi,
    October 29, 2000
DJ Screw, interview by Bilal Allah, 1995
DJ Screw, interview by Daika Bray, 1999
DJ Screw, interview by Desmond Lewis,
    2000
DJ Screw, interview by Kyu-Boi, 2000
DJ Screw, interview by unknown,
    courtesy of Chris Cooley, 2000
Dougie D, in conversation with Peter
    Beste, 2007

D-Ray, interview by Jason Culberson, 2013

Ida Mae Deary Davis, interview by Matt Sonzala, 2002

Ida Mae Deary Davis, interview by Michael Hall, 2000

K-Rino, interview by Jason Culberson, 2013

Lil' O, interview by Jason Culberson, 2013

Mr. 3-2, interview by Polow's Mob TV, accessed via YouTube, May 26, 2011

Nikki Williams, interview by Jason Culberson, 2013

Index

The abbreviation *PS* indicates an image in the photo section.